The Jewish Choice: Unity or Anti-Semitism

Historical facts on anti-Semitism as a reflection of Jewish social discord

LAITMAN
KABBALAH
PUBLISHERS

Michael Laitman, PhD

The Jewish Choice:
Unity or Anti-Semitism

Copyright © 2019 by Michael Laitman

All rights reserved

Published by Laitman Kabbalah Publishers

www.bundleofreeds.com contact@bundleofreeds.com

1057 Steeles Avenue West, Suite 532, Toronto,
ON, M2R 3X1, Canada

2009 85th Street #51, Brooklyn, New York, 11214, USA

Printed in USA

ISBN: 978-1-6718-7220-2

Library of Congress Control Number: 2019920463

Proof Reading: Mary Miesem

Associate Editors: Joseph Donnelly, Alycia Larez,
Debbie Wood, Michael Kellogg, Kathy Pirrello, Joseph Larez

Copy Editor: Mary Pennock

Cover Design: Rony Perry, Inna Smirnova

Layout: Chaim Ratz

Executive Editor: Chaim Ratz

Printing and Post Production: Uri Laitman

Cover images: Medal issued by Goebbels's newspaper *Der Angriff* commemorating head of SD Jewish Affairs Office Leopold von Mildenstein's six-month visit to Palestine.
Photos: Courtesy of Kedem Auction House

FIRST EDITION: DECEMBER 2019

Second Printing

Table of Contents

"Modern reformers, who are constructing model social systems, ... would do well to look into the social system under which the early Jews were organized."

Henry Ford

Editor's Note — Acknowledgments

Working on *The Jewish Choice: Unity or anti-Semitism*, was such an enormous task that it would have been impossible to achieve it within six months had it not been for the immensely hard work of so many people. During those months, researchers in English, German, Spanish, Italian, Russian, French, and Hebrew, worked tirelessly to comb through over one hundred books, dozens of academic papers, hundreds of letters in various languages, archived microfilms, online archives of news agencies, and other internet sites that document the fascinating-yet-tragic history of the Jewish people. Relentlessly, these precious people would dive into their task, and as soon as they completed it, would ask for yet another. But what astounded me most was that I did not approach even a single one of them; rather, they approached me and volunteered to research, edit, or assist in any way I needed. Without them, there would be no book. Below, I have listed the key researchers, but behind some of them were teams of anonymous equally dedicated soldiers.

Joe Donnelly, besides being one of the editors, dug up unbelievable heaps of materials from US government archives. Kris Dawson spent days in the UK national archive browsing through letters from the 1930s. The unbelievably diligent Mary Pennock combed books, essays, academic archives, all while editing the text, being the book's chief copyeditor. Norma Livne, besides being the content editor, raked through books, academic essays, and internet sites in her "free time," when most of us are sound asleep. Other helpful individuals were Noga Bar Noye (English and French), Kathy Pirello, and Masha Shayovich.

German was a key research language in this book, but thanks to the hard work of dedicated friends, we managed to collect the documents we needed. Alex Stetter delved into books and searched through microfilms in Germany's Bundesarchive (Germany's National Archive). Miriam Priven searched through hundreds of letters that members of the Nazi Party sent from Palestine to the SS headquarters in Berlin, while also helping in English. Elisabeth Prelog-Igler was there whenever I needed an immediate translation of German texts. Rebekka Admoni took on some of the least pleasing texts to read in both English and German, and was extremely helpful going through the Wannsee Protocol describing The Final Solution to the Jewish Question.

Russian was a big challenge, but Shelly Gaver and Misha Brushtein were extremely helpful in both finding the books we needed and digging up the relevant excerpts.

Ariana Stridi searched days and nights on her tiny phone screen for materials in both English and Italian that brought valuable insights on anti-Semitism and Christianity in Italy.

Many people offered their assistance in Hebrew. Yoel Meidan and Yuri Hechter helped in both English and Hebrew, and many others provided text and video materials in Hebrew and English. Nesi Hassid, David Malnichuck, Yaniv Si, Oren Levi, Dudi Aharoni, Leah Mendler, Ofer Nakash, Yaakov Priel, and Yoav Bernstein either sent helpful materials or were readily helpful when I needed them.

A Word about Consistency

Throughout the book, the key criteria in citing quotes were accuracy and authenticity. It was extremely important to the author that the excerpts brought in this book would be the writers' own words without any alterations. Therefore, in order to maintain authenticity, we kept the quotes untouched, and where we did have to "edit" them, we stated it explicitly, to avoid any misunderstandings.

Because the texts within the book were taken from numerous authors and sources, and from very different periods in history, inconsistencies in spelling, grammar, and even the meaning of some words are to be expected. For example, some historians spell the Russian word for "king" as "tsar" and some as "czar." Another example is the use of the word "corn" to mean all forms of grain in William Whiston's 18th century translation of the writings of Titus Flavius Josephus, or Whiston's use of the term "Greek" or "Grecian" when speaking of Romans, since their culture was Hellenism and the spoken language in the Eastern Mediterranean part of the Roman Empire was Greek rather than Latin. Nevertheless, we did not touch any of the inconsistencies in order not to tarnish the accuracy of the quotes or the authenticity of the sources.

Sincerely, the editor

Foreword: Why I Wrote This Book

I am a researcher, a scientist, and a kabbalist. But first and foremost, I am a Jew. I grew up in the former Soviet Union, and the vast majority of my family perished in the Holocaust. I have witnessed and experienced firsthand the myriad faces of anti-Semitism, tacit and overt. I have family, friends, and thousands of students in North America, Israel, and all over the world, and I see the lurking menace of another world war and another cataclysm to the Jews.

Particularly, I am very, very worried about the future of the Jews in America and Israel. I am worried about my students, I am worried about my friends, and I am worried about my family. It is this grave concern that has prompted me to write this book, a plea to all the people of my fold to wake up now while it is still possible to reverse the ominous trajectory, as the downfall is already underway. We Jews must act now since from here on, matters will only go downhill.

The "Herald Syndrome"

In ancient Athens, they would throw heralds who brought bad news into a pit where criminals condemned to death were thrown. In Sparta, they would cast them into a well and leave them to die.[1] Luckily, today it is illegal to kill bearers of unpleasant news. Yet, the "herald syndrome" of rejecting the bearer of unwelcome news still has the upper hand over most of us. The previous century has shown that in the case of Jews, denial can be deadly. If we want to live up to the motto "Never again!" the herald syndrome is not an option we should consider.

On October 30, 2014, I landed in Los Angeles. It was the start of a two week lecture tour in the US, discussing anti-Semitism and the need for Jewish unity in order to remedy it. This was not the first time, nor the second, that I spoke about anti-Semitism in the US. I had discussed it many times before, at least since my first lecture tour back in 2002, and I was always met with disbelief, smugness, and often with contempt.

Moreover, by 2014, I did not have to warn about a future danger of rising anti-Semitism. It was rampant everywhere in Europe and had pervaded universities and campuses all over the US. That October 30th, the first day of my tour, I had an online conversation with Mrs. Tammi Rossman-Benjamin, head of the AMCHA initiative to combat anti-Semitism in US colleges and universities. It was a poignant, candid dialog. Tammi was well aware of the deteriorating situation of Jewish students precisely because they were Jews. She was determined to reverse the course by increasing the awareness of university officials linked to the situation and by "working with university administrators, with legislators, or elected officials."[2] Tammi believed that "The key to solving the problem is to have university administrators solve the problem because the key to the problem is in their hands." As she put it, "We are just trying to get them to do their due diligence and their responsibility."

I, on the other hand, said that rules and regulations would not help except, perhaps, as first-aid. I cautioned Tammi that college campus anti-Semitism was only the beginning, the tip of a titanic iceberg. To me, it was evident that anti-Semitism would spread throughout the country, engulf all of the US, and that its only remedy would be for the entire Jewish community in the US to unite. I told her that the conditions in today's US are strikingly similar to those that existed in Germany prior to Hitler's rise to power (on which I will elaborate extensively later in this book), and because of it, some version of what happened there is bound to happen here.

We are not in ancient Athens, so Tammi was very polite in her rejection of my assertion. She also agreed that there is certainly a rise in anti-Semitism. But we did not see eye to eye on the solution. At least, I thought, it is a cold comfort that she acknowledged the existence of the problem. It was, nonetheless, some progress.

A few days later, on November 3, I gave a public talk at the Skirball Cultural Center Ahmanson Hall in Los Angeles, titled "Who Holds the Key for a Better Tomorrow?" To my delight, hundreds of people showed up. To my dismay, as in the past, when I began to talk about the rise of anti-Semitism in the US, many in the audience started heading for the doors. They still would not hear about it.

From LA, I flew to Washington D.C., where I was invited to give a joint lecture at the Israeli American Council (IAC) conference on the topic of "Anti-Semitism, Root, Cause and Solution." Lecturing with me was a celebrated journalist from Israel who was considered an expert on anti-Semitism. By that year, 2014, the Boycott, Divest, and Sanctions (BDS) movement had struck firm roots in college and university campuses throughout the US, staging anti-Israel Apartheid Days, die-ins, in which students simulate being shot by the Israeli army, and voicing hatred for the Jewish State—as well as for Jews— aggressively and frequently. Together with such organizations as Jewish Voice for Peace (JVP), BDS activists were active perpetrators of the incidents that drove Mrs. Rossman-Benjamin to create AMCHA.

The audience at the IAC conference consisted of Israelis living in America, and Jewish Americans supportive of Israel. Here, too, I tried to explain that there are many similarities between the conditions that drove Germany to perpetrate the Holocaust, and the current situation in America, and that the campuses were only the beginning. I stressed again that unless US Jews wake up to reality, they will be in great danger, and that they were only seeing the beginning of the wave and anti-Semitism was going to get far worse, far sooner than most people thought.

Sadly, the celebrated journalist lecturing with me asserted confidently that anti-Semitism is decreasing worldwide, that for non-Jewish Americans, "It's an honor to marry a Jew" in "all the circles of American society," and finally, that "Our situation is the best ever, especially in America." Naturally, many in the audience sided with him. The "herald syndrome" was in full force. I truly understand why no one wants to hear about problems, especially life-threatening ones, before they hit you in the face. But in the case of anti-Semitism, when it hits you in the face, it might be too late to remedy the situation.

Introduction: Lessons from Our Past

When we think of anti-Semitism, the first words that often come to mind are Nazism and the Holocaust. But where does Nazism come from? Why did it happen specifically in Germany, the birthplace of so many treasures of Western culture, and the breeding ground of so many noble ideas and works of art and science? Could a Jewish genocide happen elsewhere? Could it happen in America?

At first glance, this seems like such an unlikely notion that it should be brushed off and ignored as a momentary lapse of reason. But history tells us that we must not be complacent. Throughout history, Jews have been singled out for condemnation. They have been persecuted, expelled, and exterminated everywhere they went. It is with good reason that anti-Semitism is called "the oldest hatred."

Moreover, not only have Jews always been singled out for abuse, but the most devastating mistreatments came to them at the hands of the most developed and "civilized" nations. Egypt, Babylon, Rome, Spain, and Germany were the most scientifically, culturally, and, for the most part, economically advanced nations of their time. Yet, the most painful adversities came to the Jews specifically at their hands. The fact that today's America is the leader of the developed world in almost every aspect should certainly make us, at the very least, vigilant with regard to the Jews, as far as the sociopolitical processes that are unfolding in what is supposedly "the land of the free."

There is more to be concerned about: Today's anti-Semitism is hitting Jews from all directions, from every circle in the social and political arena, and in every country around the world. In America, today's alt-right and the anti-Semites that emerge from there should get our full attention. Since the October 2018 massacre at the Tree of Life synagogue in Pittsburgh, it has become clear that White Supremacists and neo-Nazis in America can easily become genocidal. If one of them becomes president, who knows what might ensue. At the same time, the 20th century had proven that the Left is also not immune to anti-Semitism, and of the worst kind. Joseph Stalin and Adolf Hitler both emerged from the Left, yet harbored profoundly anti-Semitic feelings and acted on them in the most demonic manner.

The bottom line is that when Jew-hatred emerges, it will cloak itself in any ideology or pretext to express itself. Today, when it is reemerging after a hiatus that lasted through the second half of the 20th century, we should take its reemergence very, very seriously.

Before the turn of the century, Harvard Law Professor Emeritus Alan Dershowitz was certain that we had reached "the end of institutional anti-Semitism, the end of Jewish persecution, and the end of Jewish victimization."[3] He stated that those who do not see "the reality of declining anti-Semitism" are suffering from "a perception gap."[4] These days, it seems that Mr. Dershowitz sees a very different picture. On April 24, 2019, for instance, he published an op-ed in The Hill where he decried the "increasing tolerance … of anti-Semitic tropes, images, and stereotypes."[5] The bottom line is that today, American Jews must open their eyes to the growing anti-Semitism all over the country, and not focus solely on one side of the political map or on one segment of American society.

The situation is not beyond repair, yet, but it is quickly getting there. If, for example, the economy takes a sharp turn for the worse, who knows what it might set off toward the Jews. We have already seen how leaders readily make Jews their scapegoats when matters turn for the worse. What guarantee do we have that an American president, Democratic or Republican, will not do the same?

From the Right and from the Left, the Jews are in the crosshairs of both. As I see it, the reactionary motion has already started. The regression is here, but it has not taken over, yet. There is a rapidly closing window of opportunity for the Jews to reverse the trend, but time is running out.

I know that my warnings are unpleasant, and I expect them to stir anger and reproof. I expect people to deride, belittle, and scorn me for my predictions. But I admit, I care too much about my people and I worry too much to mince words. It is my hope that after reading this book, you, too, will be convinced that my concern has merit, and that the time to act in unison, above all our many differences, is now.

Chapter 1: Who Are The Jews

&

Why Is There Jew-Hatred

"...If statistics are right, the Jews constitute but one percent of the human race. It suggests a nebulous dim puff of stardust lost in the blaze of the Milky Way. Properly, the Jew ought hardly to be heard of, but he is heard of, has always been heard of. ...The Egyptian, the Babylonian, and the Persian rose, filled the planet with sound and splendor, then faded to dream stuff and passed away. The Greek and the Roman followed and made a vast noise, and they are gone. Other people have sprung up and held their torch high for a time, but it burned out and they sit in twilight now, or have vanished. The Jew saw them all, beat them all, and is now what he always was. ...All things are mortal but the Jew; all other forces pass, but he remains. What is the secret of his immortality?"

Mark Twain, "Concerning the Jews"[6]

No Smoke without a Fire

Ever since they first appeared, the Hebrews, who were subsequently referred to as Israelites, and finally as Jews, have been singled out, for the most part for condemnation. In the wake of the massacre at the Tree of Life synagogue in Pittsburgh on October 27, 2018, the editorial board at *The Wall Street Journal* dedicated an article to "the oldest hatred," namely anti-Semitism. The article stated that the murders were "an awful reminder that there are human hatreds far more virulent and ancient than those that animate our current political divisions. ...This irrational hatred," asserted the writer, "is one of humanity's oldest and manifests itself in murder almost daily in the Middle East. Jews are killed simply because they are Jews, as they have been throughout history. This is why millions have sought refuge in a Jewish state, Israel, and also in the religious protections embedded in the Constitution of the United States."[7]

Jew-hatred is irrational. There are as many reasons for hating Jews as there are people. Everything that upsets, offends, hurts, or otherwise displeases people, they often attribute to the Jews. Jews have suffered from blood libels such as baking matzahs, the Passover bread, with the blood of Christian children. They have been accused of poisoning wells, dominating the slave trade from Africa to America, and disloyalty to the countries where they live.

More recently, they have been accused of manipulating the media to serve their needs. Modernity has also created a new kind of blood libel, accusing Jews of organ harvesting[8] and of spreading AIDS.[9]

Moreover, Jews are often accused of conflicting "crimes." Communists accused them of creating capitalism; capitalists accused them of inventing communism. Christians accused Jews of killing Jesus, and the French philosopher François Voltaire accused them of inventing[10] and spreading[11] Christianity. In short, any view that people disagree with, they blame its invention on the Jews. And as if all this is not enough, the Jews have also been labeled as warmongers and as cowards, racists and cosmopolitans, spineless and unbending, and so on and so forth ad infinitum.

Yet, the fact that anti-Semitism is irrational does not mean that it is without reason, a root that causes it. In fact, thinking that there is no reason for anti-Semitism is just as irrational as anti-Semitism itself. Just as there is no smoke without a fire, nothing can happen without something that causes it, and in the case of Jew-hatred, fuels the fire for millennia. Therefore, since there is clearly a cause, we should find it, treat it if we can, and cure it before flames burst once again and land another blow on our people.

To find the reason for anti-Semitism and its cure, we should look into the past, to the onset of our nation and the subsequent hatred thereof. When we understand how, and mainly why the Jewish people was founded and became a nation, we will also see why there is hatred of Jews and how we can mend it.

The Harbinger from Babylon

The Jewish nation did not begin in the land of Israel; it began in the cradle of modern civilization: Mesopotamia, otherwise known as "the land between two rivers." Mesopotamia was a vast and fertile land between the Tigris and Euphrates rivers, in today's Iraq. It was the birthplace of numerous inventions that enabled human civilization to develop. There was the invention of the wheel, the first cultivation of cereal crops, which are still the world's staple foods, and the development of mathematics and astronomy. And there was also the birthplace of a man named Abraham, who became the father of three faiths: Judaism, Christianity, and Islam.

Babylon, a kingdom at the heart of the dynamic Mesopotamian civilization, was a melting pot, an ideal substrate on which myriad belief systems and teachings grew and flourished. The Babylonians did not have a uniform belief system; they were very pluralistic in that sense. Abraham, the son of a statue builder and an idol-worshipping spiritual leader, was born in Harran, one of the major cities in the Babylonian Empire. *Sefer HaYashar* [*The Book of the Upright One*] describes the life of the Babylonians at the time, how they worshipped, and the high position of Abraham's family within that spiritual landscape: "All the people of the land made each his own god—gods of wood and stone. They worshipped them, and they became gods to them. In those days, the king and all his servants, and Terah [Abraham's father] and his entire household, were the first

19

among the worshippers of wood and stone. ... [Terah] would worship them and bow to them, and so did the whole of that generation."[12]

But Terah's son, Abraham, who then still went by the name Abram, possessed a unique trait that differentiated him from the rest of the band: He was unusually perceptive, with a zeal for the truth. Abraham was also a caring person, who noticed that his countryfolk were becoming increasingly unhappy. When he reflected on his observation, he found that the cause of their unhappiness was their growing egoism. They were becoming increasingly alienated from each other. Within a relatively short period of time, the Babylonians had gone from a prevailing sense of kinship, which the book of Genesis (11:1) describes as being "Of one language and of one speech," into vanity and alienation. From being simple-folk, happy with their lot, the Babylonians became greedy and self-centered, saying "Come, let us build us a city and a tower with its top in heaven, and let us make us a name" (Genesis 11:4).

In addition to acknowledging his people's egoism, Abraham realized that life is governed not by egoism, but by union and harmony. He discovered that there is a single force that manifests in two opposite ways: egoism and altruism, giving and receiving. The interaction between the two forces is what creates all of reality.

The Chinese call these two forces "yin and yang," and likewise, science teaches us that atoms are unstable in the absence of balance between negative-charged particles (electrons) and positive-charged particles (protons). Abraham discovered these two forces, too, but as said above, he also observed that they both stem from one, uniform root force, which then splits in two—the force of giving (positive) and the force of receiving (negative).

Human self-centeredness is a manifestation of the negative force, the force of reception, egoism. In Abraham's time, that force intensified in Babylon to the point where it dominated the positive force, the force of giving, altruism. As a result, the Babylonian society began to disintegrate as the alienation among its people increased and they grew further apart from one another. That was the reason for the vanity that had made them build the tower. But more importantly, that was the reason for their unhappiness: self-centeredness had driven them apart.[13]

In Abraham's days, his discovery that the Babylonians' egos were growing out of balance was too hard for them to swallow since it meant that they had to somehow reign in their egos or their society would tilt over and collapse. Regrettably, the Babylonians were too immersed in themselves; they could not stop the intensification of their egos, and their society was crumbling.

Abraham called his newly discovered uniform root force of nature by the name "God" or *Boreh* [Creator], from the words *Bo* [come] and *Re'eh* [see], since we come and see for ourselves how this force works.[14] In Hebrew, identicalness of meaning is reflected in the fact that the words "God" and "the nature" have the same numerical value [*Gematria*]. In other words, they are synonymous and interchangeable. The great 20th century kabbalist and thinker Rav Yehuda Leib HaLevi Ashlag, who predicted the approaching calamity of the Holocaust, placed a strong emphasis on this point in his essay, "The Peace." According to Ashlag, "It is best for us to accept … that *HaTeva* [Hebrew: the nature] has the same numerical value [in Hebrew] as *Elo-him* [God]—eighty-six. Then, I will be able to call the laws of God 'nature's commandments,' or vice-versa … for they are one and the same."[15]

Renowned 12th century scholar Maimonides describes in his momentous composition *Mishneh Torah* (*Repetition* [or *Learning*] *of the Torah*) Abraham's desperate search for answers: "Ever since this firm one was weaned, he began to wonder. ...He began to ponder day and night, and he wondered how it was possible for this wheel to always turn without a driver? Who is turning it, for it cannot turn itself? And he had neither a teacher nor a tutor. Instead, he was wedged in Ur of the Chaldeans among illiterate idol worshippers, with his mother and father, and all the people worshipping stars, and he—worshipping with them."[16]

After many days of searching, Abraham's quest succeeded and he discovered the Creator, the united source of both good and bad, giving and receiving, which creates, sustains, and drives all of reality toward its goal through homeostasis, namely balance and harmony. In Maimonides's words, "[Abraham] attained the path of truth ... with his own correct wisdom, and knew that there is one God [or Nature] there who leads... that He has created everything, and that in all that there is, there is no other God but Him."[17]

As soon as Abraham realized that his people's problem was the absence of balance between giving and receiving, he started to tell them about it. Yet, his efforts were met with ridicule and disbelief. The book *Pirkei de Rabbi Eliezer* (*Chapters of Rabbi Eliezer*), one of the most prominent *Midrashim* (commentaries) on the Torah (Pentateuch), offers a vivid description of the Babylonians' vanity: "Nimrod [king of Babylon] said to his people, 'Let us build us a great city and dwell in it, lest we are scattered across the earth ... and let us build a great tower within it, rising toward the heaven ... and let us make us a great name in the land.'"

But more important than their vanity, the commentary offers a glimpse into the Babylonians' alienation from each other: "They built it high ... [and] if a person fell and died, they would not mind him. But if a brick fell, they would sit and weep and say, 'When will another come up in its stead.'"[18]

Being a caring person, the attitude of Abraham's Babylonian contemporaries toward each other troubled him, and he would come to the construction site to observe the builders' conduct. *Pirkei de Rabbi Eliezer* continues to describe Abraham's observations of people's animosity toward each other: "Abraham, son of Terah, went by and saw them building the city and the tower." He tried to speak to them and tell them about the need to connect in order to balance their self-centeredness, "But they loathed his words," says the book. Yet, when "They wished to speak each other's language," as before, when they were still of one language, "they did not know each other's language. What did they do?" asks the book, "They each took his sword and fought one another to death. Indeed," concludes the book and describes the inevitable bloody outcome, "half the world died there by the sword."[19]

Seeing this, Abraham could not stay aloof. He tried as hard as he could to tell the Babylonians what was setting them up against each other. The 18th century book *Kol Mevaser* describes Abraham's efforts and the hostility he suffered for it in return: "We must not think that Abraham was as today's [Jewish orthodox] rabbis, sitting at home and the followers come to their homes. He, instead, would go outside and call out loud that there is one Creator to the world. ... To the people, he seemed as though he were insane, and children and grownups would hurl stones at him. Yet, Abraham did not mind any of it and kept on calling."[20]

The celebrated writer Thomas Cahill eloquently described Abraham's tenacity in speaking his truth in the face of resistance. As part of Cahill's acclaimed "Hinges of History" book series, he wrote *The Gifts of the Jews*, focusing on the contribution of Judaism and Jews to humankind as he saw it. Below he offers an intriguing perspective into Abraham's efforts: "If we had lived in the second millennium BC, the millennium of Abraham, and could have canvassed all the nations of the earth, what would they have said of Abraham's journey? In most of Africa and Europe, they would have laughed at Abraham's madness and pointed to the heavens, where the life of earth had been plotted from all eternity ... a man cannot escape his fate. The Egyptians would have shaken their heads in disbelief. The early Greeks might have told Abraham the story of Prometheus ... Do not overreach, they would advise; come to resignation. In India, he would be told that time is black, irrational and merciless. Do not set yourself the task of accomplishing something in time, which is only the dominion of suffering. On every continent, in every society, Abraham would have been given the same advice that wise men as diverse as Heraclitus, Lao-Tsu and Siddhartha would one day give their followers: do not journey but sit; compose yourself by the river of life, meditate on its ceaseless and meaningless flow."[21] Clearly, had Abraham heeded any such counsels, or had he been silenced by the stones hurled at him, human history would have been very different.

A Nation Is Born

"At forty years of age," writes Maimonides, Abraham "began to provide answers to the people of Ur of the Chaldeans, to converse with them and to tell them that the path on which they were walking was not the path of truth."[22] Perhaps unintentionally, Abraham's explanations began to build a new nation.

Yet, the beginning, as are most beginnings, was very tough, as even his own father, Terah, resisted him. *Midrash Rabbah*, a commentary written in the 5th century CE, offers an amusing glimpse into the hardships that Abraham had suffered for his discovery and his dedication to the truth, as well as to his fiery personality. "Terah [Abraham's father] was an idol worshipper [who made his living building and selling statues at the family shop]. Once, he went to a certain place and told Abraham to sit in for him. A man walked in and wished to buy a statue. [Abraham] asked him, 'How old are you?' And the man replied, 'Fifty or sixty.' Abraham told him: 'Woe unto he who is sixty yet must worship a day-old statue.' Shamefaced, the man left. Another time, a woman came in holding a bowl of semolina. She told him, 'Here, offer it to the statues.' Abraham arose, took a hammer, shattered all the statues, and then placed the hammer in the hands of the biggest one. When his father returned, he asked him, 'Who did this to them?' [Abraham] replied, 'A woman came in. She brought them a bowl of semolina and asked me to offer it to them. I offered, and one said, 'I will eat first,' then another said, 'I will eat first.' The bigger one arose, took the hammer, and broke them.' His father said, 'Are you fooling me? What do they know?' And Abraham replied, 'Are your ears hearing what your own mouth is saying?'"[23]

Abraham was invincible at arguments, but he could not stand against the Babylonian ruler. As his teaching became known, he was expelled from Babylon and left for the land of Canaan. Yet, being exiled from Babylon did not stop him from circulating his discovery.

Maimonides's elaborate descriptions tell us, "He began to call out to the whole world ... He called out, wandering from town to town and from kingdom to kingdom until he arrived in the land of Canaan ... When they [people in the places where he wandered] gathered around him and asked him about his words, he taught everyone ... until he brought them to the path of truth. Finally, thousands and tens of thousands assembled around him, and they are the people of the house of Abraham. He planted this tenet in their hearts, composed books about it, and taught his son, Isaac. And Isaac sat and taught and warned, and informed Jacob, and appointed him a teacher, to sit and teach ... And Jacob ... taught all his sons. He separated Levi and appointed him the head."[24]

To guarantee that the teachings would continue through the ages, Jacob "commanded his sons not to stop appointing appointee after appointee from among the sons of Levi, so the knowledge would not be forgotten. The lineage continued and expanded in the children of Jacob and in those accompanying them."[25]

The astounding result of Abraham's efforts was the birth of a nation that knew the deepest laws of life, or in the words of Maimonides, "A nation that knows the Lord was made in the world."[26]

Indeed, Israel is not really a name of a people. In Hebrew, the word *Ysrael* (Israel) is a combination of two words: *Yashar* (straight) and *El* (God). In other words, Israel designates a *mindset* of wanting to discover the united root, the force of life; it is a desire to attain, or perceive the Creator. Rabbi Meir Ben Gabai said about it, "In the meaning of the name 'Israel' there is also *Yashar El*."[27] Likewise, the great Ramchal wrote succinctly, "Israel—*Yashar El*." Put differently, more than a name, "Israel" designates a state of being, the direction of the desire that drove Abraham to his discoveries.

Genetically, the first Israelites were either Babylonians or members of other nations who joined Abraham's group. The meaning of their name was clear to the ancient Israelites. As Maimonides wrote, they had their teachers, the Levites, and they were taught to follow life's essential law of balance between giving and receiving, between egoism and uniting above it. Thus, the Israeli nation was established.

The Root of Anti-Semitism

Abraham's struggle to install the principle of balance was more than an attempt to save his hometown community. Abraham discovered that the egoism in humanity was an ever-growing beast, and without a working method to contain it, it would destroy everything. In the quote at the beginning of this chapter, Mark Twain mentions some of the greatest empires in history and asks how come they all declined and vanished into "dream stuff" while the Jews did not. The answer to his question is simple: Other nations succumbed to their growing egoism, which eventually disintegrated their societies and caused their downfall.

The Hebrew kings of the past and Jewish sages throughout the ages stressed the principle of fostering unity above the growing ego. They knew it was a process and not a one-time solution that would make everyone live happily ever after. King Solomon wrote in Proverbs (10:12): "Hate stirs up strife, and love will cover all crimes." The Midrash, written many centuries later, stressed, "One does not leave the world with half of one's wishes in one's hand, for one who has one hundred wants two hundred; one who has two hundred wants four hundred."[28] In the 19th century, Nathan Sternhartz, a disciple of Rabbi Nachman of Breslov, compiled the book *Likutey Halachot* (*Assorted Rules*), which his teacher had instructed. Consistent with the principle of matching hatred with love of others in order to maintain balance, Sternhartz wrote, "The vitality is mainly through unity, by all the changes being included in the source of the unity. For this reason, 'Love your neighbor as yourself' is the great rule of the Torah, to include in unity and peace. The vitality, sustenance, and correction of the whole of creation are mainly by people of different views becoming included together in love, unity, and peace."[29] In other words, we must not only cover our hatred with love, but rather keep doing so persistently. Because our egoism grows, so must our unity. Otherwise, we will disperse and dissolve just as every other nation has throughout history.

When Abraham first introduced his paradigm to the Babylonians, the bulk of them naturally rejected it and hated him for suggesting that they must rise above their egos. They rightly felt it was unnatural for people to unite above their separation. Nevertheless, Abraham was adamant that if they did not do this, their society would crumble.

The chasm that was opened then between Abraham, his students, and the rest of the Babylonians, is still open today; it is the root of this irrational hatred we call "anti-Semitism." Although for the most part, people do not know why they hate Jews, whether consciously or not, they feel that the Jews symbolize both something that they ought to do, namely to unite above their egos, and that the Jews are meant to be an exemplary nation that lives out that unity and thereby sets a role model.

At the foot of Mt. Sinai, when Moses united the fugitives from Egypt and they accepted the law we call "Torah" (which in Hebrew means "law" or "instruction"), they accepted it only because they complied with the condition to be "as one man with one heart."[30] Subsequently, they were declared a nation and were given the task to be "a light unto nations."[31] The "light" that the Jews were meant to bring was not some celestial aura, but rather the law of unity that Abraham discovered and which they, at the foot of Mt. Sinai, had committed to implement in their society. It was an approach to life that enables human beings to rise above their egos and create a balanced, thriving society that lives in homeostasis.

Ever since the Jews were given that task, hatred toward them grew when they were not united and were therefore not "a light unto nations," and diminished, or even disappeared when they conducted their relationships with one another positively, and thereby set an example that others would want to emulate.

A Radical Idea that to Our Ancestors Was a Given

Today it sounds like a radical suggestion to say that hatred for Jews depends on the Jews' own level of unity or disunity, on their level of compliance with the requirement to be "as one man with one heart." But to our sages throughout the ages, this concept was a given.

Midrash Tanah De Bei Eliyahu, an ancient commentary on the Torah, writes, "The Lord said to them, to Israel: 'My sons, have I lacked anything that I should ask of you? And what do I ask of you? Only that you love one another, respect one another, and fear one another, and that there will be no transgression, theft, and ugliness among you.'"[32]

Another seminal commentary that stresses the importance of unity among Jews as a means to avert adversity is *Midrash Tanhuma*, written in the 9th century CE. "If a person takes a bundle of reeds," the commentary explains, "he cannot break them all at once. But if he takes one at a time, even an infant breaks them. Likewise, Israel will not be redeemed until they are all one bundle."[33]

In the 18th century, Rabbi Kalonymus Kalman Halevi Epstein wrote one of the seminal books of the *Hassidut* movement, which spread through most of Eastern Europe. His book *Maor VaShemesh* [*Light and Sun*] stresses the vitality of unity for the Jews: "'That He may establish you today as His people' means that by this you will have revival; you will be saved from all calamities," he begins. "Afterwards, He [the Creator] said to them [Israel], 'Not with you alone am I making this covenant,' meaning that being saved from any harm by bonding was not promised only to Moses's generation. Rather, 'But with those who stand here with us today ... and with those who are not with us here today,' meaning that all future generations have been promised it—to pass through all the bludgeons of the covenant, and that through the unity and bonding that will be among them, they would not be harmed."[34]

In the following century, Rav Yitzhak Eliyahu Landau explicitly addressed the link between Jewish unity and what happens as a result of its absence. In his commentary on the Talmud, he wrote,

"Thus would Rabbi Eleazar ha-Kappar say, 'Love peace, and loathe division. Great is the peace, for even when Israel practice idol-worship and there is peace among them, the Creator says, 'I wish not to touch [harm] them,' as it is written (Hosea 4:17), 'Ephraim is joined to idols; let him alone.' If there is division among them, what is it said about them (Hosea 10:2)? 'Their heart is divided; now they will bear their guilt.'"[35]

And in the 20th century, the previously-mentioned Rav Yehuda Ashlag stressed the practical benefits of implementing unity in our lives: "The matter of social unity, which can be the source of every joy and success, applies particularly among bodies and bodily matters in people, and the separation between them is the source of every calamity and misfortune."[36]

Non-Jews Who Sense the Meaning of Jewishness

As the examples just shown testify, throughout the generations, our sages and leaders have written tirelessly about the need for unity as a means to keep us safe. They also wrote about how only when we are united can we be "a light unto nations." But not only Jews knew and wrote about the unique quality of our people and our task to be role models. In some cases, it came from our most ardent haters; in other cases, it came from "mere gentiles." It is said that we Jews are a stiff-necked people. Admittedly, we are. We also tend not to listen when fellow Jews talk to us about unity. But perhaps if we hear about it from the very ones who are meant to be our enemies, our ears and hearts will open to the calling.

Probably the most infamous anti-Semite in American history was industrialist and car maker Henry Ford. In his infamous composition, *The International Jew -- The World's Foremost Problem*, Ford interlaced some very curious statements that do not sound as though they came from the mind of a Jew-hater. "The whole prophetic purpose, with reference to [the people of] Israel, seems to have been the moral enlightenment of the world through its agency," he wrote in one place.[37]

Ford writes several other statements in a similar spirit about the expectation of the world from the Jews to be the agents of a positive change, but the answer as to what positive change he has in mind is found almost at the very beginning of the book. "Modern reformers, who are constructing model social systems on paper, would do well to look into the social system under which the early Jews were organized," he asserts,[38] certainly not the statement one would expect from an anti-Semite.

Not only Ford had a conscious demand from the Jews. Other anti-Semites were also keenly aware of what it was they wanted to see from the Jews. Ukraine born Vasily Shulgin was a senior member of the Duma, the Russian Parliament, before the 1917 Bolshevik Revolution. Openly and proudly, he proclaimed himself an anti-Semite, and often reiterated that statement. In his book, *What We Don't Like About Them...*, he analyzes over many essays his perception of the Jews and what he thinks they are doing wrong. Shulgin complains that "Jews in the 20th century have become very smart, effective, and vigorous at exploiting other people's ideas. However," he protests, "this is not an occupation for 'teachers and prophets,' not the role of 'guides of the blind,' not the role of 'carriers of the lame.'"[39] If this apparent contrast between hating Jews and seeing them as a people obliged to guide the blind, namely the rest of humanity, Shulgin's frequent repetition of this demand proves it is not a slip of the pen, but his genuine view. In another essay, Shulgin becomes almost poetic as he describes where the Jews can lead humanity if they only rise to the challenge: "Let them ... rise to the height to which they apparently climbed [in antiquity] ... and immediately, all nations will rush to their feet. They will rush not by virtue of compulsion ... but by free will, joyful in spirit, grateful and loving, including the Russians! We ourselves will request, 'Give us Jewish rule, wise, benevolent, leading us to the Good.' And every day we will offer the prayers for them, for the Jews: 'Bless our guides and our teachers, who lead us to the recognition of Your goodness.'"[40]

An intriguing perspective comes from a more contemporary anti-Semite: The French publisher, author, journalist, and film maker, Alain Soral is such a rabid anti-Semite. He has been tried and convicted of anti-Semitic slurs numerous times, but the fines he is repeatedly sentenced to pay seem to have no effect on his tirades. In an interview he gave on October 17, 2014, right before he entered yet another court hearing, the interviewer asked him: "What is a Jew? What does it mean to be Jewish?" Soral replied that Jews are "a people of priests, an elite, pioneers in morals and ethics." "However," he added, "there is a deviation that has become the majority. ... [The Jews] consider themselves a separate people, a state within a state." Finally, Soral speaks of the Jewish community: "I'm just showing the danger of the deviation of the community ... [and he warns] In the end, the wheel will turn against those who manipulate."[41]

Another contemporary example is the Neo-Nazi George Lincoln Rockwell. In his book *White Power*, an appalling composition, Rockwell nonetheless makes some very interesting observations regarding the Jews, and not necessarily negative ones. When he writes about unity among the Jews, he states, "In fact, the group loyalty of these Jews is perhaps the most fantastic in the history of the world. It has propelled them into near mastery of the entire world— not because they are braver, work harder, are more intelligent, or more worthy than the rest of us—but because they observe the basic laws of Nature and maintain group loyalty. While all the rest of us have fallen for their rotten 'one world,' 'we-are-all-brothers' garbage, which disintegrates our Society, the Jews maintain their society with a group loyalty such as history has never before seen, and thus they go from one triumph to another."[42] If we could use this enviable trait to the benefit of all of humanity, if we could demonstrate it in a way that everyone could emulate instead of falling for the "garbage" that Rockwell writes about, there would be no anti-Semitism to speak of; there would simply be no reason for anyone to hate Jews since people would know how to unite, and united people do not hate each other or their teachers, as Shulgin writes.

Other non-Jews, who were not necessarily anti-Semites, were also keenly aware of the role they believed the Jews were meant to play with regard to humanity. One such example is acclaimed historian

Paul Johnson, who wrote in his comprehensive composition *A History of the Jews*, "At a very early stage in their collective existence they [Jews] believed they had detected a divine scheme for the human race, of which their own society was to be a pilot."[43]

The chapters that follow will detail the Jewish struggle to maintain unity and the link we tend to overlook between our unity and our security and happiness.

Chapter 2: Self-Hatred in Antiquity

If we examine the most traumatic events in our nation's history, a disturbing recurrence emerges out of the anguish: When we hate one another, others hate us even more and eventually punish us. In the coming chapters, we will look at our nation's most harrowing tragedies and point out a common process that unfolded prior to the eruption of each calamity. Since this process is common to our nation's most traumatic episodes, if we learn how to detect it, we will be able to provide an antidote in time and prevent its recurrence in the future.

A Word about Assimilation

History shows that preceding every major crisis, there is a period where our nation becomes increasingly disunited as its members grow disenchanted with each other. In the coming chapters, I will review the generations of the Jewish nation from Egypt to the ruin of the Second Temple. As you will see, our tendency to be self-injurious has deep roots in our past.

But before we dive into the chronicles of our people, we need to understand a conspicuous phenomenon that is at the center of every adversity we have experienced throughout the generations:

assimilation. It is important to note that when ancient scriptures or historians describe a process of assimilation, it is almost invariably a symptom of declining social unity, and this fragmentation is the issue I want to address.

As mentioned earlier, when the ancient Hebrews became a nation, they were required to meet one, singular requirement: to unite "as one man with one heart."[44] Therefore, breaking away from Judaism meant first and foremost departure from this law of union above all. This is why when Rabbi Akiva, whose disciples gave us the Mishnah and *The Book of Zohar*, tried to save Jerusalem from a second ruin, he asserted, "Love your neighbor as yourself, this is the great rule of the Torah."[45]

It is no coincidence that when talking about rules, Rabbi Nathan Sternhartz, the prime disciple and scribe of Rabbi Nachman of Breslov, writes, "'Love your neighbor as yourself' is the great rule of the Torah, to include in unity and peace, which are the heart of the vitality, persistence, and correction of the whole of creation, when people of differing views are included together in love, unity, and peace."[46]

Therefore, since antiquity, and as we will see, to this day, assimilation has indicated divergence from the law of unity that had shaped us into a nation. This departure from unity is at the heart of the problem, and not one's level of strictness in observance of customs, as my teacher Rav Baruch Shalom Ashlag (RABASH) would refer to the physical commandments.

Egypt—The Tale and Toll of Brotherly Hate

The story of our exile in Egypt could hardly be more dramatic: It begins with intense hatred among brothers, continues with reconciliation and prosperity, collapses into separation and crisis, and ends in unity and a miraculous escape. And the prize for our restored union: the "official" formation of the Jewish people, along with the duty, or better put, onus, to be "a light unto nations."[47]

The seeds of the exile in Egypt were sown long before Jacob's family arrived in Egypt. It started with the hatred of Jacob's sons to their youngest brother, Joseph. The book of Genesis is quite descriptive in detailing how the brothers contrived to kill Joseph, who they scornfully referred to as "that dreamer" (Genesis 37:19).

Although the brothers eventually decide to "mitigate" their crime, avoid slaying Joseph and "settle" for dumping him in a pit, the Talmud (*Shabbat* 10b) explains that their hatred for Joseph is the reason why the children of Israel went into exile in Egypt. It writes that the brothers envied Joseph for being Jacob's favorite son and for giving him the striped shirt. Their spite was so intense that they wanted to kill him. And they would have, had it not been for the intervention of Reuben, Jacob's eldest son. This is why instead of killing Joseph, the brothers decided to throw him in the dry pit, and subsequently sold him as a slave to a caravan of Ishmaelites heading for Egypt (Genesis 37:18-28).

The correction comes through Joseph's forgiveness. Although he was now the viceroy in Egypt, and Pharaoh "took off his signet ring from his hand and put it on Joseph's hand" (Genesis 41:42), Joseph was not at all vindictive toward his brothers. Instead, he showed them nothing but compassion, love, and generosity. When they came to Egypt looking for relief from the hunger they had suffered from in Canaan, he cleverly made them bring Jacob, his father, down to Egypt, and then lavished them with the most fertile land in Egypt, the land of Goshen (Genesis 45:9-11), where they lived in prosperity for the rest of Joseph's life. In this way, he formed the union of his brothers under him, as he foresaw in his dream, which, at the time, intensified their hatred of him to the point that they wanted to take his life.[48]

Under Joseph's rule, the Israelites were united and successful. But once he died, they began to disperse and wanted to mingle with the Egyptians. "The Israelites began to conceal their Jewishness," writes Prof. Zvi Shimon of Bar-Ilan University in Israel. "They were immersed in Egyptian culture, enthusiastically attending Egyptian cultural events and adopting their modes of entertainment. Egyptian sports and theater were popular pastimes amongst the new Jewish immigrants."[49] Remember that description of assimilation as separation from unity because throughout our people's history, whenever disunity grows among us, the adoption of local culture will be the first, and one of its most conspicuous signs. While there is no harm in fun and games, when it expresses disintegration, it means we are losing the basis of our peoplehood. And because of our unique task—to present unity to the world— our separation always brings about hatred toward us.

Accordingly, and much to the Israelites' regret, the more they wanted to assimilate in Egypt, the more Pharaoh and all of Egypt turned against them. *The Book of Zohar* (*Shemot*) asks, "Why were Israel exiled, and why specifically to Egypt?" The answer that *The Zohar* gives is that "[the Creator] exiled them to Egypt, who were proud and despised and loathed Israel,"[50] and therefore did not want the Hebrews to mingle with them. The *Midrash* adds a more explicit version of the story, pointing the finger directly at assimilation: "When Joseph died, they broke the covenant and said, 'Let us be as the Egyptians.' ...Because of it, the Lord turned the love that the Egyptians loved them into hatred."[51] We tend to think of the Egyptians merely as the enemies of Israel, but this perception overlooks the beginning of Israel's stay in Egypt, when Joseph was Pharaoh's viceroy, and Jacob blessed Pharaoh, who gladly supported Joseph's decision to grant Israel the most fertile stretch of land in Egypt.

Nevertheless, the people of Israel remained fragmented until the arrival of one of the most seminal figures in world history: Moses. When he arrived, he began to reunite Israel under his leadership until, eventually, they were able to escape from Pharaoh's rule, who following Israel's disintegration as a nation, turned against them.

In the desert, at the foot of Mt. Sinai, the people of Israel solidified their unity to the point that they became as one. This is why the great 11th century commentator RASHI described them as being "as one man with one heart." That level of unity was the requirement for the aggregate of strangers who subscribed to Abraham's message to be "officially" declared a nation. There, at the foot of the mountain, was the "official" birth of the nation of Israel. Henceforth, our fate would depend on our unity. The example of disunity and enslavement vs. unity and redemption that the Israelites had experienced in Egypt was to be a lesson for them to maintain their unity no matter how intense their egoism grows. As we will see below, the linkage between disunity and adversity has not been broken since. Regrettably, nor has the lesson been learned.

With Swords in Their Tongues:
The Rise and Ruin of the First Temple

It is hardly a secret that the Jewish ego is well developed. Some will say it is too developed, but there are benefits to having a big ego, provided it is used correctly. Be that as it may, vowing to unite "as one man with one heart" is one thing; living out that vow is a very different story. It is the ultimate test to human nature, and although the ancient Hebrews were bold enough to take on the challenge, they failed left and right.

Yet, as *The Zohar* writes about our forefathers' struggles, "Anyone who wages a war in the Torah is rewarded with increased peace in the end."[52] In other words, the wars that the people of Israel fought, among themselves and against others, were over keeping the vow of complete unity. The Temple that Solomon built in Jerusalem, which we now recognize as "The First Temple," symbolizes the highest level of unity within the people of Israel.

But "The decay set in rapidly after the conquest of Joshua," writes the above-mentioned historian Paul Johnson.[53] "It again appeared under Solomon, and was repeated in both northern and southern kingdoms [Israel and Judea, respectively], especially under rich and powerful kings and when times were good."[54]

In other words, even at times of peace and abundance, there were constant strife and division, which eventually led to the ruin of the Temple. First, the nation divided into two kingdoms: Israel and Judea.

Israel abandoned their vow of unity and mingled heavily—especially the leaders—with the neighboring nations. The Talmud describes the leaders' malevolence toward each other very poignantly: "Rabbi Elazar said, 'Those people, who eat and drink with one another, stab each other with the swords in their tongues.' Thus, even though they were close to one another, they were filled with hatred for each other."[55] However, the Talmud emphasizes that "the hatred was only among the leaders of the nation, while the majority of Israel did not hate one another."[56]

The absolute hatred was to come in the Second Temple, and its horrific consequences would become a symbol of the cost of internal hatred. But even the level of separation and hatred of the ancient Israelites toward their brethren in Judea that appeared during the First Temple was enough to lead to their complete disappearance. Indeed, all ten tribes that were part of the kingdom of Israel are lost today, as is the kingdom they had built. The Jews of today are the descendants of the Hebrews who occupied the kingdom of Judea, which was but a fraction of the original people of Israel.

Meanwhile, in Judea, our forefathers did not behave much better than their now vanished siblings. The 1st century Jewish-turned-Roman historian Titus Flavius Josephus, in his meticulous style, details the misconducts of our forefathers. While the list of misdeeds is far too long for the scope of this book, it is important to realize how brutal was the hatred of the Judeans for their brethren. In *The Antiquities of the Jews*, Josephus offers some gruesome details on the foul manner with which (especially) the kings of Israel treated one another. When, for instance, Josephus writes about the anointing of King Jehoram, who ruled merely seventy years after King Solomon, who taught that "Hate stirs strife, and love will cover all crimes" (Proverbs 10:12), he says that "As soon as he had taken the government upon him, [Jehoram] betook himself to the slaughter of his brethren and his father's friends, who were governors under him, and thence made a beginning and a demonstration of his wickedness."[57] Jehoram's fate, by the way, was no better than that of his victims. He, too, was overthrown by Jehu, who "drew his bow and smote him" in the back, "the arrow going through his heart so Jehoram fell down immediately … and gave up the ghost," details Josephus.[58]

From here, matters only go downhill. When Josephus describes the atrocities that King Manasseh, son of Hezekiah, perpetrated against his own fold, he writes, "He barbarously slew all the righteous men that were among the Hebrews. Nor would he spare the prophets, for he every day slew some of them, till Jerusalem was overflown with blood."[59]

Clearly, this demeanor was not sustainable. It did take a couple more centuries of depravity for the system to finally collapse, but in the end, matters plunged to the point where calamity was clearly on the horizon. Realizing doom was nearing, King Josiah sent the High Priest Eliakim to prophetess Deborah to ask if there was anything that they could do to avert the blow. But, as Josephus reports, "When the prophetess had heard this from the messengers that were sent to her by the king, she bid them to go back to the king and say that 'God had already given sentence against them to destroy the people and cast them out of their country, and deprive them of all the happiness they enjoyed.'" Once again, internal hatred had inflicted a catastrophe on Israel, and the people were exiled to Babylon.

From Near Annihilation to Total Exhilaration: The Exile in Babylon

The ruin of the First Temple and the resultant exile were a sad chapter in our history, one of many more to come. Of the twelve tribes that formed the people of Israel that marched into the land of Israel, only the tribes of Judah, Levi, and part of Benjamin returned after the exile.

But the strength of the Jewish people was never measured by their number, but by their unity. The exile in Babylon lasted just as long as the Jews remained apart. The story of Esther tells us how that exile was to be overcome. First, the arch-anti-Semite Haman said to King Ahasuerus that the Jews were separated: "There is a certain people scattered and dispersed among the peoples in all the provinces of your kingdom" (Esther 3:8). The 17th century commentary on the Torah, *Kli Yakar*, writes that "a certain people scattered and dispersed" means that they were "scattered and dispersed from one another."[60] Likewise, the prominent interpretation of Jewish law, *Yalkut Yosef,* takes "separated" to mean that "there was separation of hearts among them."[61]

Adding that the Jews "do not observe the king's laws" (Esther 3:8), it was a no-brainer for Haman to sway King Ahasuerus into granting him permission to exterminate them.

Yet, each year on Purim, we celebrate the miracle of our survival because in the very last minute, Mordechai the Jew united all the Jews. "'Go gather all the Jews,' meaning tell them words of blandishment so they will all be in one unity. Go gather as one, the hearts of all the Jews."[62] This telling 18th century description by Haim Yosef David Azulai (the CHIDA) demonstrates the desperation of Esther and Mordechai at the prospect of seeing their entire fold obliterated.

Their last resort was unity. When they united, they saved themselves, their people, and facilitated the beginning of the return from Babylon. The book *Torat Emet* explicitly warns that "When all of Israel are in complete unity, no harm will come upon them. Indeed, wicked Haman complained about Israel that they are a scattered and separated people, that there is separation of hearts among them. Therefore, Esther suggested that they would all gather into one place and become one bundle ... and their salvation would quickly come. And as was said in the previously mentioned *Midrash Tanhuma* (*Nitzavim* 1), 'If a person takes a bundle of reeds, he will certainly not be able to break them all at once. But taken one by one, even a small child can break them.' So is the power of Israel: When they are all one bundle, when they are united together, they are rewarded and delivered."[63]

So the Jews were saved by uniting, just as they were delivered from Egypt when they united under Moses's leadership. When they came out of Egypt, they were given sovereignty in the land of Israel, though after a long and arduous journey. Now, too, once they united under

Mordechai's leadership, they regained their sovereignty and rebuilt the Temple, though again, after hardships and conflicts they had had to overcome.

But unlike Egypt, this time, they did not have to flee. Instead, they left Babylon not only with the king's blessing, but with his full moral, financial, and spiritual support: As soon as Cyrus came to power, he felt that God had ordered him to send the Jews back to their land and rebuild the Temple. He sensed he had been commanded to help them in their task. He gave the famous Cyrus Declaration which stated, "Every [Jewish] survivor, at whatever place he may live, let the men of that place support him with silver and gold, with goods and cattle, together with a freewill offering for the house of God which is in Jerusalem" (Ezra 1:4). After his order was carried out, "King Cyrus brought out the utensils of the house of the Lord, which Nebuchadnezzar had carried away [plundered] from Jerusalem and put in the house of his gods" (Ezra 1:7).

The Cyrus Declaration marked the official end of the exile in Babylon and the beginning of the era of the Second Temple, though the Temple itself had not yet been built. During that period, the Jews achieved great heights, but subsequently declined to two civil wars, the last of which was so bloody and brutal that it left the Romans aghast at the brutality of the Jews toward their brethren. As we will see later in this book, by the time the Romans entered the city and the Temple, there was very little left to ruin. The Romans merely completed the dispersion of an already disintegrated nation, and sent the people of Israel to an exile that has not ended since, despite the reestablishment of the State of Israel.

Seventy Translators Who Almost Saved the World

Whenever we Jews are given freedom, division and strife surge among us. It is our nature to be an obstinate and stiff-necked nation. My teacher's father, Rav Yehuda Ashlag, known as Baal HaSulam after his *Sulam* [ladder] commentary on *The Zohar*, poignantly described what happens when Jews "debate" (a euphemism for what the Talmud calls "stabbing each other with the swords in their tongues."[64]). Ashlag stated that when Jews argue, "They believe that in the end, the other side will understand the peril [of his own view] and will bow his head and accept their [other one's] view. But I know that even if we bind them up together, one will not yield to the other even a bit, and no [mortal] danger will interrupt anyone from carrying out his ambition."[65]

In accord with our nature, as soon as Cyrus sent us to Israel as a free people, we began to argue over the building of the Temple and the nature of our restored sovereignty. But one way or the other, the Temple was eventually built. But more importantly, for a brief period of time, *unity* was restored, and that period was a beautiful one in the pain stricken history of our people.

By the 3rd century BCE, relative calm prevailed in the nation as the people united around the Temple in Jerusalem. Three times a year they would march up to Jerusalem to celebrate the festivals of pilgrimage: Sukkot, Passover, and Shavuot (Feast of Weeks). During each pilgrimage, the sight was spectacular. The pilgrimages were intended primarily for gathering and uniting the hearts of the members of the nation. In his book *The Antiquities of the Jews*, Flavius Josephus writes that the pilgrims would make "acquaintance … maintained by conversing together and by seeing and talking with one another, and so renewing the recollections of this union."[66]

Once they entered Jerusalem, the pilgrims were greeted with open arms. The townsfolk let them into their homes and treated them as family, and there was always room for everyone.

The Mishnah relishes this rare camaraderie: "All the craftsmen in Jerusalem would stand before them and ask about their well-being: 'Our brothers, men of so and so place, have you come in peace?' and the flute would play before them until they arrived at Temple Mount."[67] Additionally, all the material needs of every person who came to Jerusalem were met in full. "One did not say to one's friend, 'I could not find an oven on which to roast offerings in Jerusalem' … or 'I could not find a bed to sleep in, in Jerusalem.'"[68]

Even better, the unity and warmth among the Hebrews projected outward and became a role-model for the neighboring nations. The philosopher Philo of Alexandria portrayed the pilgrimage as a festival: "Thousands of people from thousands of cities—some by land and some by sea, from the east and from the west, from the north and from the south—would come each festival to the Temple as if to a common shelter, a safe haven protected from the storms of life. ...With hearts filled with good hopes, they would take this vital vacation with sanctity and with glory to God. Also, they make friendships with people they had not met before, and in the merging of the hearts ... they would find the ultimate proof of unity."[69]

Philo was not the only one who admired what he saw. Those festivals of bonding served as a way for Israel to be—for the first time since they were given that vocation—"a light unto nations." The book *Sifrey Devarim* details how gentiles would "go up to Jerusalem and see Israel ... and say, 'It is becoming to cling only to this nation.'"[70]

This era in the history of our nation is probably the only time where we could see a living proof that the antidote to Jew-hatred was not assimilation but rather enhanced internal union. Historian Paul Johnson, whom we mentioned earlier, writes about that (relatively) peaceful time in our history, "The years 400-200 BC are the lost centuries of Jewish history. There were no great events or calamities they chose to record. Perhaps they were happy," he concludes.[71]

Some three centuries later, *The Book of Zohar* described succinctly and clearly the process that Israel went through: "'Behold, how good and how pleasant it is for brothers to also sit together.' These are the friends as they sit together and are not separated from each other. At first, they seem like people at war, wishing to kill one another ... then they return to being in brotherly love. ...And you, the friends who are here, as you were in fondness and love before, henceforth you will also not part from one another ... and by your merit, there will be peace in the world."[72]Indeed, being "a light unto nations" could not have been more evident than at that time.

Talking Politics

By the mid-240s BCE, at the height of that peaceful era in our history, the rumor of Israel's wisdom had reached far and wide. Ptolemy II, king of Egypt, also known as Ptolemy Philadelphus, had two passions in life: women and books. Lewdness aside, Ptolemy's passion for books led him to aspire to possess all the books in the world, especially those containing wisdom. Demetrius Phalerius, Ptolemy's librarian, was "zealously subservient" to his king's passion, wrote Josephus. When Ptolemy asked how many books he already possessed in his library, the enthusiastic servant announced festively that he already assembled 200,000 books, and that soon he would have 500,000 in his bigger-than-anybody's library.[73]

Yet, this did not satisfy the king of Egypt. He told Demetrius that he "had been informed that there were many books of laws among the Jews worthy of inquiring, and worthy of the king's library."[74] Not only did Ptolemy not have these books, but even if he did, he would not be able to read them since they were "written in characters and in a dialect of their own [Hebrew], [which] will cause no small pains to get them translated into the Greek tongue."[75]

To achieve this feat, Demetrius wrote to none other than the High Priest in Judah, asking his assistance in the matter. Ptolemy II Philadelphus "inherited" 120,000 Jewish slaves from his father, Ptolemy I Soter, who himself "received" them from his patron, Alexander the Great, who had made him ruler of Egypt. Ptolemy I was not only Alexander's companion, but also a historian, and his son, Ptolemy II, had inherited his father's fervor for knowledge and was willing to go a long way to get it.

When Ptolemy II Philadelphus ordered Demetrius to write to the High Priest in Jerusalem, one of the king's closest friends, Aristeus, reminded him that he had those 120,000 Jewish slaves under his yoke, and that perhaps, as a "trust-building" gesture, he should set them free. In fact, Aristeus did more than that: He told the king that "that God, who supports your kingdom, was the author of their laws, as I have learned by particular inquiry … and we also worship the same God, the framer of all things."[76] The conclusion of Aristeus' "campaign" was that Philadelphus ordered every single Jewish slave freed, whether they were brought to Egypt by Alexander the Great or at any other time, and that the king's treasury would recompense every slave owner by the substantial amount of a hundred and twenty drachmas. Within a week, every Jew in Egypt was a free person.

Subsequently, feeling he had paid his dues to God, Philadelphus summarily turned his attention to getting the Jewish sacred books translated. He could not wait to wrap his mind around the wisdom of the Jews and the laws of Moses. First, he wrote to Eleazar, the High Priest, telling him of the release of the Jews and of his intention to translate the Hebrew scriptures. To show his admiration for the Jews, he showered Eleazar with gold and luxurious artifacts. The High Priest replied very warmly and, naturally, accepted his request to send translators.

Seventy men were sent down to Egypt following Ptolemy's request. But the king did not send them off to work right away. First, he wanted to learn their wisdom and absorb whatever knowledge he could from them. Therefore, "he asked every one of them a philosophical question," which were "rather political questions and answers, tending to the good … government of mankind."[77] For twelve straight days, the Hebrew sages sat before the king of Egypt and taught him governance according to their laws. Along with Ptolemy sat his philosopher, Menedemus, who was in awe at how "such a force of beauty was discovered in these men's words."[78] Finally, "When they had explained all the problems that had been proposed by the king about every point, he was well-pleased with their answers." He said that "He had gained very great advantages by their coming, for that he had received this profit from them, that he had learned how he ought to rule his subjects."[79] Philo, the Jewish-Hellenized philosopher, wrote about that session that the answers of the wise men were "a feast of words full of wit and weight."[80]

Once Ptolemy was satisfied with the answers they had given him, he sent them off to an isolated location where they had peace and quiet and could focus on the translation. According to Josephus, "They made an accurate interpretation, with great zeal and great pains … while their food was provided for them in great plenty. Besides, Dorotheus, at the king's command, brought them a great deal of what was provided for the king himself."[81] When they completed their task, they handed over to the king the complete translation of the Pentateuch. Ptolemy was "delighted with hearing the Laws read to him, and was astonished at the deep meaning and wisdom of the legislator."[82]

The Talmud relates to the feat of the translation as a miracle. "King Ptolemy, king of Egypt," writes the Talmud, "assembled seventy-two elders from the sages of Israel and placed them in seventy-two separate houses. At first, he did not disclose to them why he had gathered them, so they would not consult with one another in advance. Then he went to each and every one of them [separately] and told them, 'Write for me,' meaning translate for me the law of your great sage Moses. Then God placed in the heart of each of them counsel and understanding, and they all agreed to one view. Then, not only did they translate properly, but where they changed, they made the same changes."[83]

Miracle or not, at long last, some twelve centuries after being tasked with serving as "a light unto nations," it seemed like the Jews were finally on track to being so. Now that the translation was done, King Ptolemy sent the sages back to Jerusalem with a letter to Eleazar the High Priest requesting that "he would give these interpreters leave if any of them were desirous of coming to him because he highly valued a conversation with men of such learning."[84] This, perhaps, is what Paul Johnson meant when he wrote about the society of the Jews being made as "a pilot" for humanity to emulate.[85]

Chapter 3: From the Zenith
to the Nadir

Helen the Siren: The Allure of Hellenism and Its Horrific Fallouts

The enchantment of Ptolemy with the Jewish wisdom was the heyday of the era of the Second Temple, which lasted from the people of Israel's return to their land in 516 BCE to 70 CE, when Emperor Vespasian's son and chief of staff, Titus Flavius Vespasianus, marched into Jerusalem with an army led by his regional commander, the Jew-turned-genocidal-anti-Semite Tiberius Julius Alexander. From the height of Ptolemy's reverence for the Jews, the carriers of the light for the nations began a rapid social, moral, and spiritual degeneration that bred two civil wars and ended with the Armageddon of razing the Second Temple, the slaughter of a million Jews, and enslavement of the famished and emotionally flustered relics of the Jewish people.

From being a role model to the nations, it took the Jews less than eighty years to become embroiled in the first of two civil wars. Today we call this war the Hasmonean Revolt and celebrate Hanukkah to commemorate our victory over the Greeks. But in truth, the events were far less festive than the current narrative surrounding the festival of Hanukkah.

Judea was a strategic point between the Seleucid Empire and the Egyptian Empire, both of which were Hellenistic. During the reign of Antiochus III the Great (222 to 187 BCE), Judea was ruled by the Seleucid Empire but enjoyed almost complete autonomy; the Jews could lead their lives however they chose as long as they paid their taxes to the king. In fact, Antiochus the Great was grateful to the Jews for helping him in his war against Ptolemy IV Philopator and his son, Ptolemy V Ephiphanes, and considered it his duty to guard the autonomy of the Jews. To show his appreciation for their assistance and his reverence for their way of life, Antiochus wrote a formal letter permitting the Jews to live according to their ways. He wrote, "On account of their piety toward God, [he decided to] bestow on them, as a pension for their [Temple work] ... twenty thousand pieces of silver," in addition to abundance of fine flour, wheat, and salt.[86]

When Antiochus III the Great died, his firstborn son, Seleucus IV Philopator, succeeded him. Seleucus Philopator kept the status quo with the Jews, who continued to live untroubled in Judea.

In 175 BCE, Seleucus IV Philopator died and Antiochus IV Epiphanes succeeded him. Initially, Antiochus Epiphanes had no intention to change the status quo in Judea, but some Jews had other plans, and from here matters quickly went downhill.

By the time Epiphanes came to power, many Jews were already displeased with the Jewish traditional way of life. All around the kingdom of Judea, writes Paul Johnson, cities were becoming Hellenized. It happened in Shechem, in Marissa, Philadelphia (Amman), and Gamal across the Jordan. Eventually, "a ring of such cities, swarming with Greeks and semi-Greeks, surrounded Jewish Samaria and Judah, which were seen as mountainous, rural, and backward ... antique survivors, anachronisms, soon to be swept away by the irresistible modern tide of Hellenic ideas and institutions."[87]

Seeing what was happening around them, the Jews established what Johnson called a "Jewish reform party who wanted to force the pace of Hellenization"[88] in Judea. Just as the contemporary Reform Movement that started in Germany strove to strip Judaism of Jewish customs, or at least mitigate them, and place the focus on its ethics, their forefathers strove to "reduce it to its ethical core."[89]

To accelerate the Hellenization of Judea, the leader of the archetypal Reform Movement, Jason [Hebrew: Yason], whose goals and modus operandi were very similar to today's Reform Judaism, joined hands with King Antiochus Epiphanes, who was "anxious to speed up the Hellenization of his dominions ... because he thought it would raise tax-revenues, as he was chronically short of money for his wars."[90] Jason paid Epiphanes a hefty sum of money, and in return, the latter ousted the incumbent High Priest in Jerusalem, Onias III, and handed the position over to Jason.

Jason went to work straightaway. He turned Jerusalem into a polis, renamed it Antiochia, and constructed a gymnasium at the foot of Temple Mount.[91] Just as the Reform Movement did in Germany as soon as they were given emancipation in the early 1870s, the reformers in antiquity aspired to adapt Judaism to modernity, eventually abandoning it altogether. Besides making Jerusalem more like the capital of the Seleucid Empire, Seleucia, they abandoned ancient Jewish customs that related to the Temple and stopped circumcising male babies. In the words of Flavius Josephus, "they left off all the customs that belonged to their own country and imitated the practices of the other nations."[92] But far worse than the abandonment of their customs, when the Jews turned Hellenists, they also abandoned their unity. Even among the Hellenists, fights erupted between supporters of Jason and supporters of Menelaus. The rest of the people, who preferred to maintain the Jewish spirit that had earned them such respect from Ptolemy Philadelphus and Antiochus III the Great, wanted neither leader and were growing increasingly rebellious.

In 170 BCE, Menelaus did to Jason just what he had done to Onias III before him: He paid Antiochus Epiphanes a hefty sum of money, who, in turn, anointed him the High Priest in Jerusalem. A year or so later, Jason and his supporters tried to retake the priesthood, but with the help of Antiochus, Menelaus, who was even more pro-Greek than Jason, managed to maintain his position.

Yet, Antiochus Epiphanes's help cost the Jews heavily. On his way back from a failed campaign against the Egyptian Pharaoh Ptolemy, Epiphanes entered Jerusalem without a struggle, pretending to come in peace for his supporters, the Menelaus camp. But once inside, "he spared not so much as those that admitted him into it."[93]

After slaying its people and plundering the city and the Temple of all the wealth, including even the Temple veils, Antiochus "forbade them to offer those daily sacrifices ... [and] built an idol altar upon God's altar and slew swine upon it."[94] To see that the Jews did not rebel against him, Antiochus placed a guard made of "impious and wicked" Jews who inflicted on the residents "many and sore calamities."[95]

Interestingly, Epiphanes himself was not interested in obliterating Judaism. In fact, it was most unusual for a Greek government to trample other faiths. According to Johnson, "The evidence suggests that the initiative came from the extreme Jewish reformers, led by Menelaus."[96]

Yet, in 167 BCE, when the Hellenists tried to place an idol in the Temple at Modi'in, where Mattathias the Hasmonean was the priest, the tide turned against them. The first book of Maccabees conveniently regards Antiochus IV Epiphanes as the villain in the story, describing him as the "wicked root Antiochus surnamed Epiphanes."[97]

Epiphanes certainly "earned" his reputation. In his infamous 167 BCE Antiochus's Decree, he "wrote to his whole kingdom that all should be one people, and everyone should leave his laws, so all the heathen agreed according to the commandment of the king."[98] Moreover, "many of the Israelites consented to his religion and sacrificed unto idols."[99]

But foreign leaders were never our worst enemy. Those have always come from within, and through their misdeeds, they brought upon us our most painful blows. In the case of Antiochus Epiphanes, we must not forget that it was Jason who first enticed him to force Hellenism on the Judean Jews, and his successor, Menelaus, dragged him into the war against the Maccabees.

The Second Book of the Maccabees describes Menelaus as "increasing in malice and being a great traitor to the citizens."[100] As mentioned above, he dethroned Jason from the priesthood by buying his position from Epiphanes. Yet, he did not settle for being the High Priest at the Temple; he truly wanted to make Hellenism the ruling culture and religion in Judea. To achieve this, writes Josephus, the Hellenists began to place idols inside Jewish temples all over Judea, and forced the Jews to bow before them and sacrifice to them.

One particular temple of interest to the Hellenists was the one in Modi'in, an important city not very far from Jerusalem, whose priest, Mattathias the Hasmonean, was renowned, well respected, and very adamant about his piousness. The Hellenists wanted to "compel the Jews to do what they were commanded and to enjoin those that were there to offer sacrifice [to idols]. They desired that Mattathias, a person of the greatest character … would begin the sacrifice because [so they believed] his fellow citizens would follow his example."[101]

Mattathias also thought so and precisely because he, too, believed that they would follow his example, he did the exact opposite of what the Hellenists expected. "Mattathias said he would not do it, and that if all the other nations would obey the commands of Antiochus … neither he nor his sons would leave the religious worship of their country." When another Jew stepped in to sacrifice instead of Mattathias, the enraged priest "ran upon [the Jew] with his sons, who had swords with them, and slew both the man who sacrificed and Apelles, the king's general, who compelled them to sacrifice, with a few of his soldiers."[102] When he was done with their enemies, Mattathias turned to the crowd and called out, "Anyone who is zealous for the laws of his country … let him follow me."[103]

Before long, thousands of Jews, frustrated with the forced conversion into Hellenism dealt on them by the High Priest himself, joined Mattathias and headed for the mountains of the Judah Desert. Mattathias appointed his third son, Judah Maccabee, as commander of the newly hatched militia, and from the desert, they conducted the brilliant guerilla campaign that we now know as the Hasmonean Revolt, or the Maccabean Revolt.

The Maccabean Revolt did not target the Seleucid army or any of the neighboring armies. It aimed at the Hellenized Jews and strove to intimidate them and force them back to Judaism. But since the Hellenists had the support of the Seleucid government, they turned to Antiochus and asked for his military assistance.

"Mattathias," writes Josephus, "got a great army around him. He overthrew their idol altars and slew those who broke the laws, even all whom he could get under his power, for many of them were dispersed among the nations round about them for fear of him."[104]

One year into the revolt, Mattathias passed away. Before his death, he summoned his sons and instructed how they should continue the struggle. But most of all, he commanded them to maintain their unity according to the ancient Jewish law: "I exhort you, especially, to agree one with another, and in what excellency any one of you exceeds another, to yield to him so far, and by that means to reap the advantage of every one's own virtues."[105] It is this spirit of unity and contribution of everyone's strengths to the common good that yielded the Maccabees their illustrious victory over the far greater, better equipped, and far better trained armies of the Seleucid Empire.

Three years into the insurgency, Judah was strong enough to march on Jerusalem and retake it from the Seleucids. Then, finally, in 164 BCE, the High Priest Menelaus was forced to seek refuge.[106]

As the Maccabees entered the Temple, they found it "deserted, its gates burnt down, and plants growing in the temple of their own accord, on account of its desertion."[107] The Maccabees "brought in new vessels, the candlestick ... and the altar, which were made of gold. [Judah] hung up the veils at the gates and added doors to them. He also took down the altar and built a new one... So on the five and twentieth day of the month of Kislev, …they lighted the lamps that were on the candlestick, offered incense upon the altar … and offered burnt-offerings upon the new altar."[108] To this day, we celebrate this occasion and call this festival Hanukkah.

Yet, retaking Jerusalem and resuming the worship in the Temple did not end the war. Not only did the Jews have to fight the Seleucids outside the walls, they also had trouble from within. "Throughout the period of persecution and revolt," writes historian Lawrence H. Schiffman, "the Hellenistic pagans in the Land of Israel had sided with the Seleucids and had participated in the persecutions. It was therefore natural that Judah now turned on these enemies as well as on the Hellenizing Jews who had brought on the horrible persecutions. The Hellenizers, many of them of aristocratic origins, had fought on the side of the Seleucids *against Judah*. Their center was the Acra [fortress within Jerusalem], and it was here that they finally took refuge when Judah conquered Jerusalem."[109]

"After Antiochus IV [Epiphanes] died in 164 BCE, his son Antiochus V Eupator advanced on Judea,"[110] continues Schiffman. Some of the besieged Hellenists managed to sneak out at night, writes Josephus,[111] and get to the new king, Antiochus Eupator, who was only nine when he succeeded his father. The fugitives lied to the child king, asking him "not to be neglected under the great hardships that lay upon them from those of their own nation," as they suffered "on his father's account while they left the religious worship of their fathers and preferred that which he had commanded them to follow."[112] This, of course, was completely false since it was Jason who initially approached Epiphanes and asked him to force Hellenism in Judea, contrary to the Seleucids' conduct everywhere else. The runaways also said "that there was danger lest the citadel, and those appointed to garrison it by the king, should be taken by Judas … unless he would send them assistance."[113]

As one might expect, the nine-year-old king fell for the trap and commanded to send a formidable army to Jerusalem. The Seleucids assembled "about a hundred thousand footmen, twenty thousand horsemen, and thirty-two elephants,"[114] and advanced on Jerusalem, conquering every city that came in their path. After putting a long siege on Jerusalem, and having almost starved it to death, the Seleucids suddenly found themselves under threat from Persia. Having no other choice, the king offered the besieged Jerusalemites peace, promising them freedom of worship and self-governance. The Maccabees accepted the offer willingly, and the Seleucids quickly retreated to deal with the advancing Persians. They did, however, take with them the now ousted High Priest Menelaus, as "this man was the origin of all the mischief the Jews had done them, by persuading his father to compel the Jews to leave the religion of their fathers."[115] Subsequently, Antiochus V Eupator restored the agreement of religious freedom that his great grandfather, Antiochus III the Great, had had with the Jews, and put the final seal on the Hasmonean Revolt when he executed Menelaus.

The Rise and Fall of the Hasmonean Kingdom

Despite their victory, the Hasmoneans did not translate their freedom into spiritual liberty. Instead, they focused on conquering land, forcing other nations to convert to Judaism, and gaining power and wealth. From the end of the revolt in 160 BCE, to the end of their independence, the Hasmoneans increased their territory by more than ten times. From a small region around Jerusalem, they conquered expansive territories from the Mediterranean Sea in the West to beyond the Jordan River on the East. From North to South, the Hasmonean kingdom spread from what is today's Southern Lebanon and the Golan Heights in the North, to today's Gaza strip, included, in the South, the length of several hundred kilometers.

Despite their military might, their tendency to mingle with the nations and shun Jewish unity grew stronger every day. They may have defeated the Greeks and the Hellenists in battle, but in the battle over the spirit of the nation, the Israeli spirit was losing bitterly to the Hellenists within them. Gradually, Hellenism landed deadly blows on every field of life in the Hasmonean kingdom.

Especially now, it was all the more evident that, as Paul Johnson put it, "In self-government and prosperity, the Jews always seemed drawn to neighboring religions."[116] As soon as things go well for them, they seem to forget their unique ability to forge unity above all differences, as they did at the foot of Mt. Sinai, and opt out of it and into individualistic and particularistic cultures that exalt the self.

Moreover, the Jews became imperialistic themselves. Even worse, unlike the Greeks, who allowed the Jews freedom of worship, where the Hasmoneans conquered, they forced people to convert to Judaism under threat of murder or expulsion. This completely contradicts the spirit of Judaism, since Judaism is about connection "as one man with one heart," and connection of hearts cannot be forced. It is impossible to compel one to love others. By forcibly converting non-Jews, the Hasmoneans brought into their ranks myriad "bogus" Jews who were not reared on the principle of mutual responsibility and brotherly love around which the nation was fashioned and consolidated. In doing so, they hastened the moral, spiritual, and eventually, physical collapse of the nation and the country.[117]

"Moreover," writes Johnson, "in becoming rulers, kings and conquerors, the Hasmoneans suffered the corruptions of power. ... Alexander Jannaeus [ruled 103-76 BCE] ... turned into a despot and a monster, and among his victims were the pious Jews from whom his family had once drawn its strength. Like any ruler in the Near East at that time, he was influenced by the predominant Greek modes."[118] Using his position as the High Priest and a self-crowned king, Alexander the Hasmonean was exemplary in shunning traditional Jewish customs, and thus paved the way for the populace to abandon Judaism and adopt Hellenism. When observant Jews protested his contempt for Jewish traditions, he retaliated by slaying thousands of them. "Alexander, in fact," concludes Johnson, "found himself like his hated predecessors, Jason and Menelaus,"[119] *de facto* perpetuating the civil war.

When Alexander Jannaeus died in 76 BCE, his two sons, John Hyrcanus II and Aristobulus II, struggled between them over the supremacy. Yet, Alexander "committed the kingdom to Alexandra [Salome Alexandra],"[120] Alexander Jannaeus's wife, and the sons' mother. Alexandra preferred Hyrcanus the elder to Aristobulus, but regrettably for her, he was "indeed unable to manage public affairs, and delighted rather in a quiet life."[121] Therefore, "She made Hyrcanus high priest because he was the elder, but much more because he cared not to meddle with politics."[122]

Unlike his elder brother, Aristobulus "was an active and a bold man,"[123] who had his eyes on the crown. When Salome Alexandra died in 67 BCE, Aristobulus rebelled against his older brother and defeated him in a battle in Jericho. The triumphant Aristobulus declared himself king of Judah, but he had no interest in being the High Priest and left Hyrcanus in his former position. However, regrettably for Aristobulus, his reign was to be very brief, cut short by the Romans. "The gifted rulers of the Hasmonean house would probably have carried their arms still farther," observed the celebrated historian and archeologist Theodor Mommsen, "had not the development of the power of that remarkable conquering priestly state been nipped in the bud by internal divisions."[124] Once again, disunity and internal hatred was to take its toll on the Jews.

In 63 BCE, just four years after Aristobulus captured the crown, the Roman general Pompey the Great conquered Judah as part of a much larger campaign against Anatolia (also known as Asia Minor). This began the era of Roman rule in Judah, and ended the era of Judah's independence. Perhaps Paul Johnson's concise and poignant conclusion best describes the rise and fall of the Hasmoneans' sovereignty in Judah: "The story of their rise and fall is a memorable study in hubris. They began as the avengers of martyrs; they ended as religious oppressors themselves. They came to power at the head of an eager guerrilla band; they ended surrounded by mercenaries. Their kingdom, founded in faith, dissolved in impiety."[125]

Yet, the Romans, like the Greeks before them, had no interest in forcing their beliefs or culture on the Jews. While they annexed Syria, they "left Judaea as a dependent, diminished temple state."[126] While "a heavier tribute was imposed on the Jews than on the other Syrian subjects of Rome,"[127] to avenge their insurgency, it seems as though on the whole, the Romans handed the Jews a great arrangement: A mighty empire protected them from enemies while leaving them free to lead their lives as they pleased. They could have lived peacefully and quietly under Rome's protection had it not been for the rulers of the state who arose from within their faith.

Pompey did not oust Hyrcanus from his position and left him in office as the High Priest until his death in the year 40 BCE. Pompey even declared Hyrcanus as the ethnarch of Judah, namely a ruler but with less authority than a king. Yet, to guarantee Judah's loyalty to Rome, Pompey placed the real power of governance in the hands of Antipater I the Idumaean.

Antipater, being the son of an Edomite who was forced to convert into Judaism, pledged his allegiance to his benefactors the Romans rather than to the kingdom of Judah. Antipater's rule marked the end of the dynasty of kings and rulers from the house of King David. His son Herod, who reigned after him, completely Hellenized the country, building amphitheaters, gymnasiums, and entire cities, such as Caesarea, that were completely Hellenistic. In the year 4 BCE, Herod died and the Romans divided his kingdom among three of his sons and his sister. Herod Archelaus received the biggest portion and became ethnarch of the tetrarchy of Judea at the early age of eighteen.[128]

"The people, glad of the death of the tyrant," write Gottheil and Ginzberg in the *Jewish Encyclopedia* concerning the death of Herod, "were well disposed toward Archelaus, and in the public assembly in the Temple, the new king promised to have regard to the wishes of his subjects."[129] Unfortunately, "It very soon became manifest ... how little he intended to keep his word."[130] Archelaus's reign was fraught with political intrigues, broken promises, and frequent civil unrest. In 6 CE, after ten tumultuous years, the Romans' patience had run out, and Archelaus "was deprived of his crown and banished to Vienne in Gaul. ... Archelaus was a veritable Herodian," conclude Gottheil and Ginzberg, "but without the statesman-like ability of his father. He was cruel and tyrannical, sensual in the extreme, a hypocrite and a plotter."[131] It is therefore no wonder that after banishing Archelaus, the Romans declared Judah a province of Rome and changed its name to Judea.

The Roman Province Judea

Between the years 6 CE and 66 CE, when the Great Revolt that destroyed Jerusalem and the Temple broke out, no less than fifteen Roman procurators governed in Jerusalem, sometimes for as briefly as two years. As one might expect, those years were far from tranquil. The first procurator, Coponius, was ousted after "Samaritans … threw about dead men's bodies" into the Temple.[132] Valerius Gratus, who governed from 15-26 CE, the longest term, was the first to arbitrarily appoint and depose High Priests.[133]

Following Gratus came Pontius Pilate. Pilate's term as procurator was filled with even more misdeeds than the already high level of offenses that Roman procurators had committed. Josephus writes that Pilate started off by placing "images of Caesar that are called ensigns" in the Temple,[134] and Philo adds that Pilate did this "not so much to honor Tiberius [Caesar] as to annoy the [Jewish] multitude."[135] The Jews sent an urgent embassy to Caesarea, where Pilate's palace was located, and "appealed to Pilate to redress the infringement of their traditions caused by the shields and not to disturb the customs which throughout all the preceding ages had been safeguarded without disturbance by kings and by emperors."[136] Yet, when Pilate, "naturally inflexible, a blend of self-will and relentlessness, stubbornly refused, they clamored, 'Do not arouse sedition, do not make war, do not destroy the peace; you do not honor the emperor by dishonoring ancient laws. Do not take Tiberius as your pretext for outraging the nation; he does not wish any of our customs to be overthrown. If you say that he does, produce yourself an order or a letter or something of the kind so that we may cease to pester you and having chosen our envoys may petition our lord.'"[137]

In the end, the Jews sent a letter of complaint to Tiberius, who became infuriated with his incompetent procurator and ordered him to remove the ensigns and place them in Caesarea. Toward the end of his term, Pilate also ordered the crucifixion of Jesus. To summarize, Philo defined Pilate's term as full of briberies, insults, robberies, outrages, wanton injuries, constantly repeated executions without trial, and ceaseless and supremely grievous cruelty.[138]

Seeking to quiet the tumultuous province, the Romans kept replacing procurators. Their ambition proved impossible to achieve. In 44 CE, Rome appointed Cuspius Fadus as procurator. During his time, "a certain magician, whose name was Theudas, persuaded a great part of the people to ... follow him to the river Jordan, for he told them he was a prophet and that he would, by his own command, divide the river and afford them an easy passage over it."[139] But Procurator Fadus would not permit them to do this. He "sent a troop of horsemen out against them, who ... slew many of them... They also took Theudas alive and cut off his head, and carried it to Jerusalem."[140]

In response to the reckless cruelty, the Romans quickly deposed this yet another failed procurator, Fadus, and in 46 CE appointed the Alexandria born Jew Tiberius Julius Alexander as procurator "in the belief that a born Jew would be welcome to the Jews."[141] Tiberius's term, however, was just as short as the others. On the positive side, he made "no alterations of the ancient laws" of the Jews, which "kept the nation in tranquility," writes Josephus.[142] On the other hand, he had no interest whatsoever in Judaism or in the Jews. In fact, he detested his native fold and was to become the worst genocidal murderer ever to emerge from the Jews, and he would perform his genocide against his own people, including his hometown. Still, during his term he made no provocations and left in peace as he had come, seeking to advance his military career in the Roman army.

Ventidius Cumanus, who succeeded Tiberius Alexander in 48 CE, was to be the procurator under whom matters began to accelerate the decline toward calamity, "and the Jews' ruin came on,"[143] culminating in the Great Revolt that began in 66 CE, and the final destruction of the Temple four years later.

Following Cumanus, the Roman Emperor Claudius appointed Marcus Antonius Felix as the procurator in Judea. Either out of hatred for Jews or simply out of indifference, Claudius appointed a freedman (former slave) as the ruler in Judea. That was clearly a poor choice. The Roman senator and historian Tacitus writes that "Antonius Felix practiced every kind of cruelty and lust, wielding the power of king with all the instincts of a slave."[144]

Josephus, on the other hand, chose to focus on "those actions of [Felix's] time in which the Jews were concerned."[145] Josephus dedicates Chapter Thirteen in Book II of *The Wars of the Jews* to detail the disastrous results that one incompetent procurator can inflict on a whole nation (however contentious) within just eight years. Initially, it did not seem as though Felix's term would be so turbulent. He began by purging the country of the robber Eleazar, his accomplices, and so many criminals who plagued the country that "were a multitude not to be enumerated."[146] But the promising start soon turned out to be mere wishful thinking, as Felix's "inimical attitude toward the people"[147] manifested, despite his Jewish wife Drusilla of Judea.

Worse than the licentiousness and abuse of power that Tacitus reported, Felix's term was fraught with violent crimes perpetrated by rogue, rebellious, and blood-thirsty groups. First, once the country has been purged of Eleazar and his lot, "there sprang up another sort of robbers in Jerusalem, which were called Sicarii."[148] The Sicarii, an extremist fringe group of the Zealots, were cunning dagger wielders who would stab stealthily, then sneakily join the appalled crowd protesting the stabbing. Their first victim was none other than the High Priest Jonathan, but following him, "many were slain every day." In this way, the Sicarii spread such terror in the country that "the fear men were in … was more afflicting than the calamity itself, and everybody expected death every hour, as men do in war." People could not even trust their friends, "but in the midst of their suspicions and guarding of themselves, they were slain."

The Sicarii certainly earned the title "First Century Terrorists"[149] that Dr. Amy Zalman gave them, or "Ancient Jewish 'Terrorists,'"[150] as Prof. Richard Horsley called them. Yet, they differ from contemporary terrorist organizations that act against Jews or the State of Israel in that the Sicarii came from within their own fold. They were not an underground movement that sought to overthrow the government and chose violence as a means to force down the government. Rather, they sought to intimidate and physically eradicate people from their own faith of whom they did not approve, either because they viewed them as submissive to the Romans or for whatever other reason. The division between the Zealots and the rest of the nation was the seed of the bloodbath that the people of Israel inflicted on themselves during the Great Revolt a few years later, but the diabolic assassinations of the Sicarii deepened the hatred and suspicion among the factions of the nation to levels that sealed the fate of the Jews.

As though this were not enough, "There was also another body of wicked men gotten together," continues Josephus his harrowing description of the miseries of the Jews under the procurator Felix.[151] This body was "not so impure in their actions, but more wicked in their intentions, which laid waste the happy state of the city no less than did these murderers." These people pretended to be prophets and visionaries and would lead people into the wilderness "pretending that God would there show them the signals of liberty." Regrettably for them, Felix, plagued by distrust and ill-will, suspected that they might be starting yet another revolt, "so he sent horsemen and footmen, both armed, who destroyed a great number of them."[152]

One of these false prophets was such a successful con artist that he "got together thirty thousand men that were deluded by him."[153] He brought them all to the Mount of Olives and intended to break into Jerusalem and conquer it. As would be expected, Felix charged the hapless people with Roman soldiers accompanied by many other people, who were not part of the fool-hearted band. The resolute false-prophet's believers fought back, and in the battle, the "[prophet] ran away with a few others while the greatest part of those that were with him were either destroyed or taken alive."[154]

Josephus compares the Jewish nation to a diseased body. He writes that when the riots over the false prophets quieted, "another part was subject to an inflammation."[155] According to Josephus, "A company of deceivers and robbers got together and persuaded the Jews to revolt, and exhorted them to assert their liberty, inflicting death on those that continued in obedience to the Roman government, and saying that such as willingly chose slavery ought to be forced from such desired inclinations. …They parted themselves into different bodies and lay in wait up and down the country, plundered the houses of the great men, slew the men themselves, and set the villages on fire … till all Judea was filled with the effects of their madness. And thus the flame was every day more and more blown up till it came to a direct war."[156]

Even in Caesarea, the procurators' own city of residence, Felix could not force order. Jews and Syrians living in Caesarea disputed over who owned the city, completely ignoring the fact that the Romans owned it and governed it. The Jews argued that the city was theirs since Herod built it, and he was a Jew. They conveniently ignored the fact that Herod was a Jew only because his grandfather was forced to convert into Judaism, and during Herod's time, even the Jews did not regard him as fully Jewish. The Syrians agreed that Herod was Jewish, but contested that it is nonetheless a fact that he did not build a Jewish city but "a Grecian city, for that he who set up statues and temples in it could not design it for Jews."[157] Once again, the feud got out of control and "came at last to arms, and the bolder sort of them marched out to fight."[158] Finally, Felix gave up trying to discipline the rebellious factions and sent ambassadors from both sides to Emperor Nero, so he would sort it out. This tactic ended the feud, but it also ended Felix's term as ruler of Judea.

Porcius Festus, whom the *Jewish Encyclopedia* describes as "more just than his predecessor,"[159] was a very short relief (relatively).

Josephus writes that Festus "made it his business to correct those that made disturbances in the country so he caught the greatest part of the robbers and destroyed a great many of them."[160] Unfortunately, Festus died while still in office, having completed a mere two years.

Festus's successor, Lucceius Albinus, summarily and wholly corrupted the little good that his predecessor had managed to do. Albinus stole, plundered, and imposed exaggerated taxes on the whole country. He released so many criminals from prison for ransom that "nobody remained in the prisons but he who gave him nothing."[161]

In Jerusalem, seditions broke out as gangs of bloodthirsty criminals would buy their freedom from Albinus "while he himself, like an arch-robber ... made a [fortune] among his company and abused his authority over those about him in order to plunder those that lived quietly."[162] As a result, concludes Josephus, "Nobody dared speak their minds, tyranny was tolerated, and at this time were those seeds sown which brought the city to destruction."[163]

Despite all the hardships they had suffered from the Roman procurators, and despite the belligerent sects among them, "Still the Jews' patience lasted until Gessius Florus became procurator [succeeding Albinus]: In his time war began," writes Tacitus.[164]

Prof. Helen K. Bond writes that "Florus ... made Albinus appear by comparison a paragon of virtue."[165] Josephus, who lived at the time when the events took place, does not settle for one-sentence insinuating portrayals. He dedicates chapters fourteen through seventeen to describe the provocations, slaughter, plundering, and devastation that Florus inflicted on the Jews precisely in order to provoke them to rebel and start a war against Rome.[166] In Chapter 18, Josephus describes a surprise and massive pogrom that the Caesarea Grecians inflicted on the Jews. "In one hour's time," he writes, "above twenty thousand Jews were killed, and all Caesarea was emptied of its Jewish inhabitants."[167] This carnage is what Paul Johnson refers to when he writes that "The revolt itself began in 66 AD not in Jerusalem but in Caesarea ... with a pogrom in the Jewish quarter, while the Greek-speaking Roman garrison did nothing."[168]

The Great Revolt – A Self-Inflicted Genocide

All that has been said thus far about the cruelty of the Jews toward each other will soon be dwarfed by the horrors that the Jews inflicted on themselves during the Great Revolt. While the official enemy of the Jews was the Roman legion, the most unspeakable, inconceivable, and inhuman agonies came to the Jews at the hands of their coreligionists. The bottom line of the atrocities of the Great Revolt is as our sages put it, "The Second Temple ... why was it ruined? It was because there was unfounded hatred in it,"[169] and because of how that hatred manifested.

When Titus, the victorious Roman general, finally conquered Jerusalem, he was astounded by its fortifications. Looking from within at the towers, the walls, and the size and exactness of the bricks, he felt that he could not attribute his victory to his own military craftiness or to his army's might. Instead, he said, "We have certainly had God for our assistant in this war, and it was no other than God who ejected the Jews out of these fortifications; for what could the hands of men or any machines do towards overthrowing these towers?"[170]

Titus continued to speak about his observations with his friends, writes Josephus, and although he razed the walls, he "left the towers [standing] as a monument of his good fortune" and as proof that he had "auxiliaries that enabled him to take what could not otherwise have been taken by him."[171] Even when he returned to Rome, he still maintained that it was not his doing that had gotten him the victory, but the hands of God. Johnson writes that the Greek sophist Philostratus "asserted in his *Vita Apollonii* that when Helen of Judaea offered Titus a victory wreath after he took the city, he refused it on the grounds that there was no merit in vanquishing a people deserted by their own God."[172]

The idea that in this war, the Romans had "superior" help did not emerge when Titus first saw the walls of the city from within. The war against the Jews was so gruesome and filled with Jewish self-inflicted cruelty that it made the Romans think that God was actually on their side. At the beginning of the siege, looking at the Jews fighting one another inside the city, "the Romans deemed this sedition among their enemies to be of great advantage to them, and were very earnest to march to the city," writes Josephus.[173] "They urged Vespasian," the newly crowned emperor, "to make haste, and said to him that 'The providence of God is on our side by setting our enemies against one another.'" The Roman commanders wanted to take advantage of the situation for fear that "the Jews may quickly be at one again," either because they were "tired out with their civil miseries" or because they might "repent them of such doings."

However, the Emperor was very confident that the hatred of the Jews for one another was beyond repair. "Vespasian replied," writes Josephus, "that they were greatly mistaken in what they thought fit to be done," adding that "If they stay a while, they shall have fewer enemies because they will be consumed in this sedition, that God acts as a general of the Romans better than he can do, and is giving the Jews up to them without any pains of their own, and granting their army a victory without any danger; that therefore it is their best way, while their enemies are destroying each other with their own hands, and falling into the greatest of misfortunes, which is that of sedition, to sit still as spectators of the dangers they run into, rather than to fight hand to hand with men that love murdering, and are mad one against another. ... The Jews are vexed to pieces every day by their civil wars and dissensions, and are under greater miseries than, if they were once taken, could be inflicted on them by us. Whether therefore any one hath regard to what is for our safety, he ought to suffer these Jews to destroy one another."[174]

The siege on Jerusalem was the end of a four-year battle. When it began in 66 CE, after the earlier mentioned pogrom in Caesarea, violence broke out throughout the province. If during the Hasmonean Revolt, the fighting was between Hellenized Jews and militant Jews who remained faithful to their religion, now the fighting was only among "proper" Jews, among various sects of the militant Zealots, and moderate Jews, who strove to negotiate peace with the Romans.

Yet, the unfounded hatred that surfaced among Jews during the revolt was far worse than even the already intense odium that the factions in the nation felt for one another before its outbreak. Initially, writes Josephus, "All the people of every place betook themselves to rapine, after which they got together in bodies, in order to rob the people of the country, insomuch that for barbarity and iniquity, those of the same nation did no way differ from the Romans. Nay, it seemed to be a much lighter thing to be ruined by the Romans than by themselves."[175] This statement, that what the Jews did to each other, even the Romans did not do to them, would repeat itself throughout Josephus's elaborate and graphic descriptions of the revolt. Clearly, he spared no effort to stress that, as our sages said, it was our own hatred of each other that destroyed us rather than our enemies' war machines.

And while the Jews were at each other's throats, the Roman residents did not stand by. They, too, participated in the killing and the looting. Johnson writes that as a result of the fighting that erupted everywhere, "Jerusalem was filling up with angry and vengeful Jewish refugees from other cities where the Greek majority had invaded the Jewish quarters and burnt their homes."[176] The Jews, who were already in a fighting mood, did not take the Romans' blows quietly. In the struggle between the more peace seeking Jews and the more pugnacious ones, the pogroms inflicted by the Romans "turned the tide in favor of the extremists, and the Roman garrison was attacked and massacred."[177]

Worse yet, the domination of the militant Zealots and Sicarii prevented any chance of moderation or negotiation with the Romans, even when the latter asked for it. The extremist approach not only caused more lives to be lost in battle, but made the civil war within Jerusalem far more vicious. "As the city was engaged in a war on all sides, from these treacherous crowds of wicked men," concludes Josephus, "the people of the city, between them, were like a great body torn in pieces."[178]

After more than three years of fighting throughout the land of Israel, in the spring of 70 CE, the majority of Jews were gathered in

Jerusalem, either because they had fled there, or because it was the festival of Passover, a pilgrimage when every Jew with regard to the Jewish customs would come up to Jerusalem to congregate, bond, and study together. Because of these two reasons, reports Josephus, when the siege began, the population within the city numbered no less than "two million seven hundred thousand and two hundred persons."[179] Even by today's standards, a city of nearly three million people is a very big city. In those days, it was humongous. To get some perspective on the size of ancient Jerusalem, consider that a population of 2.7 million is about the same as the population of Chicago, IL, the third largest city in the US.[180]

Moreover, since the Jewish pilgrims and refugees were already inflicting "barbarity and iniquity" on each other in a manner that "did no way differ from the Romans," they not only joined the civil war already raging in the city, they brought more of it with them as they came to the city. Josephus writes that "this quarrelsome temper caught hold of private families, who could not agree among themselves, after which those people that were the dearest to one another broke through all restraints with regard to each other, and everyone associated with those of his own opinion and began already to stand in opposition one to another, so that seditions arose everywhere."[181] As we will see below, this estrangement among family members would lead to some of the most horrific chapters in this civil genocide known as the Great Revolt.

Despite the vast number of people in Jerusalem, there should have been no shortage of food. Being a regular place of congregating, the city was well prepared for feeding very large gatherings for extended periods. Its enormous food depositories should have outlasted the ability of the Romans to maintain the siege. Yet, as Johnson writes, "The Jews were ... irreconcilably divided."[182] They were so engrossed in mutual destruction that they could pay no thought to the future, not even to the following day. As a result, as part of their all-out war, "Simon and his party ... set on fire those houses that were full of corn [namely all forms of grain] and of all other provisions. The same thing was done by Simon when, upon the others' retreat, he attacked the city also, as if they had, on purpose, done it to serve the Romans by destroying what the city had laid up against the siege, and by thus cutting off the nerves of their own power."[183] As a result, "Almost all that corn was burnt, which would have been sufficient for a siege of many years. So they were taken by the means of the famine."[184]

William Whiston, the 18th century historian and mathematician, is also the best known translator of the writings of Titus Flavius Josephus from the original Greek into English. In a comment on the burning of the food-warehouses, Whiston concludes, "Nor ... could the Romans have taken this city had not these seditious Jews been so infatuated as thus madly to destroy."[185]

As terrible as burning each other's food supplies is, the cruelty of the Jews toward each other went further, much further than that. First, without explicitly mentioning to which camp they belonged, Josephus describes the desecration of the High Priesthood as a means to bring people to despair. He speaks of robbers who plundered the city and did with its population and government whatever they wanted. "In order to try what surprise the people would be under," he writes, "and how far their own power extended, [the robbers] undertook to dispose of the high priesthood by casting lots for it."[186]

Although he does not use the specific name very often, it is clear that when Josephus speaks of robbers, he means the militants, who were the various sects of Zealots, the Sicarii, until they fled into the Judah Desert and settled in Masada, and, to a lesser extent, the Idumeans. Still, the sensation that permeates through all the descriptions is one of complete eradication of the value of human life and human dignity, and therefore absolute carelessness for one another, and often even glee at the destruction and tormenting of others.

In order to take over the city, the Zealots set up fake tribunals where they held bogus trials. They would frame the rich and powerful and sentence them to death so they would not threaten their control. Once they were executed, they would also take their possessions. In this way, they turned Jerusalem into "a city without a governor."[187]

As always in such states, the rank and file people suffered most. Seeing that the situation was heading for a disaster, many Jews wanted to get out. But the guards, fearing that people would join the Romans or be caught by them and give them information about the situation inside the city, would not let anyone escape. The exception, as always, was "he who gave them money [got to] clear off, while he that gave them none was voted a traitor. So the upshot was that the rich purchased their flight by money while none but the poor were slain."[188]

Meanwhile, within the city and in the roads leading to it, the cruelty of the militants surpassed anything conceivable. "Along all the roads, vast numbers of dead bodies lay in heaps ... But these zealots came at last to that degree of barbarity as not to bestow a burial either on those slain in the city, or on those that lay along the roads, as if they had made an agreement to cancel both the laws of their country and the laws of nature. ...They left the dead bodies to putrefy under the sun. ... The terror was so very great that he who survived called them that were first dead happy, as being at rest already ... [and] those that lay unburied were the happiest."[189]

"The aged men and the women were in such distress by their internal calamities that they wished for the Romans, and earnestly hoped for an external war ... [for] their delivery from their domestic miseries. ... The ... fighting was incessant, both by day and by night. ...Nor was any regard paid to those that were still alive, by their relations; nor was there any care taken of burial for those that were dead. ...They fought against each other while they trod upon the dead bodies as they lay heaped one upon another, and taking up a mad rage from those dead bodies that were under their feet, became the fiercer thereupon. They ... omitted no method of torment or barbarity."[190]

Trapped between the fighting parties, the regular "people were their prey on both sides," and "were plundered by both factions."[191] The misery grew to such extremes that in the end, according to Josephus, people welcomed the conquest and "those that took it did it a greater kindness, for I venture to affirm that the sedition destroyed the city, and the Romans destroyed the sedition."[192] Moreover, and here Josephus writes as a Jew lamenting the fate of his people, destroying the sedition "was a much harder thing to do than to destroy the walls, so that we may justly ascribe our misfortunes to our own people."[193]

Hatred and Apathy in the Extreme

Worse than all the horrors of war, killing, and plundering, nothing turned the people of Jerusalem into animals more than the self-inflicted famine. "The more powerful had more than enough, and the weaker were lamenting [for want of it]. …Children pulled the very morsels that their fathers were eating out of their very mouths, and what was still more to be pitied, so did the mothers do to their infants. …And when those that were most dear were perishing under their hands, they were not ashamed to take from them the very last drops that might preserve their lives. And while they ate after this manner, yet were they not concealed in so doing."[194]

The hungrier people became, the madder they were. Since people hid whatever food they had left in their homes, "the robbers came … and searched men's private houses. … If they found any, they tormented them because they had denied they had any. And if they found none, they tormented them worse because they supposed they had more carefully concealed it."[195]

If people did not snatch food from their own kin and from their children, the fighters did it. "The seditious everywhere came upon them immediately and snatched away from them what they had gotten from others; for when they saw any house shut up, this was to them a signal that the people within had gotten some food, whereupon they broke open the doors and ran in, and took pieces of what they were eating almost up out of their very throats, and this by force. The old men, who held their food fast, were beaten, and if the women hid what they had within their hands, their hair was torn for so doing. Nor was there any commiseration shown either to the aged or to the infants, but they lifted up children from the ground as they hung upon the morsels they had gotten, and shook them down upon the floor. But still they were more barbarously cruel to those that had prevented their coming in, and had actually swallowed down what they were going to seize upon, as if they had been unjustly defrauded of their right. They invented terrible methods of torment to discover where any food was [hidden inside people's bodies], and they were these to stop up the passages of the privy parts of the miserable wretches, and to drive sharp stakes up their fundaments, and a man was forced to bear what it is terrible even to hear, in order to make him confess that he had but one loaf of bread, or that he might discover a handful of barley-meal that was concealed." Even worse, "this was done when these tormentors were not themselves hungry … but … to keep their madness in exercise."[196]

When the food ran out, the blockaded Jews turned to human flesh. Tacitus writes that "The Jews, being closely besieged and given no opportunity to make peace or to surrender, were finally dying of starvation, and the streets began to be filled with corpses everywhere. …Moreover, [they were] made bold to resort to every kind of horrible food, they did not spare even human bodies."[197]

Josephus, who by now had become part of the Roman legion, was present at the scene when it happened. As a result, his documentation of the cannibalism is often graphic and deliberately revolting, in order to show how unbearable was his people's suffering, and at the same time how morally low they had stooped. In the following description, for instance, Josephus uses his report on cannibalism to stress that the Jews boasted in their savagery. "They drank the blood of the populace to one another, and divided the dead bodies of the poor creatures between them. …Although … they contended with each other, yet they very well agreed in their wicked practices, for he that did not communicate what he got by the miseries of others, to the other tyrant seemed to be too little guilty."[198]

Sometimes, the weak ones, who could not rob or tolerate eating human flesh, "were driven to that terrible distress as to search the common sewers and old dunghills of cattle, and to eat the dung which they got there." The hunger had reduced them to a state where "what they of old could not endure so much as to see, they now used for food."[199]

But the most inhuman chapter in this orgy of monstrous hatred called the Great Revolt is an episode that left even the crassest of the robbers aghast, dumbfounded, and downright horrified. It did not involve any men or fighting, but only one tormented soul of a caring mother, driven to insanity by starvation. The book *Lamentation* (4:10) mentions it very briefly and succinctly: "The hands of compassionate women cooked their own children."

Josephus, too, had serious doubts as to whether he should report what he had found out. He writes that he was afraid he "might not seem to deliver what is so portentous to posterity."[200] But since he had "innumerable witnesses to it," and since he believed that his nation, the Jewish people, "would have had little reason to thank me for suppressing the miseries that she underwent at this time,"[201] he had decided to tell the story of the fall of Mary, the eminent woman from Bethezob. Below, I bring the inconceivable report of Josephus as he wrote it, and as William Whiston translated it: "Her name was Mary. Her father was Eleazar, of the village Bethezob. …She was eminent for her family and her wealth, and had fled away to Jerusalem with the rest of the multitude, and was with them besieged therein at this time. What [food] she had treasured up … had been also carried off by the rapacious guards, who came every day running into her house for that purpose. This put the poor woman into a very great passion, and by the frequent reproaches and imprecations she cast at these rapacious villains, she had provoked them to anger against her. But none of them, either out of the indignation she had raised against herself, or out of commiseration of her case, would take away her life. And if she found any food, she perceived her labors were for others, and not for herself. And it was now become impossible for her … to find any more food, while the famine pierced through her very bowels and marrow, when also her passion was fired to a degree beyond the famine itself. Nor did she consult with anything but with her passion and the necessity she was in.

"She then attempted a most unnatural thing, and snatching up her son, who was a child sucking at her breast, she said, 'O thou miserable infant! For whom shall I preserve thee in this war, this famine, and this sedition? As to the war with the Romans, if they preserve our lives, we must be slaves. This famine also will destroy us, even before that slavery comes upon us. Yet these seditious rogues are more terrible than both the others. Come on, be thou my food, and be thou a fury to these seditious varlets [archaic: evildoers], and a by-word to the world, which is now wanting [only] to complete the calamities of us Jews.' As soon as she had said this, she slew her son, and then roasted him, and ate the one half of him, and kept the other half by her concealed.

"Upon this the seditious came in presently, and smelling the horrid scent of this food, they threatened her that they would cut her throat immediately if she did not show them what food she had gotten ready. She replied that she had saved a very fine portion of it for them, and withal uncovered what was left of her son. Hereupon they were seized with horror ... and stood astonished at the sight. She said to them, 'This is mine own son, and what hath been done was mine own doing! Come, eat of this food, for I have eaten of it myself! Do not you pretend to be either more tender than a woman, or more compassionate than a mother. But if you be so scrupulous and do abominate this sacrifice of mine, as I have eaten the one half, let the rest be reserved for me also.' After this, those men went out trembling."[202]

The Morbid Numbers of the Self-Annihilation

By the time the Romans finally breached the walls and stormed Jerusalem, there was no longer anything left to desecrate. The Romans killed whoever still had the urge or energy to fight, set aflame the little that had not been burnt, and took captive and into slavery the rest of the city's inhabitants.

Within a mere five month period, out of a population of 2.7 million strong who inhabited Jerusalem at the beginning of the siege,

"The number of those that perished during the whole siege [was] eleven hundred thousand [1.1 million], the greater part of whom were indeed of the same [Jewish] nation."[203] And the vast majority of the Jews were slain by people of their own fold. Tacitus, who documented the unfolding solely from the perspective of the Romans, had similar estimates to those of Josephus regarding the number of casualties. He counted just short 1.2 million Jews, but he also included in his estimate Jews who were exiled.[204]

Whether the number is one, 1.1, or 1.2 million Jews, one thing is clear: As inconceivable as this may be, with the exception of a few months during World War II, even Nazi Germany, during the Final Solution phase of the Holocaust, did not outpace the killing rate that the Jews had inflicted on themselves at the time of the siege in Jerusalem. Moreover, they slew one another not with gas chambers or machine guns, but with knives, swords, and spears, looking at their victims straight in the eye, or simply by starving them to death. Often, they knew their victims personally or were even their own spouses, parents, or children.

When the Roman soldiers and generals entered the city and saw what the Jews had done to their own people, they were appalled and disgusted beyond belief. Perhaps now we can understand why Philostratus wrote that Titus declined to wear the "victory wreath after he took the city ... [since] there was no merit in vanquishing a people deserted by their own God."[205]

On the 9th of the Hebrew month of *Av* [August or September] each year, Jews commemorate the fall of Jerusalem. But those among us who acknowledge what had happened do not commemorate the conquest of the city, but the conquest of the evil inclination over the hearts of our people. We, the nation that formed under the condition of uniting "as one man with one heart," and was tasked with being a light unto the nations, a beacon of unity, have given the world a lesson in self-hatred that will not be forgotten. When our sages speak of the Second Temple being ruined by unfounded hatred, they are referring to the just described atrocities we had committed on ourselves.

A Father of the World

When Titus stormed Jerusalem and destroyed what was left of the Temple, he not only wished to extinguish the revolt, he wished to exterminate the Jewish people altogether. By the beginning of the Common Era, the Jews had already spread throughout the Roman Empire, and Titus did not like Jews. The book *Jewish Life and Thought Among Greeks and Romans*, edited by acclaimed scholar of Hellenistic civilization, Prof. Louis H. Feldman, writes that the Greek geographer and historian Strabo said that Jews are to be found everywhere in the world.[206] According to the book, by 86 BCE, some 150 years before Titus stormed the walls of Jerusalem for the last time, "This people has already made its way into every city, and it is not easy to find any place in the habitable world that has not received this nation and in which it has not made its power felt."[207]

According to Tacitus, the Romans were indecisive about whether they should raze the Temple. They "deliberated whether [Titus] should destroy such a mighty Temple ... a consecrated shrine which was famous beyond all other works of men." But not the high commander: "Titus himself opposed [to preserving the Temple], holding the destruction of this temple to be a prime necessity in order to wipe out more completely the religion of the Jews." He also wanted to eliminate the budding religion Christianity, but maintained that it "nevertheless sprang from the same sources; the Christians had grown out of the Jews: if the root were destroyed, the stock would easily perish."[208]

Similar to the Spaniards in the years leading to the expulsion from Spain, the Germans leading to the accession of the Nazi Party to power, and America's current anti-Semites, Titus did not want Jewish influence to be so prominent in the Roman Empire. In an attempt to eliminate Jewish influence, he was driven to attempt to eliminate the Jews. Once again we see how the symptom of Jewish disunity—the drive of Jews to assimilate among the nations instead of maintaining their unique spirit and historic task—results in the world turning against them.

Still, Titus, like many great leaders before him and after him, did not, and in fact, could not succeed. You can kill every Jew that you can put your hands on but you will never destroy the entire nation, since the Jews have an obligation to the world, and until they carry it out, they cannot be destroyed. That said, until they carry it out, they will continue to be tormented, hated, admired, and despised, all at the same time, and often by the same people. Adolf Hitler, perhaps the symbol of satanic anti-Semitism, wrote in his book *Mein Kampf* [*My Struggle*]: "When over long periods of human history, I scrutinized the activity of the Jewish people, suddenly, there arose in me the fearful question whether inscrutable destiny, perhaps for reasons unknown to us poor mortals, did not … desire the final victory of this little nation."[209]

What Hitler did not know was that the victory of the Jews would not be a physical one but a spiritual one, a victory expressed in the unification of humanity under the law of unity and love of others. And no one expressed that law better than Rabbi Akiva, who suffered from such disclosures of hatred that his "flesh [was] torn from his body by iron combs."[210]

Akiva ben Yosef, better known as Rabbi Akiva, was born around the year 50 CE, and lived until approximately 136 CE. Not much is known about his life. Maimonides writes that his father, Joseph, converted to Judaism.[211]

Rabbi Akiva was a simple man, pasturing the herds of Kalba Savua, whose daughter Rachel he later married. Yet, at some point, while already an adult, he went through a transformation and decided not only to study the essence of Judaism, but to dedicate his entire life to studying it. He developed such a thirst for the laws of life, the same laws that Ptolemy II Philadelphus learned from the ancient sages, that he dropped everything and went to learn with the sages of his time. Indeed, Rabbi Akiva was so prodigious in his learning that his teacher soon regarded him as a maker of rules, and he became the most illustrious teacher of all time, with no less than 24,000 disciples.

What Rabbi Akiva taught was very simple: The greatest rule in the Torah [Jewish law] is "love your neighbor as yourself." Yet, even the great Rabbi Akiva could not save his disciples from internal hatred and its ramifications. The Talmud writes that all but five of Akiva's 24,000 disciples "died at the same time because they did not treat each other with respect,"[212] since they could not love one another as their teacher had instructed them.

The Jerusalem Talmud referred to Rabbi Akiva as one of the fathers of the world.[213] Yet, his righteousness, his love for others, his efforts to reinstate love in the people of Israel, all those merits could not help even Rabbi Akiva as long as his disciples did not uphold his most fundamental tenet: Love others as much as you love yourself. Moreover, they could not carry out even its less demanding version, which Hillel proposed. The Talmud tells us that "When a proselyte came to Hillel and asked him to teach him the whole Torah while he was standing on one leg, meaning very quickly, Hillel replied, 'That which you hate, do not do unto your neighbor. This is the whole of the Torah, and the rest is its commentary.'"[214] Is it any wonder then that eventually, the Romans got their hands on this "father of the world" and raked his flesh to death with iron combs?

Nevertheless, Rabbi Akiva's teaching was not in vain. Five out of the 24,000 disciples survived, since they were not afflicted by the unfounded hatred that had plagued the rest of their friends. Those disciples wrote both the Mishnah and *The Book of Zohar*. The Mishnah, with its commentary, the Talmud, served throughout the centuries as the foundation of Judaism, and was the basis for maintaining the existence of the Jewish people, while *The Book of Zohar* is the seminal book in what is known as the "internality of the Torah," or "the wisdom of Kabbalah." Without these writings, there would not be Jews today, and, more importantly, no knowledge of how to bring unity and peace to the world.

While Rabbi Akiva did not succeed in reestablishing the Jewish people on its original foundation, he did enable the nation to continue to exist so that eventually, it would achieve its vocation and would be a light of cohesion and love of others unto the nations of the world.

The Swan Song

During Akiva's time, yet another, final revolt against the Romans took place. In 132 CE, Simon bar Kokhba attempted one last time to restore Jewish sovereignty in the land of Israel. He waged what was known as The Third Jewish-Roman War or The Third Jewish Revolt. It was a futile, hopeless attempt, yet both Rabbi Akiva and his close disciple Rabbi Shimon Bar Yochai, author of *The Book of Zohar*, supported the revolt,[215] although they probably did not participate in the fighting itself.

Johnson writes that initially, the revolt was quite successful "and created a great deal of trouble for the Romans."[216] It lasted no less than four years, and for some time, the Jews even regained control of Jerusalem, but without walls around the city, it was not defensible. In the end, the Roman army overwhelmed the rebels, Rabbi Akiva was executed, and Bar Kokhba died, too, probably from a lethal snake bite.[217] This effectively ended the history of the Jewish state in antiquity.

The land that was intended to foster a nation built on love of others ejected its people precisely because they had become a symbol of baseless hatred. As such, they were unworthy of statehood, peoplehood, or sovereignty. Officially, they have retained the title Jews, but the essence of Jewishness, which lies in the tenet "love your neighbor as yourself," was no longer existent among them. They broke the vow they had made some seventeen centuries earlier, to be "as one man with one heart" and project that oneness to the world so that humanity would be as one, as well. And once they broke it, they stopped being a nation and regressed into a collection of strangers who bear the same name. Today, Jews come together only when the hatred of the world compels them. Now that the world blames them for everything that is wrong and painful, this hatred keeps this fold alive. Without the nations' animosity, we would have ceased to exist many generations ago.

As we will see below, history will not let our people vanish. Nor will it let us live in peace until we carry out our task. Even in exile, the principle of unity as our remedy holds true, and every time we forget it, we pay a heavy toll.

Chapter 4: Spain — Former Jews vs. Present Jews

"Intensification of assimilationist tendencies in Jewry has always caused intensification in anti-Semitism, and, in particular (which sounds particularly paradoxical), an increase in accusations of particularism."[218]

Prof. Solomon Lurye

As we saw in the previous chapters, in antiquity, our greatest woes were always our internal conflicts. Even in exile, we can detect (a different form of) the same phenomenon: Whenever there is a noticeable movement of Jews outside of their fold and toward mingling with their host culture, the host culture rejects their attempt. Usually, and paradoxically, it also blames them of not assimilating, which is exactly what they would do had the host culture not rejected them.

Like everything else about anti-Semitism, there is no logic in this paradox, only a gut feeling on the part of the gentiles that the Jews are to blame for whatever hurts them at that moment. The only thing that changes is the blame, the pretext for the hatred. Classic anti-Semitism, modern anti-Semitism, anti-Semitism in antiquity—these are all different titles of the same phenomenon: hatred of Jews. The pretexts only give it different names but it is the same Jew-hatred under different cloaks.

The ruin of the Second Temple and the horrors that Jews inflicted on themselves while fighting against the Romans were the last straw in the demise of Jewish unity. Despite the anti-Semites' claim that Jews stick together, we have not restored our unity since it disintegrated two millennia ago, at least not to the level that we were tasked with achieving at the foot of Mt. Sinai, and which we achieved for a while, before the ruin of the Temple.

During the exile in Babylon, the majority of our people , who were no longer able to maintain unity above differences, assimilated in the Babylonian culture and all but two tribes disappeared. During the Seleucid rule over the kingdom of Judah at the time of the Second Temple, the majority of Jews became Hellenized and gradually disappeared. But since the ruin of the Second Temple and the dispersion of our people, the tendency to dissolve into the host culture has intensified to the point where it has become our most dominant trait. Were it not for anti-Semitism, our tribe would have been long gone, as have all the ancient nations.

The paradoxes that surround anti-Semitism also surround the tenacious existence of the Jewish people. Numerous poets, authors, and historians throughout the centuries have pondered the conundrum of Jewish perseverance against all odds. Even Jews themselves, in every generation, saw themselves as a dying creed. The eloquent Polish born Jewish American philosopher Simon Rawidowicz beautifully conveyed that state. In his aptly titled book, *Israel, the Ever-Dying People*, Rawidowicz writes, "He who studies Jewish history will readily discover that there was hardly a generation in the Diaspora that did not consider itself the final link in Israel's chain. Each always saw before it the abyss ready to swallow it up. There was scarcely a generation that while toiling, falling, and rising, again being uprooted and striking new roots, was not filled with the deepest anxiety lest it be fated to stand at the grave of the nation...

Each generation grieved not only for itself but also for the great past that was going to disappear forever, as well as for the future of unborn generations who would never see the light of day."[219]

However, despite their fear, the Jews are here. "As far as historical reality is concerned," continues Rawidowicz, "we are confronted here with a phenomenon that has almost no parallel in mankind's story: a people that has been disappearing constantly for the last two thousand years, exterminated in dozens of lands all over the globe, reduced to half or third of its population by tyrants ancient and modern—and yet still exists... There is no people more dying than Israel, yet none better equipped to resist disaster."[220]

The last time we had some form of self-governance, albeit short-lived and limited, was during the Bar Kokhba Revolt, which ended in 135 CE. Since then, we have been in exile. During the exile, we have been expelled or exterminated (or both) in our host countries more than 800 times![221] There is virtually no place on Earth where Jews did not live, and there is virtually no place on Earth from which they were not, at some point, ruthlessly ejected or simply annihilated.

The End of *Convivencia*

Out of all the persecutions and expulsions, a particular one stands out. The story of the rise and fall of Spanish Jewry has been an emblem of the Jewish experience in exile—combining great achievements and a bitter end. Until the Holocaust, the Jewish expulsion from Spain was *the* tragedy of world Jewry after the destruction of the Second Temple. Even after the horrors of the Holocaust, the story of the *Sephardim* [Spanish Jews] is still an open wound in the collective memory of the tribe.

Yet, as we will see, it bears distinct similarities to all the major downfalls that our nation has experienced over the ages. Therefore, the immersion in Spain and expulsion from it should be looked upon as part of Jewish history rather than as a unique event. Doing so will help us better understand and put our current situation in the global arena into context.

The presence of Jews in Spain began very early. Professor of Jewish History at the City University of New York Jane Gerber writes that "Jews had probably reached the westernmost edge of the Mediterranean [Iberian Peninsula, roughly today's Spain and Portugal] in antiquity, when the Second Temple still stood in Jerusalem."[222] The beginning of the Jewish settlement in Spain was also the beginning of the complicated Judeo-Christian relationship. Yitzhak Baer, an acclaimed historian and expert on medieval Spanish Jewish history, writes that "The first Jews to settle in Spain were part of the ancient Diaspora which was dispersed throughout all corners of the Roman Empire. Already the apostle Paul intended to visit Spain, undoubtedly to establish contact with a Judeo-Christian community in existence there."[223]

Prof. Gerber writes that after two centuries of persecutions of the Jews in Spain, the beginning of the 8th century marked a new era in the lives of Spanish Jews. The year 711 marks the end of the Visigothic Kingdom in Spain, which was virulently anti-Semitic. Gradually, a unique relationship developed where three Abrahamic religions—Judaism, Christianity, and Islam—developed a positive coexistence that enriched all three, and at the same time respected the customs of each religion.

Norman Roth, Professor of Jewish History at the University of Wisconsin, describes the extraordinary relationships among Jews, Christians, and Muslims at that time: "So unusual, one may say unique, was the nature of that relationship," he writes, "that a special term is used in Spanish for it ... *convivencia* [roughly meaning, 'living together in affinity']. In truth, the real extent of *convivencia* in medieval Christian Spain has not yet been fully revealed."[224]

The *convivencia* in Spain continued for many centuries. In *Conversos, Inquisition, and the Expulsion of the Jews from Spain*, Roth continues to elaborate on the subtle implications of *convivencia* among the three faiths in Medieval Spain. "The special situation of the symbiotic relationship between Jews, Muslims, and Christians in Spain is given a special term, untranslatable into English: *convivencia*. To call this 'living together,' or coexistence, as is sometimes done, is wide of the mark, for people may live together and yet not like each other. There was, in fact, an *interdependence* of the three peoples in medieval Spain, a phenomenon that survived the Christian 'Reconquest' of Muslim Spain which was completed in the thirteenth century. Muslims, too, then lived intermingled with Christians, though to a less extensive degree than the Jews. The Christians found themselves heavily indebted, culturally and in daily life, to Muslims and Jews."[225]

However, the tide began to turn against the Jews when the Jews began to abandon their own roots and turn against their former coreligionists. The basic rules concerning the Jews did not change simply because they were exiled from the land of Israel. Jewish unity as a condition for success, and Jewish disunity as an instigator of adversity, has, is, and always will be the guiding principle for the Jewish people. When we forget that, we are reminded by the nations, and we call that reminder "anti-Semitism."

When Jews were united in antiquity, before they began to adopt Hellenism, Ptolemy II Philadelphus said about their teachings that "he had learned how he ought to rule his subjects."[226] When they were united, the nations would "go up to Jerusalem and see Israel ... and say, 'It is becoming to cling only to this nation.'"[227] But when Jews disunited and wanted to leave their tribe, it has "always caused intensification in anti-Semitism, and, in particular ... an increase in accusations of particularism,"[228] as paradoxical as this may sound. Simply put, a society that was built to be "a pilot," as Paul Johnson put it, cannot opt out of its task.

We the Jews, as I have shown above, formed our nation out of fragments of foreign, often rival nations, tribes, and clans that lived in ancient Mesopotamia and the Near and Middle East. Abraham united us under the rule, "Love will cover all crimes" (Proverbs 10:12). When Moses united us above all our many differences and disputes, we were given a task: to show the world how to rise above conflicts through unity and love of others, and in this way, be "a light unto nations." Since then, as long as we kept our unity, we thrived; when we abandoned it, we were beaten until we barely survived.

In the middle of the 14th century, intensifying alienation from their fold induced in Jews in Spain an accelerated process of assimilation and abandonment of their religion. We have not been united since before the ruin of the Second Temple, but complete assimilation, conversion to another faith, means the denial of the chance to restore unity, and this, we will not be permitted to do. Accordingly, at the same time when Spanish Jews began to convert, anti-Semitism began to grow apace.

Michael Grant, English classicist, author, and professor at Cambridge University, observed the inability of Jews to mingle even in antiquity: "The Jews proved not only unassimilated, but inassimilable," he writes. "...The demonstration that this was so proved one of the most significant turning points in Greek history, owing to the gigantic influence [of the Jews] exerted throughout subsequent ages by their religion, which not only survived intact, but subsequently gave birth to Christianity."[229]

Anti-Semites, philo-Semites, and other individuals throughout the centuries who were intrigued by Judaism have noticed that the Jews survive under circumstances that other nations would have long succumbed to. They ponder this perseverance but they cannot explain it. They often know that it has to do with the vocation of the Jews, but they cannot put their finger on the nature of that vocation—that it is to bring unity to the world by means of rising above all crimes.

One of the most poetic quotes in this regard is attributed to the famous Russian author Leo Tolstoy. The *Jewish World* periodical published it back in 1908, and whether or not Tolstoy actually wrote it, the excerpt reflects the wonder of the nations at the resilience of the Jews. Below is the slightly truncated excerpt: "What is the Jew? ...What kind of unique creature is this whom all the rulers of all the nations of the world have disgraced and crushed and expelled and destroyed; persecuted, burned and drowned, and who, despite their anger and their fury, continues to live and to flourish? … The Jew is the symbol of eternity. …He is the one who for so long had guarded the prophetic message and transmitted it to all mankind. A people such as this can never disappear."230

Speaking of Russians, in the early 20th century, Vasily Shulgin, the self-proclaimed anti-Semite and senior member of the Duma [Russian Parliament], was probably one of the most perceptive individuals with regard to the role of the Jews in the world, and how they performed it in antiquity. In his earlier-mentioned book, *What We Don't Like About Them...* (ellipses in the original title), he writes, "I don't feel goodness in Jewry. Cut me to pieces; do what you want; I do not feel it! I would be happy to feel it. I would be happy to bow before the apostles of the Jews again, as we had bowed before [in antiquity]. … But where are these individuals, who stopped being humane since the spirit of holiness ceased shining the aura over their heads?"231 Reading these words from the pen of a rabid anti-Semite, who, apart from a few excerpts, dedicated his entire book to tirades and rants about how Jews use and abuse humanity, should make us pay close attention to his words since he does not only hate Jews, he also tells us how he would love us if we only led humanity to the good, to the real vocation of the people of Israel.

But in the middle of the 14th century, to get back to the topic of this chapter, the Jews in Spain began to drift from Judaism at an accelerated rate. As a result, anti-Semitism quickly intensified and by the end of the century, it became full blown persecutions.

"In the summer of 1391, a series of attacks on Jews spread throughout Castile, and soon spread to Aragon, Catalonia, Majorca, and Valencia," writes Norman Roth. "Much robbing and looting took place, and some Jews were killed."232 According to the Jewish Virtual Library, "On June 6 [1391], the mob attacked the Juderia in Seville from all sides and murdered 4,000 Jews; the rest submitted to baptism as the only means of escaping death. During the months-long riots, the Cordova Juderia was burned down and over 5,000 Jews ruthlessly murdered regardless of age or sex. Again, more Jews converted as the only way to escape death. ...After the persecutions of 1391, many Jews converted, and still thousands more continued to practice Judaism in secret (these people were known as Marranos). On account of their talent and wealth, and through intermarriage with noble families, the converts [which became known as *conversos*] and Marranos gained considerable influence and filled important government offices."[233]

But the massacre of 1391 only exacerbated a preexisting problem: accelerated Jewish conversion. "Until 1391, conversion in the face of persecution had been literally unthinkable in Christian lands," writes Jane Gerber. "When Jews faced the fury of the mobs in the Rhineland during the first and second Crusades in 1096-1147, they unhesitatingly chose martyrdom, becoming an example that echoed in Jewish liturgy and shared memory ... Their martyrdom ... was considered the norm. Given the context of long-standing Judaic tradition, then, the collective conversion in 1391 of nearly 100,000 Jews ... is evidence of enormous erosion of faith."[234] And because the dispersion of Jews turns the nations against them, "The presence of these new converts, known as *conversos*, would be a source of prolonged anguish for the Jews and of mounting antagonism from the Christian population," concludes Gerber.[235] In some places, such as Córdoba, hardly any Jews remained. The rest had converted to Christianity.

As it always happens, the assimilation instigated "mounting antagonism," as Gerber put it. Christians became increasingly hostile toward Jews, and especially toward *conversos*, whose sincerity of conversion they doubted, and because these *conversos* began to climb up the social ladder, even among the clergy.

Possibly in order to prove their loyalty to their new faith, or because they genuinely loathed their former one, many *conversos* not only became prominent clergymen, they also developed virulent anti-Semitism. Some *conversos* even became very active in leading the campaign against the Jews which culminated in the expulsion, and were among its most avid supporters.

The most commonly known story, of course, is that of Tomás de Torquemada, the Inquisitor General who is said to be "himself from a converso family."[236] It is said that Torquemada was "the nephew of a celebrated theologian and cardinal, Juan de Torquemada, who himself was a descendant of a *converso*."[237]

While there are some who dispute the reliability of the sources that attest to the Jewish roots of Torquemada, there is no dispute that many Jews, especially Jewish scholars and rabbis, became high ranking clergymen in the Spanish Catholic Church. "The conversion of Solomon ha-Levy, a rabbi of Burgos, and with him his entire family, took place some time *before* the events of 1391," writes Norman Roth. "This is an example of conversion motivated not by fear but by sincere belief."[238] Rabbi Solomon ha-Levy became Bishop Pablo de Santa Maria whose example "inspired others, such as his former disciple Joshua al-Lorqi, also to convert. What such conversions meant to the larger Jewish community can well be imagined," concludes Roth.[239]

Later, Roth describes the collaboration between anti-Semitic Christian born clergymen and *conversos*. "One of the most notoriously anti-Jewish of the medieval popes was the Spaniard Benedict XIII, the 'antipope' of Avignon whose jurisdiction was recognized by all of Spain. In 1413 he instituted yet another disputation [debate between Jewish and Christian clergymen aiming to ridicule the Jews and cause them and their followers to convert] in Tortosa in Catalonia, in which major Jewish rabbis and thinkers were 'invited' to participate. The primary spokesman for the Christians was none other than [the former disciple of the now Bishop Pablo de Santa Maria] Joshua al-Lorqi, who upon his conversion had taken the name Jeronimo de Santa Fe and who became, in fact, a leading Christian theologian. The result of this disputation, which lasted well into the following year, was again the conversion of large numbers of Jews, including many rabbis and prominent leaders, among whom were some of those who took part in the disputation itself."[240]

In fact, writes Roth later in the book, "The most important *conversos* who were bishops, Church officials, and theological writers for many years to come were members of the Santa Maria-Cartagena family. These included Pablo, bishop first of Cartagena and then Burgos, his son Alonso de Cartagena, who succeeded his father in both positions, and many others. Juan Diaz de Coca, son of Alonso Diaz, one of Pablo's sons, was bishop of Calahorra. Another important member of this family who was a bishop was Juan Ortega de Maluenda."[241]

But the rapid ascent of *conversos* did not prove advantageous, neither for them nor for the Jews. Gerber already noted that the presence of these new converts was "a source of prolonged anguish for the Jews and of mounting antagonism from the Christian population." British historian Cecil Roth elaborates on the issue, stating that "The forced and voluntary conversions of that period liberated tens of thousands [of former Jews] from legal, cultural and religious constraints that had kept them as a class apart when they were Jews. The Spanish *Conversos* entered Catholicism and Christian society vigorously and enthusiastically, quickly penetrating the Castilian middle and upper classes and occupying the most prominent positions in the royal administration and church hierarchy."[242] However, just as it was observed by historian of antiquity and author of *Anti-Semitism in the Ancient World*, Prof. Solomon Lurye—whom we quoted in the beginning of this chapter—the paradox of anti-Semitism emerged. On one hand, the Catholic Spaniards grew antagonistic toward Jews. On the other hand, they detested those who converted. The tragic results of this paradox, concludes Roth, was that "The hostility of the masses to the New Christian elite [*conversos*] led first, around the middle of the 15th century, to the notorious 'Purity of Blood Statutes' [an 'antecedent' of the Nazi race laws] and then, in 1478, to the establishment of the Spanish Inquisition."[243] The latter, again, paradoxically, was initiated and promoted by "veteran" *conversos* of previous generations such as Tomás de Torquemada.

In other words, both the Purity of Blood laws and the Spanish Inquisition did not target Jews, but rather those they called "crypto-Jews" or "Marranos." According to Prof. of History Robert A.

Maryks, "Purity of blood (*pureza [limpieza] de sangre*) was an obsessive concern that originated in mid-15th-century Spain on the basis of the biased belief that the unfaithfulness of the 'deicide Jews' (God-killing Jews) not only had endured in those who converted to Catholicism, but also had been transmitted by blood to their descendants, regardless of their sincerity in professing the Christian faith. Consequently, Old Christians 'of pure blood' considered New Christians impure and therefore morally inadequate to be members of their communities."[244]

Anti-Semitic *Conversos*

Although the Spaniards did not trust the *conversos*, many *conversos* did reach very high positions in both the government and the church. They became bishops, confessors to the Spanish nobility and royalty, and treasurers wherever they lived in Spain.

The *conversos* who had ascended the hierarchical ladder in Spain often became rabid anti-Semites themselves, either in order to prove their piety or because they genuinely loathed their former faith, or both. According to Jane Gerber, as earlier mentioned, "One of the most famous [among them] was Solomon HaLevi. This former rabbi of Burgos, who became bishop of the city under his baptismal name of Pablo de Santa Maria, became best known, unfortunately, for his anti-*converso* attitudes and programs. Even more prominent [on the Catholic Church hierarchy] were Bartolomeo Carranza, who became archbishop of Toledo and then primate of all Spain, and Hernando de Talavera, who became archbishop of Granada."[245] Finally, "There is an even more astonishing example of devout conversion: the patron saint of Spain, Theresa of Avila was of *converso* descent."[246]

According to Norman Roth, "It sometimes seems to be as difficult for some modern Christians as for Jewish historians to accept the simple fact ... that the overwhelming majority of the Jews who converted did so because they sincerely believed in Christianity and just as sincerely were convinced of the falseness of the Jewish faith. ... It is not surprising that many *conversos* chose a career in some form of religious life, and this is a further indication of the sincerity of their Christianity. Many [even] entered monasteries and convents."[247]

Numerous cases of anti-Semitism or anti-Judaism—as *conversos* often refer to it—have been documented. One such case was that of the "blood libel" of 1468. In that year in Segovia, a case was presented to court, accusing Jews of killing Christian boys to use their blood. The bishop of Segovia was the *converso* Juan Arias Davila. According to Roth, he "ordered the arrest of sixteen Jews, no less, supposedly 'guilty' of this crime. Some were condemned to death by burning, others imprisoned, and one youth saved himself by accepting baptism."[248]

Initially, King Ferdinand and Queen Isabella had a favorable attitude toward Jews. However, the *conversos* turned the king and queen against the Jews, which ultimately resulted in the expulsion from Spain. According to Prof. Roth, "The question of whether these *converso* officials had anything to do with Fernando and Isabel's favorable attitude toward Jews can be answered in the negative, of course. Like the majority of *conversos*, they were ardent Catholics and most were vehemently anti-Jewish (especially was this true with *converso* clergy, but also with the officials)."[249]

Another case of actively anti-Semitic *conversos* was the family of Azarias. "All of the brothers of Azarias (Luis) converted with him, and one of these, Martin de Santangel, was no less than the Inquisitor General of Aragon."[250]

But there was another dominant family in Aragon: the de la Cavalleria family. "One of the most important members of the family," writes Roth, "was Jaime de la Cavalleria, judge of the 'Holy Brotherhood' of Zaragoza."[251] According to Roth, the brotherhood was actually a long standing organization in Castile whose purpose was to protect the peace, but which in truth was reorganized under the Catholic Monarchs into a powerful quasi-religious, quasi-military institution which often caused problems for Jews and *conversos*. "Directly contradicting the express orders of the king and queen," writes Roth, "the Inquisitors and officials of Zaragoza prohibited the Jews from taking any of their goods or property when they were expelled in 1492."[252]

Gerber supports Roth's words regarding the infamous de la Cavalleria family. She writes that a surviving fragment of a Hebrew chronicle of the de la Cavalleria family, written immediately after the expulsion, "suggests that court intrigue involving some malevolent *conversos* in the family may have helped foster the decree [of expulsion]. They were *conversos* 'accustomed to the evil of sinning, starting with the days of Fra Vicente [Ferrer],' who 'thought evil of God's nation' and 'conspired to destroy the name of Israel from the land.'"[253]

Another case I would like to mention, out of many like it, is that of Hernando de Talavera. De Talavera was a monk who became the Archbishop of Granada and confessor of Queen Isabella herself. He, too, was of *converso* origin. Roth writes that de Talavera was "a severe critic of Judaism."[254] That is, he objected to Judaism as a religion, to the existence of the Jewish religion. As such, he opposed the Inquisition against *conversos* and wanted to focus the persecutions against Jews. But as soon as they converted, they should be left in peace, he maintained. In his view, he was not anti-Semitic, but rather anti-Judaism.

Alfonso was another member of the earlier mentioned de la Cavalleria family. "In 1484, Fernando wrote ... that the 'devoted Inquisitors' [Alfon-so de la Cavalleria, vice-chancellor of Aragon, and Garcia Sanchez, ...also a *converso*] had informed him that Jews in the village of Cella, near Teruel, did not live separate from Christians as they were supposed to, and therefore great 'dangers in offense to divine majesty and damnation of the souls of Christians' result from the 'participation and conversation' between Christians and Jews. The king thereupon ordered that all Jews leave the village within eight days, and that in whatever place they went (in Spain) they wear a colored badge."[255]

But the most vitriolic and anti-Semitic of all *conversos* was undoubtedly the Grand Inquisitor Tomás de Torquemada. Although matters grew worse for both Jews and *conversos* as the Inquisition raged throughout Spain, the Jews remained relatively unharmed as long as they stayed within the confines of their living areas and did not attempt to mingle with Christians or *conversos*. But in the eyes of Torquemada, the only option to guarantee that *conversos* would not become Marranos, meaning crypto-Jews—who pretend to be avid Christians but are secretly practicing Judaism—was complete expulsion of all Jews from Spain, and killing the ones who refused to leave.

King Ferdinand and Queen Isabella were not wholly convinced that there was no alternative, but Torquemada, being the queen's confessor for many years, had critical influence on the royal couple. Early in 1492, he managed to persuade them to issue an edict of expulsion for all the Jews. The edict, which was to become known as the Alhambra Decree, was prepared very carefully and made sure all details were included and clarified.

When the Jews heard that an edict of expulsion was in the making, they did their best to ward off the calamity. When they could not persuade the king and queen to cancel it, they attempted to "buy" their freedom. There are many versions of the story of how the decision to publish the decree was finally made, but all of them depict the critical influence of Torquemada in the completion of the decree. According to the Jewish Virtual Library, "Don Isaac Abravanel ... offered Ferdinand and Isabella 600,000 crowns for the revocation of the edict of expulsion. As the story goes, Ferdinand hesitated, but was prevented from accepting the offer by Torquemada, the grand inquisitor, who dashed into the royal presence, threw a crucifix down before the king and queen, and asked whether, like Judas, they would betray their Lord for money."[256]

Prof. of Jewish History Jacob Rader Marcus came across a more dramatic depiction of the events leading to the announcement of the decree, though the general outline and the result are the same. In his book *The Jew in the Medieval World*, Prof. Marcus details the events. He writes that the agreement permitting the Jews to remain in Spain on the payment of a large sum of money was almost completed when it was frustrated by the Prior of Santa Cruz, Tomás de Torquemada.

"Legend relates that Torquemada, Prior of the convent of Santa Cruz," writes Marcus, "thundered, with crucifix aloft, to the King and Queen: 'Judas Iscariot sold his master for thirty pieces of silver. Your Highness would sell him anew for thirty thousand? Here he is [pointing to the cross], take him, and barter him away.'"[257] King Ferdinand was indeed dumbfounded by the zealous speech, which foiled any hesitations he might have had about the implementation of the decree.

However, what happened next was even more amazing. Marcus writes that Queen Isabella, who was present in the room when Torquemada stormed in, "gave an answer to the representatives of the Jews, similar to the saying of King Solomon [Proverbs 21:1]: 'The king's heart is in the hand of the Lord, as the rivers of water: He turns it wherever He wills.' She said furthermore: 'Do you believe that this comes upon you from us? The Lord has put this thing into the heart of the king.'"[258] Subsequently, concludes Marcus, the Jews "saw that there was evil determined against them by the King, and they gave up the hope of remaining."[259]

The Edict of Expulsion

As in antiquity, the Spanish Jews suffered because of their lack of unity. Their attempts to convert inflicted on them the Inquisition, which ended with all Jews and untrustworthy *conversos* (in the eyes of the inquisitors) being expelled from Spain or slain.

As in antiquity, by the time calamity struck, the level of animosity between Jews and *conversos*, and the mistrust of the Spaniards toward Jews and *conversos* alike, were too intense to overcome. It is hard to place the finger on the point of no return, but beyond a certain level of internal alienation among Jews, the wheel cannot be turned back. As Gerber woefully notes, "Unfortunately, the persistent and growing anti-Jewish sentiment across the land could not similarly succeed in melding the Jews ... into one strong communal organization."[260] Some 450 years later, we will see the same scenario unfolding in Nazi Germany, but with far more tragic consequences than the outcome of the disunity of Spanish Jewry, and, in fact, far worse than anyone could have imagined until it actually happened.

Interestingly, the Alhambra Decree to expel all Jews from Spain does not sound hateful, but rather quite pragmatic, more like a legal notice. The included translated excerpts, quoted from the meticulous work of Dr. David Raphael, convey how banal horror can sometimes sound: It begins very politely, "Don Ferdinand and Dona Isabel, by the grace of God King and Queen of..."[261] naming all the kingdoms over which Ferdinand and Isabella ruled. From there the decree goes on to name all the people to whom it is meant to be delivered, "Count and Countess of Barcelona and the lords of Biscay and Molina, Dukes of Athens and Neopatria, Counts of Rosellon and of Sardinia," and many others. The king and queen even formally address "Prince Don Juan, our dear and beloved son."

From there the decree goes on to address nearly every class, title, and occupation in the country. Finally, the edict addresses the Jews directly, and in such a practical manner that it does not even begin a new sentence: "...and bishoprics and dioceses of our reigns and seignories [domains of feudal lords], and to the communities of the Jews of the said city of Burgos, and to all the cities and villages and places of our said reigns and seignories, and to all the Jews and their singular persons, thus men and women of whatever age, and to all other persons of whatever legal status, dignity, or preeminence, or condition to which that contained below in our letters [decree] appertains or may appertain in any manner." Subsequently, the edict concludes the opening salutations with a greeting: "health and grace unto you."

After the cordial address, the king and queen explain the "crimes" of the Jews, namely that they think that Jews are trying to draw *conversos* back to Judaism: "We were informed that in these our kingdoms there were some bad Christians who Judaized and apostatized from our holy Catholic faith, this being chiefly caused by the communication of the Jews with the Christians. ...We ordered that the said Jews be separated in all the cities, villages, and places of our kingdoms and seignories, and that they be given Jewish quarters and separate places where they could live, hoping that this separation would remedy [the problem]. Moreover, we have sought and given the order that an inquisition be conducted in the said kingdoms and seignories which ... has been done and is continuing, and on account of it, many guilty individuals have been found, which is notorious."

After describing the situation, the edict describes the harms that the king and queen see: "It is evident and apparent that the great damage to the Christians has resulted from and does result from the participation, conversation, and communication that they [*conversos*] have had with the Jews, who try to always achieve by whatever ways and means possible to subvert and to draw away faithful Christians from our holy Catholic faith and to separate them from it, and to attract and pervert them to their injurious belief and opinion ... giving them books from which to read their prayers" and numerous other Jewish customs that they ostensibly entice the *conversos* to observe, "which has redounded to the great injury, detriment, and opprobrium of our holy Catholic faith."

Despite all the detriment that the king and queen saw coming from the Jews to the *conversos*, they admit that initially, they did not plan to expel the Jews. "Notwithstanding that we were informed of most of this beforehand, and realizing that the true remedy for these injuries ... was in breaking of all communication of the said Jews with the Christians and to eject them from our kingdoms, we sought to content ourselves in ordering them out of all the cities and villages of Andalusia where it appeared they had done great damage, believing that this would be sufficient, so that the other cities and villages and places of our kingdoms and seignories would cease to do and commit the aforesaid. And because we are informed that neither that nor the punishments meted out to some of those said Jews found culpable in the said crimes and transgression against our holy Catholic faith will suffice as a complete remedy to obviate and terminate such great opprobrium," they reason the edict of expulsion, "...Therefore, with the counsel and advice of some prelates, grandees, and cavaliers of our kingdoms and other persons of knowledge and conscience of our

Council [the most prominent of whom being Torquemada], having had much deliberation upon it, resolve to order all and said Jews and Jewesses out of our kingdoms and that they never return nor come back to any of them."

Subsequently, the edict specifies the date of expulsion. The edict was issued on March 31, 1492, and stated that "by the end of July of the present year [1492]," merely four months from the date of issue, "all Jews and Jewesses of whatever age ... who live and reside and are in the said kingdoms or seignories, natives and non-natives alike, who by whatever manner or whatever reason may have come or are to be found in them," must "leave the said kingdoms and seignories with their sons and daughters, male and female servants and Jewish domestics ... of whatever age they may be."

Afterwards, the edict grows stern and foreboding, stating "that they dare not return unto them [kingdoms or seignories], nor be in them, nor be in any part of them, neither as dwellers nor as travelers, nor in any other manner whatsoever, upon punishment that if they do not thus perform and comply with this ... they incur the penalty of death and confiscation of all their belongings." Moreover, continues the edict: "Such penalties they shall incur by the very deed itself without trial, sentence, or declaration."

If this was not enough, anyone who helped the Jews was to be severely punished, too. "We command and maintain that no one in our said kingdoms of whatever status, conditions, or dignity they may be, dare to welcome, harbor, protect, either publicly or secretly, any Jew or Jewess after the said deadline at the end of July has passed." If they do, the edict states that they will suffer the "pain of losing all their belongings, vassals, fortresses, and other landed properties and, moreover, lose whatever sums they may have from us."

Finally, the edict states that the decree should be circulated everywhere, and everyone must tell about it to everyone in their families and everyone they know "so that this may come to the notice of all, and no one may pretend ignorance [of the decree]." Any Christian who did not comply with any of the parts relating to Christians was punishable by confiscation of all their belongings and wealth.

To Spanish Jewry, the Alhambra Decree was their Final Solution. As we will see later in the book, despite the obvious differences between Spain and Germany, and between the Alhambra Decree and the Nazi Final Solution, there are many critical similarities between the process that unfolded in Spain and the one that unfolded in Germany. These similarities, when we superimpose them on the process currently unfolding today in America, Western Europe, and in Israel, should light up big warning signs. If we are to avert yet another catastrophe in the pain-strewn history of our people, we must not ignore them.

Despite the similarities, the events leading up to the Holocaust present a much more complicated picture than the one that led to the expulsion from Spain, as painful as it was. Contemporary forms of anti-Semitism are highly connected to global trends and ideologies that spread throughout Europe, and later the world over. For this reason, to see the full picture of the attitude of Nazi Germany toward its Jews and toward Judaism as a whole, we must also consider what had been unfolding elsewhere in the world around that time, and particularly in Palestine. To do that, we will need to look at the roots of Zionism in the Russian Empire and how it is related to the tragedy of European Jewry. This will be the topic of the following chapter.

Chapter 5: Storms in the South

&

The Genesis of Zionism

When we examine the events leading up to the Holocaust, it is hard to keep from wondering why German Jewry did not simply emigrate from Germany. The Nazis clearly did not want the Jews around them, and many Jews did indeed realize that they had no future in Germany and fled. But far more of them stayed, and of those who remained in Germany, the vast majority perished.

The answer that one often hears when asking why the Jews did not leave is that they had nowhere to go since no one would take them in. Indeed, no country opened its doors to them. However, when you look at the circumstances in the countries where Jews wanted to go (and they would not go just anywhere), a very complex picture emerges.

When Hitler came to power in January 1933, the first, and most obvious place to go for German Jewry should have been Palestine. The Zionists were already in the midst of building "a national home for the Jewish people" in Palestine, as stated in the 1917 Balfour Declaration, and after the League of Nations gave the British Empire the mandate to carry out their statement in July 1922, the easiest solution to the "Jewish question" should have been a mass emigration to Palestine. This would have given a big boost to the "national home" and at the same time resolve the "Jewish question" for the Germans. But a mass emigration did not happen, and the reasons for it lie neither with the Arab inhabitants of Palestine nor with the British Empire. Surprisingly, the answer lies with the Jews themselves.

Two Jewish entities partook in the drama that unfolded when the Nazis first came to power: the Zionists in Palestine and German Jewry. The building of the "national home" began far from Palestine or from Germany; it began in Russia, in 1881. On April 15 of that year, a long, deadly, and vicious series of pogroms and riots against Jews erupted in the city of Elizavetgrad (today's Kropyvnytskyi), and spread through most of Southern Russia, in the area of today's Ukraine.

What triggered the pogroms, which lasted over a year and became known as "The Storms in the South," after their location in Southern Russia, was the murder of the Russian Tsar Alexander II, who was, ironically, very positive in his attitude toward the Jews. Anti-Semites spread a rumor that the Jews had killed the Tsar, and from here the anger quickly became violent. "The subsequent anti-Semitic pogroms," writes Friedrich Battenberg on the *European History Online* website, "resulted in a discontinuation of [Jewish] emancipation efforts ... and, simultaneously, the genesis of Zionism."[262]

Nicholas I and Alexander I—the Afflicting Tsars Who Kept the Jews Together

To understand the Jewish emancipation and the emergence of Zionism, we must travel back to early 19th century Russia. "In the final years of Alexander I's reign," writes acclaimed Israeli historian Israel Bartal, "after the Napoleonic wars, Russian policy took an extreme turn in relation to the Jews. ...The Christian orientation reemerged with greater vigor, and Alexander acted resolutely in cooperation with religious organizations that had missionary aims. Now he believed, contrary to his previous view, that the Jews could be integrated into the Russian state if they converted to Christianity."[263]

To implement his vision, Alexander I founded in 1817 "the Society of Israelite Christians, which promised converts land for settlement in the areas of New Russia. He also cooperated with the London Society for Promoting Christianity among the Jews and supported the activity of the British missionary Lewis Way."[264]

In 1825, Alexander I died of typhus while on a voyage in Southern Russia, though some rumors maintain that he became a monk named Feodor Kuzmich. Either way, his successor, his younger brother Nicholas I, who ruled from the time of his brother's death until 1855, continued his late brother's efforts to impel the Jews to convert to Christianity as a means to integrate them into the general Russian society.

Under Nicholas I, the government went beyond attempting to convert Jews. The tsar attempted to turn the Jews away from their traditional occupations and integrate them in the general economic life of Russia. He also imposed on the Jews a painful mandatory "conscription of Jews into military service [as] an effective means of 'correcting' their character."[265]

Following conscription and the economic reformations came even worse steps: attempts to reform Jewish education! "From the early 1840s, Czar Nicholas took steps to introduce a comprehensive reform in the status of the Jews and to intervene in their internal cultural life. Traditional education and its key text, the Talmud, became the major target. To the czar and his ministers, the Jewish religion was an extremely influential element that prevented the Jews from becoming integrated into the Russian state. They believed that the religious-intellectual pursuits of the Jews—in particular, their intensive study of the Talmud and rabbinical literature—engendered xenophobia, offensive traits, and economic damage. In other words, Jewish scholarship was officially perceived as a political element hostile to the state. The negative, almost demonic image of the Talmud as hostile to Christianity and spreading hatred of human society in general ... became ... a major issue in the various texts describing the behavior of Jewish society."[266]

Earlier, we mentioned the paradox Prof. Solomon Lurye observed: When Jews turn their backs on their coreligionists and attempt to assimilate, they arouse anti-Semitism, which, paradoxically, blames them of being separatists and reluctant to assimilate. But the opposite paradox works just as well: When Jews unite among themselves and increase their cohesion, anti-Semitism decreases. Whenever they are attacked, they restore their ancient bond, which was shattered along with the walls of Jerusalem back in the first century CE. And even though their restored unity is currently self-serving and transient, contrary to their vocation to spread the light of unity to the nations (see Chapters 1 and 9), it is nonetheless powerful enough to maintain their survival, though certainly not unscathed.

Very few leaders noticed that recurrence in history, and therefore fell for the trap of attempting to force their will on the Jews, and Nicholas I was no exception. "Paradoxically," writes Bartal, "the czar achieved the very opposite of what he had intended [to disperse the Jewish society]. …Frameworks of social organization and cohesion continued to operate, preserving the distinctive identity of the Jewish ethnos. What the Russian government sought to eradicate through formal integration grew in strength and found other channels of continuity."[267]

Thus, "Despite all the efforts of the Russian government … the majority of Jewish society maintained traditional lifestyles. The government introduced comprehensive reforms, both in the legal status of the Jews [by] incorporating them in the urban estate, and in their self-rule [by] abolishing Jewish autonomy. [The government] attempted to limit traditional communication through the channels that disseminated beliefs and doctrines [through] control over books, censorship, and limitations on printing. In fact, the government's intervention did not achieve real results: the number of Hasidim did not decrease, the study of the Talmud was not discontinued, and the knowledge of the state language was limited … to a very small group of wealthy merchants. Thirty years of Nicholas I's rule did not give rise to a decisive change in the relationship between the Russian government and the Jews."[268] On the contrary, it created suspicion and hostility that became the basis for future radicalism to appear among the Jews since "the traditional political basis on which Jewish autonomy had rested for centuries—their fundamental loyalty to the government as such—was shaken."[269]

Alexander II—the Great Reformer

In March of 1855, Nicholas I died and his eldest son, Alexander Nicolaevich, better known as Alexander II, succeeded him. "Up to the moment of his accession in 1855," writes Donald Mackenzie Wallace in the 1910 edition of *The Encyclopedia Britannica*, "No one ever imagined that he would be known to posterity as a great reformer. … In the period of thirty years during which he was heir-apparent, the moral atmosphere of St Petersburg was very unfavourable to the development of any originality of thought or character. It was a time of government on martinet principles, under which all freedom of thought and all private initiative were as far as possible suppressed vigorously by the administration. … Political topics were studiously avoided in general conversation, and books or newspapers in which the most keen-scented press-censor could detect the least odor of political or religious free-thinking were strictly prohibited."[270] Additionally, "To the disappointment of his father, in whom the military instinct was ever predominant, [Alexander] showed no love of soldiering and gave evidence of a kindliness of disposition and a tender-heartedness which were considered out of place in one destined to become a military autocrat."[271]

But Alexander II will not be remembered for his kindness or tenderness, but rather for his calculated boldness to reverse his father's policies on educational, social, and economic affairs, including his attitude toward Jews. Alexander II's boldness earned him great admirers, brought him significant achievements, but eventually also led to his untimely passing. On March 3, 1861, the sixth anniversary of his accession, he signed and published the law of emancipation of the serfs. Soon after, he installed a new penal code of law and reformed the Russian army. Alexander II emancipated the rural districts, which now acted much more freely.

However, Alexander II was a very cautious tsar and would not take rash steps that were not thoroughly calculated. The reforms he intended to take for the betterment of the country progressed slowly, often evoking impatience and agitation rather than excitement. "Thus appeared ... two extreme groups: on the one hand, the discontented Conservatives, who recommended a return to a more severe disciplinarian regime; and on the other, the discontented Radicals, who would have been satisfied with nothing less than the adoption of a through-going socialistic program. Between the two extremes stood the discontented Moderates, who indulged freely in grumbling without knowing how the unsatisfactory state of things was to be remedied."[272]

Gradually, the very people who most enjoyed Alexander's reforms—the young and energetic students, who could finally learn hard sciences and modernize the country—turned against their benefactor. They formed revolutionary movements that "gradually assumed the form of terrorism, and aimed at the assassination of prominent officials, and even of the emperor himself. [...] The struggle between the Terrorists and the police authorities became more and more intense, and attempts at assassination became more and more frequent."[273] Finally, on March 13, 1881, the revolutionaries succeeded. On that day, near the Winter Palace in St. Petersburg, a bomb exploded next to Alexander II, mortally wounding him, setting off a new and dark era in Russia as a whole, and the "Storms in the South" for the Jews.

Alexander II and the Jews

As Tsar Alexander II was revolutionary in his approach toward education, military, law, and the economy in Russia, so he was toward the Jews. Acclaimed historian and 1970 Nobel Prize Laureate in Literature Alexander Isayevich Solzhenitsyn writes that Alexander II "expressed his intention to resolve the Jewish Question—and in the most favorable manner. For this, the approach to the question was changed drastically. If during the reign of Nicholas I, the government saw its task as first reforming the Jewish inner life, gradually clearing it out through productive work and education with consequent removal of administrative restrictions, then during the reign of Alexander II the policy was the opposite: to begin with the intention of integrating this population with the native inhabitants of the country [Russians/Ukranians]."[274]

As the restrictions imposed by his father Nicholas I were lifted, the Jews began to move out of the Pale of Settlement (Russian territories in which Jews were permitted permanent settlement) and migrated toward the big cities. "Under Alexander II ... the Jewish population of Moscow began to grow rapidly," writes Solzhenitsyn. In fact, everything that his father, Nicholas I, and Alexander I before him tried to achieve by force, namely the integration of the Jews in the general population, Alexander II achieved by simply lifting the restrictions and opening the doors to universities and occupations that Jews were hitherto forbidden to practice.

Jews against Jews

Another benefit for the Russian authorities from opening the doors of academia to the Jews was that the new *maskilim* [proponents of the *Haskalah* (Enlightenment) movement], who strove to become part of the Russian society, now saw their own establishment of Orthodox Jewry as their enemy, instead of the Russian government. Alexander II succeeded in disintegrating the Jews precisely because he stopped fighting them and let them do what they wanted. Because ever since the ruin of the Temple—when hatred overcame the nation and caused the Jewish people to perform a self-inflicted genocide (see Chapter 3)—what most Jews want is to integrate themselves into the host culture (and at times even altogether disappear as a distinct faith-tradition). This was what we saw in 19th century Russia. The same process that unfolded before the ruin of the Second Temple, before the expulsion from Spain, before the Holocaust in Germany, and is unfolding now in America, also happened in 19th century Russia and ended with the pogroms we now call the "Storms in the South."

For a while, the *maskilim* were delighted to be among the Russians, partake, and even take a leading role in Russia's political arena. Unlike the Jewry of 15th century Spain, which had no option of integration other than conversion, Russian Jews in the age of Alexander II could remain Jews, but in a modernized version and adapted to the Russian culture. Therefore, Prof. Bartal explains that "The *maskilim* did not want to see Jewish society disappear, nor did they aspire to bring about the disappearance of the Jews as individuals. What they wanted to do was to 'reform' the Jews. The image of the future society that the *Haskalah* wanted to mold had been and remained a society of 'reformed Jews,' not one of 'non-Jews' integrated into a universal society."[275]

But tolerance among Jews was never one of our strengths. We became a nation when we learned to unite *above* our differences, not diminish them. So once we lost the ability to rise above our disputes and unite, we were left with disputes, but with no unity. As a result, "the *maskilim* were not very different from the Orthodox, who hated them and whom they hated in return,"[276] and in short, neither could tolerate the other, much less form any kind of union.

"The attitude of the *maskilim* toward Hasidism provides a telling example of the difference between one area and another," continues Bartal. "The Galician *Haskalah*, which was distinctly rationalistic in nature, placed an emphasis on its struggle against Hasidism. It is not surprising that the leading *maskilim* in Galicia, the authors Joseph Perl and Isaac Erter, devoted a considerable portion of their writing to scathing parodies and satires of the Hasidic movement. In this sense, the *Haskalah* in Lithuania had a totally disparate character. Although the Lithuanian *maskilim* advocated a platform similar to that of the Galicians, their activity was not centered around vigorous opposition to Hasidism. Instead, they focused on the argument that the traditional Jewish society as a whole, not merely part of it, was deficient and in need of reform."[277]

Another indication of the opprobrium of the Jewish *Haskalah* movement toward its roots was "The attitude of the members of the

Haskalah movement toward Yiddish: From the second half of the eighteenth century, they regarded it as a flawed, degenerate language that ought to be banished from Jewish culture."[278]

At times, the hatred of Orthodox Jewry toward *maskilim* took on a very personal tone. If a prominent *maskil* [proponent of the *Haskalah*] were to express himself openly in its favor, the Orthodox establishment would punish him severely. Such was the case of Moses Leib Lilienblum, "who dared suggest to the rabbis of Lithuania that they ought to adapt the demands of *halakha* [Jewish law] to the conditions of the modern era. Lilienblum wrote: 'We have come upon fine times and here we are following the life of the land, to live like all other men, and that will require many changes in our lives, and you will stand against us as if nothing at all had happened. . . . Why do you not remove some of the many restrictions from us, those added by the more recent rabbis, which lay heavy upon us like the sand upon the shore?' The response was not long in coming. The brave young man who had dared to publicly air his opinion about the need to adapt the Jewish religion to the era of reform in Russia was ostracized and excommunicated in his city. In a letter to his friend the poet J. L. Gordon, he described the harrowing experience: 'On the festival of Shavuot, a meeting was convened in the home of the community rabbi for the purpose of depriving me of a livelihood and driving me from the town. The government-appointed rabbi informed me the day after the festival that the leaders of the town had resolved to write a letter of slander about me to the governor of the province in Vilna. . . . All my acquaintances have distanced themselves from me. I cannot come to their homes nor they to mine, for fear of their parents. If I should come to the house of prayer, I am regarded as one of God's accursed; no one greets me, nor am I allowed to join a minyan of ten for prayer. When I walk in the town streets, I am surrounded by a flock of boys yelling at me: 'Heretic! Apostate!'"[279]

The *maskilim*, for their part, were no better. "In the eyes of the *maskilim*, Hasidism [adherents of the Hassidut movement] not only embodied the evil of irrationality, but also inhibited progress. They did all they could to convince the authorities in Russia, Austria, and the autonomous regions of Poland that the spread of Hasidism should be halted, because it posed a political danger and even the threat of rebellion against the kingdom."[280]

Indeed, to many Russian assimilationist Jews, "their own indigenous society," namely Orthodox Judaism, and even the more lenient Jewish bourgeois community, was "a world of hypocrisy, oppression, ignorance, and religious fanaticism," writes Professor of History Erich Haberer.[281] "We were..." Haberer quotes Grigorii Gurevich, a leader of one of the circles of emancipated Jews, "assimilationists, determined to fight against the Orthodox and the oppressors of the community. The old *kahal* [Orthodox community leadership] was for us a horrible picture that showed the community leader ... making a living out of Jewish misery."[282] In the eyes of the assimilationists, Orthodox Judaism "accounted for their spiritual and intellectual stagnation, and their people's isolation from 'universal humanity' in general, and Russian society in particular."[283] Many years later, this animus toward their Jewish roots would play a key role when the Zionist movement in Mandatory Palestine determined its policy toward their coreligionists oppressed in Nazi Germany and anti-Semitic Poland.

Because of the assimilationist tendencies among Jews, they resented their coreligionists who aspired to maintain their traditional way of life. They wanted to shatter all remnants of religious facets, and felt more comfortable among anti-Semites than among Jews. "There were certainly anti-Jewish prejudices [in Russian revolutionary circles], but these were also prevalent among Jewish socialists," concludes Haberer.[284]

Indeed, there were no righteous in the war between the vying factions of the Jews in Russia. "Throughout the nineteenth century, the two rival movements were locked in an uncompromising struggle, in which neither side was loath to engage in persecutions, informing to the authorities, and even physical violence. ...It was an extremely blatant struggle ... between two spiritual streams, each claiming a monopoly over the definition of the 'true Judaism.'"[285]

Sowing Internal Hatred Reaps Rising Anti-Semitism

As ever, so now, when Jews manifest hatred toward each other and therefore attempt to assimilate, the nations manifest hatred toward them. The Russian people were no exception. As mentioned earlier, when Alexander II acceded to the crown, he did his best to acculturate the Jews into the Russian society on *their own terms*, rather than force Russian education on them like his two predecessors tried unsuccessfully. During the reign of Alexander II, according to Aleksandr Solzhenitsyn, Russia conducted itself with regard to the Jews as "the most powerful, solitary support of a progressive society. It may have become so against the backdrop of oppression and pogroms, but nevertheless, in no other country ... was it so complete. Our broad-minded freedom-loving intelligentsia has put beyond the boundaries of society and humanity not only anti-Semitism, but even [one] who did not support loudly and distinctly, and especially ... the struggle for the equal rights of Jews, was already considered a 'dishonest anti-Semite.' The bourgeois—conscientious, acutely sensitive Russian intelligentsia—tried to fully heed and learn precisely the Jewish understanding of the priorities of all political life... Russian society not only staunchly defended the Jews against the government, but forbade itself, and everyone, to show even the slightest shadow of any criticism of the behavior of an individual Jew."[286]

Nevertheless, when the Jews turned against each other, anti-Semitism soon followed. At first, it manifested mostly in writing. Prof. Bartal writes that "The Jewish press in Russia ... had to cope with the anti-Semitic writings that grew more numerous and more strident in the 1870s, and to come to the defense of Jewish society that was severely attacked from time to time."[287]

The Jewish *maskilim* were locked between conflicting feelings: On one hand, they were Jews and therefore dreaded the perils of anti-Semitism. On the other hand, "many members of the new Jewish intelligentsia agreed with the harsh criticism of the anti-Semites about the role of the Jews in the Eastern European economy."[288] The solution that many of the Jewish *maskilim* found was to seek to

109

"change the Jew outside the boundaries of the empire, in agricultural colonies overseas."[289] This idea of reforming the Jews through agriculture coincided with the growing awareness among Jewish *maskilim* that their tribe needed its own sovereign state, as we will see later in this chapter.

From Assimilationists to Revolutionaries to Terrorists

Another factor that contributed to the rise of anti-Semitism was the fact that once the Jews were given freedom to merge with the local population, many of them not only shunned the Orthodox society of their youth, but also rushed to join the ranks of socialist and communist circles and became radical revolutionaries. As previously mentioned, many assimilated Jews became liberals and espoused the *Haskalah* [enlightenment] movement. Erich Haberer wrote what Prof. Norman Naimark of Stanford University described as "The first serious book to examine systematically the most important questions related to Jewish participation in Russian radicalism."[290] Haberer asserts that the Russian Jews transformed "the old *maskilic* [relating to the *Haskalah*] intelligentsia into a Russian educated intellectual elite whose outlook and aspirations were closely tied to contemporaneous liberal and radical elements in Russian society."[291]

Haberer also analyzes the integration and growing fascination of Jews with radicalism and revolutionary circles. According to him, by 1872, the process had already begun, though "it was not until the end of 1873 that their activity assumed a revolutionary coloring."[292]

In fact, at the height of their emancipation in tsarist Russia, many Jews became so radicalized that some of them became outright terrorists. Leizer Ioselevich Tsukerman, for example, joined the terrorist organization *Narodnaya Volya* [the People's Will] in 1879, and served as its principal printer of underground publications.[293] This organization consistently attacked the highest levels of government in Russia, and eventually, in March 1881, assassinated Tsar Alexander II himself, who had been so welcoming and open to the Jews.

But Tsukerman was not the first, or even the most ardent Jewish militant. Mark Andreevich Natanson, a freshman at St. Petersburg University, "quickly became absorbed in extra-curricular activities,"[294] "The merits of Natanson as a revolutionary and founder of the circle of Chaikovtsy in 1871, and the secret society of' *Zemly i Volya* in 1876, is incomparable with the activity of anyone else in this time. In [forming] the society of' *Zemly i Volya*, he selected with utmost skill and clarity of vision the original group of members and, so to speak, infused them with his own spirit of action and conspiracy... His work can only be compared with that small group of innovators, Morozov, Kviatkovskii, and Al[eksandr] Mikhailov, who in 1879 ... [originated] *Narodnaya Volya*."[295] When fourteen years later, that group committed the assassination of the Tsar, it ignited the "Storms in the South," inflicting horrendous suffering on all the Jews of southern Russia and parts of Poland, which in turn engendered the Zionist movement.

Often, the Russians frowned upon the radical tendencies of the Jews and their assimilationist aspirations. According to Solzhenitsyn, the Russian philosopher and theologian Vladimir Solovyov, for instance, objected to the complete merger of Jews into the non-Jewish society. Solovyov believed that until now "we have hushed up the peculiarities of ... the Russian people, and that bringing them out is not anti-Semitism or suppressing other nationalities, such as the Jewish nationality."[296] In Solovyov's view, "Between nationalities there should be harmony and not fusion."[297]

Yet, to many Russian Jews, even harmony between Russians and Jews was not enough. They wanted complete merger. Moreover, many of them aspired for complete obliteration of all nationalities, complete cosmopolitanism. Aron Samuel Liberman, a leading member of the revolutionary Vilna Circle, "wished nothing more than [that] under the pressure of a popular socialist workers' revolution, all national divisions should disappear together with the [capitalist] monopoly *in all* its expressions in the life of humanity. Indeed, like all his fellow socialist Jews, he rejoiced in the prospect that the Jews, because of their cosmopolitan character and their ever increasing assimilationist tendency, would pioneer the integration of all mankind into a worldwide, nationless workers' republic." Moreover, Liberman felt that "until then, it was necessary—especially in Russia—to speed up this process in that 'propaganda must begin by uprooting national pride and exclusiveness.'"[298]

A Jew Is a Jew, Is a Jew

While the socialist and communist Jews aspired to make all Russians the same, the revolutionary circles in Russia viewed matters quite differently. Because Jews are not like all other nations, they are always excluded. Just as today's progressive movements in America, such as the Dyke March,[299] excluded Jews, so did the progressive and revolutionary movements in 19th century Russia. The Jews, who in many cases were among the founders of revolutionary organizations, learned the hard way that even though they regard themselves as Russians, to the Russians, a Jew is a Jew, is a Jew. For many revolutionary Jews, this was a bitter pill to swallow.

According to Haberer, "Historians ... agree that the loss or retention of 'faith in socialist cosmopolitanism' was a crucial factor in deciding whether or not a Jewish Populist remained loyal to the Russian revolutionary movement. This faith, so the argument continues, had been seriously challenged by the massive anti-Jewish riots ... and even more so by the fact that two major revolutionary parties showed clear signs of sympathy with the [1881] pogroms. In other words, popular anti-Semitism and corresponding sentiments in the principal revolutionary groupings of Russian Populism—*Narodnaya Volya* and *Chernyi Peredel*—compelled Jewish socialists to reconsider their allegiance to revolutionary Populism, for these parties had dismally failed to live up to their professed internationalism in the face of brutal anti-Jewish persecution."[300]

Moreover, not only did the revolutionary movements fail the Jews, the authorities also blamed the Jews of establishing the revolutionary organizations, which, to an extent, was true. In fact, according to Haberer, "blaming the Jews for undermining established authority through the propagation of socialism and terrorism was already current in the late 1870s."[301]

As in 15th century Spain prior to the expulsion of the Jews from there, the growing presence of Jews in positions of power had a detrimental impact on the Jews. Even worse was the fact that in 19th century Russia, Jews not only climbed the ranks of government; they sought to topple it altogether and replace it with a socialist, communist regime. "The ever growing Jewish participation in the revolutionary movement, and its increasing visibility, as Jews became more frequently linked to highly publicized acts of terrorism," stresses Haberer, "was duly registered by those who had least to gain from it—the government officials. ...The general feeling was that from time immemorial, the 'Hebrew race' had been an alien and subversive element in society and that its decomposing powers [a reflection of the alienation among themselves] had reached epidemic proportions due to the influx of Jews into Russian society via educational, professional, and commercial channels. This feeling gained in force as more and more Jewish names appeared conspicuously on the pages of government reports and newspaper articles dealing with political subversion in general and terrorist plots in particular. ...This gave rise to a new anti-Semitic myth which attributed the revolutionary unrest of the 1880s and of the following decades to the Jewish people. ... Both fact and prejudice induced and enabled [Russian anti-Semitic thinkers] to contrive a rationale for explaining the 'revolutionary cancer'" that is Judaism.[302]

The execution of Ippolit Mlodetskii was a blatant case of the anti-Semitism that Jewish involvement in politics stirred up. On February 22, 1880, "Ippolit Osipovich Mlodetskii was publicly executed in St. Petersburg for attempting to assassinate Count Loris-Melikov, the newly appointed 'crisis manager' of the empire. Although anti-Semitic motives seem to have played no role in this case, it occasioned an unprecedented display of anti-Semitic rhetoric in the Russian conservative press. The huge crowd of some 40,000 spectators who watched Mlodetskii's spectacular execution knew of course that the 'criminal' was a Jew, and those who did not know yet that he was merely a manifestation of a general Jewish conspiracy were enlightened by reading in the pages of *Novoe vremia* that 'these Jews, being from time immemorial the representatives of the revolutionary spirit, stand now at the head of Russian Nihilists.'"[303]

After the murder of the tsar, anti-Jewish feelings grew so intense that a burst of pogroms became just a matter of time. "The pogroms ... began several weeks after the tsar's assassination," writes Prof. Bartal. "For an entire year, assaults were repeatedly made on the Jewish population in towns, cities, and villages. In the larger pogroms, there were several instances of murder, and in some Ukrainian cities, some Jewish women were raped." The attacks "occurred in several waves, spread over an entire year. Some assert that the pogroms continued until 1884, but the major violent attacks against Jews took place between April 1881 and April 1882. The period of the 'storms of the south' opened with three waves of pogroms in the spring of 1881, in April and early May, in the six provinces of central and south Ukraine. One of the largest pogroms took place in Odessa in the first days of May. ...At the end of 1881, a large pogrom was carried out in Warsaw, very far from Ukraine, during the Christmas season." Subsequently, "there was a respite for several months until in late March of 1882 during Passover, a dreadful pogrom—perhaps the largest in terms of the number of casualties—broke out in Balta in Ukraine."[304]

The prevailing view in Israel regarding the "Storms in the South" is that they erupted all of a sudden without apparent forewarning or a process that had led to it. Bartal clearly disagrees with this presentation of the events. "In some historical literature as well as in several textbooks used in Israeli schools," he writes, "1881 is described as the year in which the *maskilim*, who had cherished such optimistic hopes, were suddenly disillusioned by the Russian government's reaction to anti-Semitism. ... But things were quite different. As we saw earlier, a continual process had been taking place for close to ten years before the pogroms in Russia. In this sense, the pogroms that broke out in 1881 were the culmination of a process, not a sudden, surprising event that the *maskilim* could not have foreseen."[305] Indeed, however traumatic, the pogroms did not appear out of the blue. They were a long time coming. While Jews are not the culprits or perpetrators of the crimes against them, the linkage between their disdain for each other and the nations' aversion toward them is plainly evident, not just in the case of Russia, but throughout Jewish history. In Germany, this will become even more evident, and infinitely more disastrous.

The continual obliviousness of Jews to their role of setting an example of unity, and their incessant engagement in divisive activities, bear harsh consequences and always lead to tragedy. We Jews must recognize our responsibility to behave in such a manner that will produce affinity toward us rather than enmity. And we can achieve this *only* by striving to unite among us rather than by patronizing, deriding, and detesting other Jews merely for disagreeing with us.

The candid words of the earlier-mentioned Ukraine born prominent member of the Russian parliament in the early 20th century, Vasily Shulgin, who declared that he was an avowed anti-Semite, clearly show what the Russians were searching for in emancipating the Jews, and what they did not find. "In order to surrender to the Jews as leaders, in order to calmly and joyfully look at Jewry capturing the commanding heights of the psyche, something more is needed. One must feel their moral superiority over oneself. We must feel that they are not only stronger but also better than us. We must feel that … they are imbued with wisdom, which always leads to Love. …In one aspect or another, they must be above us. Not individual Jews, but Jews in general, as a nation, Jews, as a race."[306]

The Dawn of Zionism

In the final chapter of his book, Bartal describes the emergence of national awareness in Russian Jewry in the wake of the "Storms in the South." He, too, observes the connection between "integration," which is how he refers to assimilation, and the rise in anti-Semitism. Following is Bartal's description of the impact of the pogroms and the process that led to the birth of Zionism: "The year 1881 was a milestone in modern Jewish history. It marked the largest shift toward the emergence of the modern movements that influenced that chapter in Jewish history. As a result of the open anti-Jewish policy adopted by the government of the new czar, Alexander III, members of the *Haskalah* movement rarely tended to cooperate with the state any more. The social class [in Jewry] that had acculturated and identified with the Russian urban milieu was struck a hard blow by the glaring change in the government's policy vis-à-vis the Jews. Their disillusionment with the cold, hostile reaction of Russian intellectuals during the pogroms and the following years led many radicals among the Jewish intelligentsia to develop a national Jewish consciousness. In the new Jewish nationalist thinking, a historical model was shaped that attempted to explain the emergence of the Jewish nationalist movement. This model, which would reproduce itself many times throughout the twentieth century in every attempt by Jews to cope with hostility toward them, had three stages: it opened with the hope of integration, continued with the outright rejection by the non-Jewish side, and culminated in a renewed awakening of the old Jewish identity in a new national guise. ... For many years, this model played a key role in Zionist historiography and directly connected the period of the pogroms in Russia to the inception of the new settlement in Palestine."[307]

If we look back at the events leading to the expulsion from Spain, the similarities are patent. The first two stages are identical: 1) the hope of integration, and 2) the outright rejection by the non-Jewish side. The third stage—the advent of aspirations for national sovereignty—is absent in the expulsion from Spain. At that time, before Napoleon and before the "Spring of Nations," the concept of national self-determination was not on anyone's mind and the Jews regarded Spain as their homeland. But now that they were flogged once more by the very people with whom they sought to merge, the socialist Russian Jews realized that they had to find a place where they could be the sovereign, where they could realize their dreams of establishing a socialist society.

In that regard, we should look into the insightful words of Prof. Haberer concerning the "Storms in the South": "The Jewish response to the pogroms of the early 1880s has been of great interest to historians concerned with the rise of modern Jewish national consciousness and its politico-cultural expression, Zionism. To some, this response was akin to a revolution, to a sharp break with previous assimilationist tendencies, which necessarily undermined the authority of groups most clearly identified with Jewish adaptation to Russian life."[308] Indeed, as previously mentioned, the Jews' "faith in socialist cosmopolitanism had been seriously challenged by the massive anti-Jewish riots," which in turn "compelled Jewish socialists to reconsider their allegiance to revolutionary Populism."[309]

Just as is happening in the US today—where Jews are excluded from the progressive groups which they themselves were leaders in creating—the Russian parties "had dismally failed to live up to their professed internationalism in the face of brutal anti-Jewish persecution. Thus, according to conventional interpretations, anti-Semitism—particularly among Gentile revolutionaries—undermined a Jewish socialist's cosmopolitan world view and forced him either to renounce his Russian-centered revolutionary convictions or, paradoxically, confirm them anew in [a] cosmopolitan-assimilationist fashion."[310]

"That renunciation rather than reconfirmation of the 'faith' was the prevalent reaction of Jewish radicals," continues Haberer.[311] Historian Louis Greenberg succinctly expressed this view when he wrote, "Most of the Jewish *Narodniki* [members of the socialist movement in Russia] were stunned by the open anti-Semitism revealed in the ranks of their Russian comrades, a sentiment directed even against the Jewish socialists. Because of this hostility Jewish revolutionaries left the ranks of the *Narodniki*, some even joining the newly formed Zionist groups. Clearly, for Greenberg 'revolutionary antisemitism' was the decisive variable in the set of circumstances which drove many, if not most Jews to abandon the revolutionary movement."[312]

Indeed, Zionism provided the answer to many socialist and radical Jews. It created a new vision in which Jews were masters of their own fate and could build the ideal society in a state of their own, without fear of persecution.

However, the onset of Zionism was not easy. The Jewish Orthodox community had already been completely alienated from the socialist Jews. Additionally, the whole idea of Zionism conflicted with the notion that the return to the land of Israel should be an act of Messianic intervention and not the work of mere mortals.

On the secular sphere, the idea of Zionism also sounded odd to many intellectuals. According to Solzhenitsyn, Jewish Austrian philosopher Otto Weininger, who later converted to Protestant Christianity, argued with Theodor Herzl about the feasibility of the Zionist dream. In Weininger's view, "Zionism and Jewry are incompatible because Zionism seeks to force the Jews to take responsibility for their own state, which contradicts the essence of the Jew."[313]

"In Russia in 1899," continues Solzhenitsyn, "[journalist and author] Iosif Menassievich Bikerman vigorously opposed Zionism," describing the whole idea as "ghostly, born of anti-Semitism, reactionary in spirit, harmful in essence." It is necessary "to reject the illusions of the Zionists and, by no means abandoning the [Jewish] spiritual individuality, to fight hand in hand with the cultural and progressive elements of Russia in the name of the revival of a common homeland."[314] Evidently, some Jews were so alienated from their own people that it was hard for them to abandon the idea of merger and acculturation even in the face of brutal anti-Semitism.

Indeed, in its first decades, Zionism was the unwanted child of persecuted Judaism. Orthodox Jewry detested it, and, as we will see later in the book, assimilationist Western societies, such as in England and Germany, scoffed at it.

Clearly, when the matter of bringing Poland's Jews to Palestine came up, thereby saving them from the looming menace in Europe, the Zionists were strongly disinclined. After all, these were the very same Orthodox Jews who had so vilified Jewish socialist secular radicals at the onset of the movement in Russia. Chaim Weizmann, who was to become the first President of Israel, was seven years old when the "Storms in the South" broke out, but he grew up in a socialist, Zionist home. According to Prof. of Jewish studies Chimen

Abramsky, Weizmann's father was "an early adherent of the Hovevei Zion ["Lovers of Zion," a Zionist movement in Russia], and he imbibed warm feelings toward Palestine from childhood on."[315] Weizmann grew up on the writings of such assimilationist Jews as Pinsker, Lilienblum, and particularly Ahad Ha'am. He stated very lucidly that "the aim ... was to attract to Zionism the productive forces in Judaism."[316] In light of the decades long animosity and struggles between Orthodox Jewry and assimilationist, and later Zionist Jews, it is no wonder that even in the face of genocide, knowing full well the danger that was coming, Chaim Weizmann had very little compassion toward his coreligionists. On August 4, 1937, in a speech at the 20th Zionist congress, he said the following chilling words about European Jewry, mainly the Orthodox: "The old ones will pass; they will bear their fate or they will not. They are dust, economic and moral dust in a cruel world." After acknowledging that there were six million Jews in Europe, he added, "Two million, and perhaps less: *She'erit Hapleita* [the survivors], only a remnant shall survive. We have to accept it."[317]

Acclaimed historians Jehuda Reinharz and Yaacov Shavit quote the poet Uri Zvi Greenberg, who was born in the Ukraine to an Orthodox family but became a Zionist and came to Mandatory Palestine in 1923, in their book *The Road to September 1939*. In his poem, Greenberg wrote about the Orthodox Polish Jewry with great disdain: "Now that the gates to all the countries are shut, the dark hour has come; the Polish peddlers have finally remembered Palestine, the end to all exiles. It is a sign that all hope is lost."[318]

"Such expressions of distaste were not uncommon in the 1920s," the authors add, "and even in the second half of the 1930s one could still hear people supporting the principle of selection, that is, giving preference to 'pioneers' and 'workers,' and the image was still prevalent of the lower-middle-class Polish Jew who was 'a little bit of a matchmaker, a little bit of a tout and a little bit of a trader.'"[319]

Religious Jewry in Palestine, for its part, garnered its own abhorrence toward Zionist socialists. In her essay, "The Religious

Motifs of the Labor Movement," Prof. Anita Shapira writes that "The deeply religious colonists in Petah Tikva demanded that all Jews maintain a religious way of life. They refused to hire the young socialist workers on religious, cultural, and economic grounds, employing Arab laborers in their fields instead."[320] As one might imagine, "The young socialists, in turn, regarded these Orthodox Jews as the epitome of hypocrisy, disguising class interests and prejudice by sanctimonious piety."[321]

Even the most prominent Zionist leader, David Ben-Gurion, was tainted by ill feelings toward observing Jews. He "described the farmers of Petah Tikva as having installed an idol in the Temple and desecrated the land by idolatry. His imagery captures the young socialist view of traditional society: religion came to be identified with all that was abhorred. The struggles within the Jewish community in Palestine over such issues as the *shmitah* (sabbatical year) or the effects by Rabbi Abraham Isaac Kook to compel the workers to observe the religious commandments heightened the tension and sharpened the antireligious convictions of the youth in the labor movement."[322]

Clearly, the closer we come to our time, the more poignantly we must ask ourselves if and how our own relations with the members of our tribe impact our lives, and indeed our survival. As we will see in the following chapters, German Jewry went through a similar process of assimilation and rejection at around the same time. But in Germany, the consequences were beyond anyone's worst nightmare.

Chapter 6: The Unification of Germany

&

The Dissolution of German Jewry

Like all Golden Eras in Jewish history—the First Temple, Second Temple, the Spanish *convivencia*, and even, to a lesser extent, the integration of the Jewish intelligentsia in Russia—the emancipation of the Jewish people in Europe and their integration into the general society started out as a great promise, and ended in a cataclysm.

In the case of German Jewry, that tragedy entailed near annihilation not only of German Jewry, but of European Jewry altogether. Within six years, in the course of World War II (1939-1945), though in truth, mainly during the years 1942-1945, during the implementation of the Final Solution plan, European Jewry was gassed to death, shot to death, and suffocated in cars of animal trains to the point of near extinction. The Holocaust, which wiped out nearly 150 years of Jewish efforts to acculturate themselves into the European society and culture, nearly wiped out the Jews themselves.

Since the collapse of love of others within Israel leading up to the destruction of the Second Temple, the hallmark of separation and alienation has been the desire to assimilate and merge with the host country. As described in the previous chapter, this trend usually accompanies a wave of rejection of traditional Judaism, rifts between Jews, and anger among and within Jewish communities. The aspiration to renounce one's Jewishness, and sometimes Judaism altogether, wears many attires, but the bottom line is that assimilation always entails a drift from the root of Judaism, namely love of others. Instead, Jews adopt local values and morals, strive either to convert or to "reform" Judaism in order to adapt it to the surrounding milieu, and develop local patriotism, making their host country their "new Jerusalem."

But since the Jews are not an ordinary nation, but one with a vocation that haunts its members and demands its fulfillment—as the anti-Semites quoted earlier in the book articulated so eloquently— our efforts to merge and dissolve in the host culture never succeed. Instead, those efforts backfire, painfully.

This chapter focuses on the trends leading to the rise of Nazism in Germany, illustrating the changing attitudes toward Jews since the "Spring of Nations" through the unification of Germany, the subsequent official emancipation of the Jews, the dissolution of the Jewish community, and finally the painful letdown as the most civilized nation in Europe turns its back in arrogant disdain to the desperate-for-acceptance German assimilationist Jews.

Early Signs of Intolerance

Nineteenth century German Jewry displayed once more the familiar pattern of a growing drift from cohesion, which is the root of Judaism, and intensifying anti-Semitism. The difference between the Holocaust and prior calamities that befell the Jewish people is that the Holocaust was a premeditated attempt to physically exterminate the Jews. Other cataclysms, even the most deadly, such as the destruction of the Second Temple, were not calculated attempts to obliterate the existence of the Jewish people (although Titus did express his wish that it would happen, see Chapter 3). Rather, they were attempts to expel or convert the Jews.

In order to understand how Germany, the most educated, civilized, and cultured nation in Europe at the time, ended up committing the most heinous atrocity, we must go back to the early 19th century, shortly after the release of Germany from Napoleon's grip. In the wake of the French Revolution and the spirit of liberalism it brought with it, the Jews, who had been excluded from Christian European society for centuries, enthusiastically embraced the new zeitgeist. "Jews throughout Europe lobbied their respective governments for emancipation," explains an essay in the *Jewish Virtual Library*.[323] "Having for centuries been regarded as non-citizens without any rights, the Jews ... began to demand from their rulers citizenship and treatment equal to that of non-Jewish residents," continues the essay.

As one might expect, "The cause of emancipation, which began to be implemented on a permanent basis in the mid- and late-nineteenth century, was greatly hurt in 1819 by a series of anti-Jewish disturbances known as the 'Hep! Hep! Riots.'"[324] In either case, the slogan became a widespread one in 1819 when German Jews were the targets of widespread rioting. In that same essay, the Jewish Virtual Library asserts that "The immediate cause of these riots probably lay in the Jewish demands for civil rights." This is the important point to note: the evident, ever-emerging connection between the attempts of Jews to blur, or even veer off from their origin, and the reaction of their host nation. "The Jewish representatives who attended the 1815 Congress of Vienna formally demanded emancipation," continues the essay, "and German academics and politicians alike responded with vicious opposition."[325] In other words, the opposition was not to the Jews, but to their attempt to merge with the Germans.

Austria born Jewish journalist and author Amos Elon describes the Hep! Hep! Riots in his book *The Pity of It All: A Portrait of the German Jewish Epoch, 1743-1933*. While he does not make the connection between Jewish assimilation and anti-Jewish riots, he is sincere enough to admit bewilderment. "In early August 1819, a sudden wave of riots struck the Bavarian city of Würzburg," Elon writes. "For two or three days, frenzied mobs ran through the streets looting and demolishing Jewish homes and shops, screaming *Hep! Hep! Jude verreck!* (Death to all Jews!) The rioting began at the local university. During an academic ceremony, an aged professor who had recently come out in favor of civic rights for Jews had to run for his life as angry students assaulted him. The riots then spread to the streets. The students were joined by shopkeepers, artisans, and unemployed workers. Two people were killed and some twenty wounded. The material damage was considerable. With cries of *Hep! Hep!*—an acronym of the Latin *Hierosolyma est perdita* (Jerusalem is lost)—the mob broke into shops and homes, wrecking doors and furniture. The army was called in, preventing a massacre. The Jewish population fled the city and spent the next few days in tents in the surrounding countryside."[326]

Yet, this was only the beginning: "From Würzburg the riots swept through other Bavarian towns and villages and from there to central and southwest Germany—to Bamberg, Bayreuth, Darmstadt, Karlsruhe, Mannheim, Frankfurt, Koblenz, Cologne, and other cities along the Rhine—and as far north as Bremen, Hamburg, and Lübeck," Elon details. "In Franconia, Jews were chased out of their homes. In Hamburg, hundreds fled the city to seek refuge across the nearby Danish border. The riots appeared to be entirely spontaneous. Some thought they had been triggered by economic crisis. The year 1816 had been one of drought and hunger, rising bread prices and widespread unemployment. Others claimed that Jews were scapegoats for oppressive reactionary regimes of the post-Napoleonic era. Why Jewish residents of Würzburg or Koblenz would have been held responsible for unemployment or the arrests of liberal militants was unclear. The search for 'rational' reasons was widespread and, of course, useless. Some 90 percent of German Jews were poor or very poor; 10 percent of the latter were said to be beggars. More rich Jews lived in Prussia than anywhere else, yet in Prussia there were no riots at all."[327]

Similar to the forced conversions in Spain, or the voluntary assimilation in Russia, "The riots had two simultaneous effects on the German Jews. In many cases, the violence sped the Jews' attempts to assimilate and integrate in the secular society. Proponents of emancipation refused to be dissuaded, and believed that only if Jews became fully 'German' would they be treated as such." On the other hand, "The riots also led some Jews to form even more tightly knit groups in response to the animosity from without."[328]

Because the assimilation efforts of the early 19th century Jews were largely unsuccessful, the riots were relatively mild—if quite impactful—and quickly died down. However, the aspiration of German Jews to assimilate and become European rather than Jews lingered in their hearts. "Eventually," continues the *Jewish Virtual Library* essay, "emancipation was achieved." However, the outcome was that "even more virulent expressions of anti-Semitism became prevalent."[329] While the Jews were celebrating their "victory," the seeds of their ruin were being sown and watered by their rapid ascent to prominence, similar to their ascent in Spain's clergy and government ranks.

Assimilating Despite the Warning Signs

The Hep! Hep! Riots did not deter the Jews for long. The 1848 revolutions in Europe, also known as the "Spring of the Nations," brought with them a new spirit of freedom and a revival of liberal ideals. A Minnesota State University essay concisely concludes that "In exchange for greater legal rights and greater acceptance in society, Jews in France, Britain, Germany and elsewhere discarded many of their older customs. Ironically," continues the essay, "this 'assimilation' helped give rise to a newer form of anti-Jewish prejudice. As Judaic historian Robert Seltzer has noted, the new prejudice 'was a backlash against Jewish success upon entering the mainstream of European society, and in that, [just as the *conversos* were targeted in Spain] the acculturated rather than the traditional Jew was the main focus of fear.'"[330]

Historians Jonathan Frankel and Steven Zipperstein offer an expressive description not only of the extent of Jewish assimilation during the mid-19th century, but also of the desire of many Jews to untie their connections to Judaism altogether. "Although legal emancipation was incomplete before 1871, the corporate and national character of Jewish life was well on the way to dissolution before then. German Jews were embracing gentile patterns of thought and behavior and abandoning traditional religious customs. Old loyalties and allegiances were weakening and new identities being forged," write Frankel and Zipperstein.[331] As a result, when German Jews immigrated to Britain, they were already "accustomed to participating in spheres of activity outside the confines of Jewish social and business networks. Few had received a traditional education or grown up in homes in which regular synagogue attendance and observance of the dietary laws were the norm. [...] The immigrants' prior acculturation to gentile standards and habits and complete or partial estrangement from Jewish beliefs and customs, as well as their exposure to the pervasive anti-Semitism of their homeland [due to the aforementioned backlash to assimilation], profoundly influenced their communal and religious behavior once settled in England. Many held aloof from any formal identification with Judaism, while those who affiliated with synagogues remained for the most part haphazard in their attendance at services and lukewarm in their observance of domestic rituals. ...Most either passed out of the Jewish community altogether, through conversion or intermarriage, or established such a weak connection to it that their children or grandchildren eventually did so."[332] As a conclusion, Frankel and Zipperstein state that it is "abundantly clear that the majority of immigrants from Central Europe [chiefly Germany] in the Victorian period [referring to mid-19th century England] took advantage of their new surroundings to shed or dilute their Jewishness."[333]

In the introduction to this book, I mentioned acclaimed Professor of Law Alan Dershowitz, who stated that those who do not see "the reality of declining anti-Semitism" are suffering from "a perception gap,"[334] and that he now sees a very different picture. Dershowitz is not the first, second, or third to make that mistake. In the 19th and 20th centuries, the majority of German Jews made it, and at an incomprehensible cost to themselves and to all European Jewry.

In her book *Hitler, Germans, and the Jewish Question*, Sarah Ann Gordon writes that "During the revolution of 1848, Jews and liberal Christians alike advocated Jewish emancipation. Although the revolution failed, and therefore did not realize its goals," she writes, "German liberals retained their commitment to equality for all citizens."[335] In order to achieve their goals, the Jews were ready and willing to shed their "Jewishness," oblivious to the lessons from the past, that assimilation brings intensification of anti-Semitism. Echoing the words of Frankel and Zipperstein, Gordon writes that "Many German and Jewish liberals believed that Jews could never become true citizens of the state until they abandoned their distinctive customs."[336] Many Jews embarked on an effort to become Germans and shed their Jewishness emphatically and unequivocally. According to Prof. of History Glenn R. Sharfman, "One Jewish liberal became so enthralled by the promise of emancipation that he wrote: 'The messiah, for whom we prayed these thousands of years, has appeared and our fatherland has been given to us. The messiah is freedom, our fatherland is Germany.'"[337] Finally, Sarah Gordon concludes, "Their aspirations were fulfilled by the legal emancipation of 1869, which was extended to all of Germany under the German Constitution of 1871."[338]

Alas, Jew-hatred has its own laws. As we have seen throughout the history of our people, the backlash to emancipation never fails to come. Soon after the Jews in Germany were legally emancipated, a wave of sinister anti-Semitism struck the hopeful liberals. "Just as liberal thinkers began to believe that anti-Jewish tendencies would gradually fade, renewed prejudice appeared in France, Britain, and elsewhere,"[339] such as in Germany.

In March 1879, Wilhelm Marr, who espoused in his twenties communist ideals, wrote the anti-Semitic essay, "The Victory of Judaism over Germandom." In it, he coined the term "anti-Semitism."[340] In his essay, "Marr argued that acculturated Jews would eventually subvert traditional German culture; they would corrupt 'all [German] standards ... dominate commerce, [and] push themselves ever more into state services,'"[341] states the above-mentioned Minnesota State University essay.

Marr's anti-Semitism was a new incarnation of Jew-hatred. Probably the foremost researcher on German anti-Semitism, the late Prof. Robert S. Wistrich, former head of the Vidal Sassoon International Center for the Study of Anti-Semitism at the Hebrew University in Jerusalem, pointed out that Wilhelm Marr "vehemently emphasized that his antisemitism was *not* motivated by religious hatred [emphasis in the source]. A veteran radical democrat of 1848, convinced ... that Hebrew monotheism was 'a malady of human consciousness' and the root of all tyranny and evil, Wilhelm Marr's antisemitism was also virulently anti-Catholic," continues Wistrich to explain Marr's ideology. Moreover, "Wilhelm Marr believed that no Christian could be a genuine anti-Semite since Christianity was itself based on Jewish racial tradition," concludes Wistrich.[342]

Indeed, Marr's ideas mark the advent of racial anti-Semitism, the most lethal kind of Jew-hatred history has ever known. Here the seeds of the Holocaust were sown. Acclaimed historian Francis Nicosia concisely worded the dismal conclusion from the atrocities that eventually unfolded: "That one could be both German and Jewish ... had been a basic premise of Jewish emancipation, one that ultimately proved untenable in modern Germany between 1871 and 1945."[343]

But anti-Semitism has always been part of the lives of Jews in the Diaspora. They could not tell that Marr's type of hatred would lead to a far more savage result, one that even a sincere conversion could not appease, one from which there was no escape because you could not "undo" the race into which you were born.

The attempts of Jews to become part of the new "fatherland" had the expected adverse consequences. The Germans did not approve of the Jewish integration in their midst, and many of them became increasingly anti-Semitic. Worse yet, politicians learned to use anti-Semitism to their benefit. "Hermann Ahlwardt ... epitomized this newer brand of ... hooligan anti-Semitism which was threatening to undermine Junker hegemony in agrarian Germany. Ahlwardt's election in the Conservative stronghold of Friedeberg-Arnswalde on 24 November 1892, was one of the high points of the *völkisch* movement. Anti-Semites in the 1893 Reichstag elections received 263,000 votes, a fivefold increase over their results a few years earlier. This increase in support coincided with a disastrous slump in the number of Liberal Progressive deputies from 67 to 37. There were now 16 anti-Semitic deputies in the German Parliament. Moreover, on 8 December 1892, the Conservatives adopted for the first time an openly anti-Semitic plank in their Tivoli program, in order to stem the *völkisch* tide which was moving against them."[344]

Otto Böckel was another politician who had succeeded in politics using anti-Semitism. "His proto-Nazi agrarian populism idealized peasants as the backbone of the German nation, the repository of its 'racial' purity and of 'Germanic' virtues such as hard work, loyalty, and strong character. This *Blut und Boden* (blood and soil) ideology drew much of its strength from the negative effects of liberal economic reforms in the Second Reich, rampant anti-Prussianism, as well as the Jewish emancipation of 1870–71."[345]

In this way, Jews had become political tools for electoral gain. Some forty years later, Hitler would perfect the use of anti-Semitism in politics to rise to power.

As always when there is an increase in anti-Semitism, intensified division within the Jewish fold precedes it. In the case of Germany, one of the most prominent proponents of Jewish self-hatred was the renowned poet, playwright, journalist, and essayist Heinrich Heine, who was born to a Jewish family but converted to Lutheranism at age 28. Journalist and author Amos Elon, whom we mentioned earlier in this chapter, describes Heine's manifest disdain toward the religion of his birth: "In the summer of 1823, Heine returned to Göttingen, in the kingdom of Hanover, to prepare for his doctoral exams. He continued to maintain a lively correspondence with his friends at the society. His year of participation in its work had sobered him. 'We no longer have the strength to grow a beard, to fast, to hate, and, through hate, to abide,' he wrote to Immanuel Wohlwill, a society colleague who supported reform of synagogue worship."[346] In fact, Heine was very negative even toward the budding Reform Judaism. In his eyes, the modifications made by Reform rabbis to the Orthodox customs "were merely imitative of Christianity and offered only a 'new stage set and decor.' The new rabbis (Heine called them *souffleurs*— prompters) wore a Protestant parson's 'white band' in their collars. Reform Judaism was like mock turtle soup, he thought, 'turtle soup without the turtle.'"[347]

Perhaps the most patent display of the sensitivity of non-Jews to Jewish lack of unity is the words of the Jewish people's worst evil-doer of all time: Adolf Hitler. In *Mein Kampf*, Hitler expressed specifically his abhorrence toward the Jews for their hatred of their brethren, regarding it as a sign of absence of culture. In Hitler's own words, "As soon as egoism becomes the ruler of a people, the bands of order are loosened and in the chase after their own happiness men fall from heaven into a real hell. Yes, even posterity forgets the men who have only served their own advantage. ... In the Jewish people ... as soon as the common enemy is conquered, the danger threatening all averted and the booty hidden, the apparent harmony of the Jews among themselves ceases, again making way for their old causal tendencies. The Jew is only united when a common danger forces him to be or a common booty entices him; if these two grounds are lacking, the qualities of the crassest egoism come into their own, and in the twinkling of an eye the united people turns into a horde of rats, fighting bloodily among themselves. If the Jews were alone in this world, they would stifle in filth and offal; they would try to get ahead of one another in hate-filled struggle and exterminate one another."[348]

Despite the backlash expressed in escalating anti-Semitism, the attempts of German Jews to acculturate themselves in the German society only intensified. Acclaimed researcher Steven M. Lowenstein described the efforts of Jews to become part of the German society through marriage. His research, titled "Jewish Intermarriage and Conversion in Germany and Austria," is an enlightening report that sheds light on that same age-old phenomenon that Hitler noticed: When Jews do not unite above their differences, they strive to disperse.

Unlike Spain, which forced Jews to choose between banishment, death, or conversion to Christianity, Germany was affected by liberalism and therefore permitted Jews, who had by now been emancipated, to have no religion whatsoever. Moreover, they could merge with the non-Jewish while still remaining Jews, and even wed non-Jews without relinquishing their birth religion.

As a result, Jews began to intermarry as soon as they were emancipated, albeit initially in very small numbers. In the first years after the emancipation, the percentage of intermarriage among Jews, where Jews married either Protestant or Catholic Germans, was less than five percent.[349] Yet, by 1933, when the Nazis came to power, it was almost thirty percent, with some years peaking even higher.[350]

Another interesting point to make in regard to Jews leaving the fold through wedlock was that when the general number of weddings declined, such as at times of war, the number of weddings with spouses outside the tribe declined far less. For example, in 1915, at the height of World War I, when Jewish weddings were far fewer than usual due to the tensions of the war, marriages outside the fold were far less affected and amounted to no less than 34.2 percent of marriages that involved Jews.[351] When the number of weddings picked up again, so did the number of interfaith marriages, but proportionally less than the general number of weddings. As a result, although the percentage of interfaith marriages dropped, the absolute number of mixed marriages continued to climb.[352]

Furthermore, among intermarried couples where the wife was not Jewish, less than eight percent of the wives converted into Judaism. Because in Judaism, the mother determines the child's religion, this meant that more than 92 percent of the children of intermarried couples where the wife was not Jewish were also not Jewish. When the case was reversed and the wife was Jewish, again the numbers were leaning toward consequent conversion. Fifty-five percent of the Jewish women in intermarried couples left the Jewish faith, and less than one half percent of the Christian husbands converted into Judaism.[353] These are not mere statistics; these never-before-seen levels of intermarriage indicate the aspiration of the Jews to abandon their roots and make their host country—which in this case was Germany—their "new Jerusalem." As Lowenstein put it, it reflected the "desire of Jews to escape the Jewish community."[354] As we will see, this desire is also precisely what Nazis stressed in their distinction between Zionist Jews and assimilationist Jews, in favor of the former.

The Treaty of Versailles and the Weimar Republic

World War I devastated most of Europe. To Germany, however, it meant far more than losing a war. According to the online *International Encyclopedia of the First World War*, the number of German war casualties and wounded was the highest of all the countries that participated in the war. Some two million soldiers died in battle, with another one million civilian casualties, and over four million soldiers were wounded.[355]

Despite the devastation, and although "Jewish Germans died at the same rate as non-Jewish Germans," in some ways, World War I was a boon for the German Jewry. "For most of the war," writes Prof. David Mikics of the University of Houston, "German Jews and gentiles stood proudly together in defense of their country. Jews welcomed the war as a fight for justice, freedom and, most important of all, German culture. Gertrud Kantorowicz wrote in August 1914, when the conflict broke out, that 'the war itself is pure greatness … my being relates to Germany as a life's breath relates to the body out of which it arises.'"[356]

Yet, Germany was defeated in the war, and the 1919 Treaty of Versailles, in which Germany officially capitulated to the Allies, was a devastating blow to German pride. As it always happens, at times of crisis, the Jew is the default go-to scapegoat.

Consequently, to many anti-Semitic Germans, the war was a great opportunity to prove that the assimilated Jews were not really assimilating—a striking similarity to the accusations made by anti-Semitic Spaniards preceding the onset of the Inquisition, which eventually led to numerous executions and the complete expulsion from Spain. According to Mikics, the Germans could not understand why Germany surrendered. After all, no army invaded, much less conquered Germany, and reports from the front did not disclose the grimness of the situation. As a result, "There was only one possible explanation: Germany had been betrayed by Socialists and (you guessed it) Jews."[357] Once again, the paradox of assimilated Jews being accused of *not assimilating enough* blew the wind out of the sails of the perpetual Jewish effort to become "a normal people," belonging to the nation where they lived.

Just as it happened in 15th century Spain and in 19th century Russia, the growing anti-Semitism did not stop the efforts of Jews to assimilate. If anything, it invigorated these efforts. Lowenstein writes that after the war there were "many indications that anti-Semitism in Weimar Germany was far worse than it had been before World War I... If ... the initiating party in marriages was usually the man, then the growing gap between male and female intermarriage during the Weimar Republic indicates that while many Jewish men wanted to marry non-Jews, fewer non-Jewish men wanted to marry Jewish women. This would indicate a greater desire of Jews to escape the Jewish community than of non-Jews to accept them."[358]

Germany after World War I was a wreck. Internally divided, violent clashes erupted in Berlin between right-wing paramilitary organizations against left-wing agitators. As if the casualties of war were not enough, in March 1919, 15,000 Germans died in just nine days of street fighting.

In addition to violence, the German economy was shattered. The high reparations payments and costs of war had devastating consequences. The cost of living in Germany rose twelve times between 1914 and 1922. When the government sought to pay reparations simply by printing more money, the value of the German mark rapidly declined, leading to hyper-inflation. In January 1920, the exchange rate was 64.8 marks to one dollar; by November 1923, it was 4,200,000,000 (4.2 billion!) to one.[359]

But in the midst of the turmoil, Germany had managed to establish a genuine—albeit short-lived—democracy. During those few years of existence of the Weimar Republic, there were real freedom of speech, freedom of occupation, and freedom of worship. Thanks to this liberalism, and despite increasing anti-Semitism, German Jewry in post World War I democratic Germany quickly climbed the ranks of society. Once again, the similarities between the rise of Germany's assimilated Jewry and the Spanish *conversos* are striking, even if in the case of Germany, the bloom was far shorter. Thus, over a mere decade and a half, German Jewry thought it had it all.

Moreover, not everything was dismal in the struggling republic. In the cultural arena, Germany experienced its own "Roaring Twenties." Urban centers like Berlin became some of the most socially liberal places in Europe. Berlin had a thriving nightlife full of bars, cabarets, and even numerous gay and lesbian bars. In fact, "Sexual liberation was a very real phenomenon, complete with a gay and lesbian rights movement led by [the Jewish] Dr. Magnus Hirschfeld who ran an Institute for Sexual Science."[360]

Women, too, were given full voting rights, even before the US and the UK. Artists were given freedom of expression, and Germany became the cultural hub of Europe.

The Killing of the Jewish Minister

Now that they had been unfettered, Jews quickly ascended the ranks of government and industry. But no person represents the rise and fall of German Jewry better than the slain foreign minister Walther Rathenau. In "The Assassination of Walther Rathenau," historian

Nigel Jones tells the story of the man whose fall heralded the fall of his entire creed.

"Rathenau was one of the most formidable figures in early 20th century Germany. A Jewish industrialist, thinker and diplomat, he built the enormous AEG electronics and engineering conglomerate into a powerhouse of the German economy. During the First World War, when Britain's naval blockade was starving Germany of vital raw material imports, Rathenau became his nation's economic overlord.

"...Rathenau husbanded Germany's dwindling resources and directed its industrial production, brilliantly improvising to give a lease of life to its failing war effort. His work, according to some historians, prolonged German resistance by months or even years. It also sowed the seeds of hatred in the minds of Germany's anti-Semitic nationalists, who saw in Rathenau, not a great patriot brilliantly managing scarcity, but a rich Jew cornering markets.

"After the war, the infant Weimar Republic sought out the talented Rathenau, making him foreign minister. [...] Rathenau duly stoked the Right's rage in 1922 by negotiating the Treaty of Rapallo with the nascent Soviet Union, while insisting that Germany had to fulfill the provisions of the deeply unpopular Treaty of Versailles. [...] They [fanatical Right] tramped the streets yelling hymns of hate: 'Knock down Walther Rathenau. The God-forsaken Jewish sow!' Some prepared to do just that. On June 24, 1922, a rogue right-wing terrorist group called Organisation Consul (OC) … murdered Rathenau as he drove to his office from his home in Berlin Grunewald district."[361]

Rathenau's assassination did not crush the infant republic, but it was a clear sign that the Germans would not agree to Jewish acculturation among them. It proved that for all their efforts, Jews were still pariahs.

When the Great Depression hit the US in 1929, it was horrendous for America. But for the fledgling German democracy, the shock waves that rippled through all of Europe were a fatal blow. The government had no choice but to employ "an austerity program which cut spending and those programs designed precisely to help those most in need. Economic hardship combined with a general distrust of the Weimar system to destabilize parliamentary politics. ... Coalitions in the Reichstag were difficult to form among an increasing number of extremist parties, left and right. Elections were held more and more frequently," until the Weimer Republic finally disintegrated.[362]

In the bleak atmosphere of a hapless democracy, one charismatic man knew how to patch the factions of the broken German nation. Adolf Hitler pinned it all on the Jews, and the most civilized, educated, and cultured nation on the planet cheered *Sieg Heil...*

Chapter 7: Nazism, the Holocaust, & Very Hard Questions

On May 8, 1945, Germany submitted its unconditional surrender to the Allies and the Second World War officially ended in Europe. By then, the evidence of the genocide that the Nazis had committed against European Jewry was overwhelming. Even the captured Nazis did not try to deny it.

Not only the death camps, concentration camps, forced labor camps, and mass graves were exposed. What constituted the most damning evidence were not the camps, but the documents that the Nazis themselves had so meticulously produced and kept. Every train that was sent to the death camps was documented, including the number of people on board. Every shipment of Jews from place to place, every killing, by gas or by bullets, was written down and sent to Berlin to be archived. Every piece of jewelry, shoe, golden tooth, even hair, was stripped off, piled up, and documented for later use in the efficient, demonic Nazi killing machine. In all of history, there has never been a more premeditated and carefully executed extermination of one nation by another.

The majority of my own family perished in the Holocaust. I grew up with the specter of this genocide, but I never received any answers. Simply, no one seemed to have any.

How did the Germans come to this? Was it fate or could the Holocaust have been avoided? These are two of the many questions we will tackle below. There may not be unequivocal answers, but there are certainly facts that the predominant narrative often overlooks and which should be stated so we may explore new perspectives on the Holocaust and learn new lessons from this tragedy, if we truly want it to never happen again.

Two Kinds of Jews

The November 1932 elections in Germany were indecisive. Adolf Hitler's National Socialist German Workers Party-NSDAP, better known as the Nazi Party, captured 230 out of 608 seats in the Reichstag, the German parliament, and became the biggest party in Germany. However, it did not have a majority and could not form a government without a coalition with another party. Nevertheless, Hitler would not share power with the Socialists, who got 20 percent of the vote, or with the Communists, who got 17 percent. Finally, on January 30, 1933, the exasperated President Paul von Hindenburg exercised his emergency powers and appointed Adolf Hitler as interim chancellor.

"The Nazis had promised that upon assuming power they would rebuild Germany's economy, dismantle its democracy, destroy German Jewry, and establish Aryans as the master race—in that order," writes Edwin Black in his groundbreaking book *The Transfer Agreement: The Dramatic Story of the Pact Between the Third Reich and Jewish Palestine*. "Yet many Western leaders saw only the economic value of Nazism. Hitler seemed the only alternative to a Communist state, a man who might rebuild the German economy and pay Germany's debts. That would be good for all Western economies. As for the threat to Germany's Jews, that was [considered] a domestic German affair."[363]

So, undeterred and virtually undisturbed—except for unsuccessful attempts by Jewish organizations to boycott German goods—the Nazis went straight to make good on their word. Almost immediately, they began to put pressure on the Jews and eliminate the opposition. On February 27, 1933, the Reichstag building caught fire. "By the next morning," writes Black, "the German public was convinced that the fire ... was in fact the beginning of a Jewish-backed Communist uprising. Hitler demanded and received temporary powers suspending all constitutional liberties."[364]

However, what is less known is that in the eyes of the Nazis, not all Jews were equal. Nazi Germany made clear distinctions between assimilationist Jews, who saw Germany as their fatherland, and Zionist Jews, whose goal was to drive as many Jews as possible out of Germany and into the Land of Israel, which was then called "Palestine," as part of the efforts to establish a national home for the Jewish people. As early as 1920, "at a Munich beer hall, while Hitler was preaching his doctrine of Jewish expulsion, someone from the crowd hollered something about human rights. Hitler answered sharply, 'Let [the Jew] look for his human rights where he belongs: in his own state of Palestine.'"[365]

Alfred Rosenberg, one of the chief Nazi theoreticians—who was not Jewish, despite his Jewish sounding name—also regarded Palestine as a good solution. In 1920, he wrote, "Zionism must be actively supported so as to enable us annually to transport a specific number of Jews to Palestine, or, in any case, across our borders."[366]

Accordingly, when the Nazis came to power, they implemented two completely opposite policies toward assimilationist Jews and toward Zionists. Alongside persecution of assimilationist Jews, as later prescribed in the Nuremberg Laws, they encouraged Zionism and Zionist activities with the same zeal that they persecuted assimilationists.

In fact, acclaimed historian and Professor of Holocaust Studies at the University of Vermont, Francis R. Nicosia, writes that a June 1934 SS internal position paper "proposed a positive effort by the government and Party to encourage Zionist efforts in Germany designed to instill a sense of Jewish consciousness and identity in German Jews and to promote emigration to Palestine. Jewish schools, athletic groups, institutions and culture—in short, all Jewish organizations and activities promoting Jewish self-awareness— were to be encouraged. These efforts, along with the occupational retraining centers established by the Zionists throughout Germany for Jewish emigrants going to Palestine, were to be favorably treated by the SS."[367]

Not Just the Jews but the Entire World Would Benefit

Kurt Tuchler, an active Zionist, was acquainted with several members of the Nazi Party, some of whom were quite senior. Among them was his good friend, Austria-born SS officer Baron Leopold von Mildenstein. To solidify Nazi support for Zionism, Tuchler asked Mildenstein to write favorable newspaper articles about the Zionist enterprise in Palestine. Mildenstein agreed but stipulated his consent on visiting Palestine and exploring first-hand the Zionist efforts to build a national home for the Jews.

"In late April 1933," writes Black, "both men and their wives boarded an ocean liner for Palestine. The Nazi party and the ZVfD [*Zionistische Vereinigung für Deutschland* (Zionist Federation of Germany)] each had granted permission for the joint trip. Von Mildenstein approved of what he saw in the kibbutzim and in Tel Aviv. He even learned a few Hebrew words. Many photographs were taken, numerous mementos were dragged back to Germany. An elaborate illustrated series was published about eighteen months later in *Der Angriff* (Images 1, 2 [p 142]) under the title 'A Nazi Travels to Palestine.' Goebbels's newspaper was so proud of the series that a commemorative coin was struck in honor of the voyage. On one side was a swastika; on the other side a Star of David (Image 3 [p 143])."[368]

In 1980, historian Jacob Boas published an essay about Mildenstein's little known but important story in the prestigious magazine *History Today*. Aptly titled "A Nazi Travels to Palestine," the essay reads, "The possibility of a significant Jewish return [to Palestine] existed despite Palestine's underdeveloped economic base, provided that, von Mildenstein cautioned, Jews 'create their own homeland by working their own land.' From such a return, concluded von Mildenstein in his final article, not just the Jews but the entire world would benefit, in that 'it points the way to curing a centuries-long wound on the body of the world: the Jewish question.'"[371]

Image 1: A microfilm image of "A Nazi Travels to Palestine" banner advertising the article series on the top right corner of *Goebbels's Der Angriff* newspaper from October 3, 1934.[369]

"In Palestine," writes Boas, "von Mildenstein encountered a Jew that he liked, a Jew who cultivated his own soil, the 'new Jew.' ...There he saw a Jew who was struggling against great odds to reestablish his roots in the land of his forefathers.... Of this Palestinian Jew von Mildenstein painted a highly flattering portrait." Indeed, adds Boas, "the image of the 'new Jew' projected by von Mildenstein must have left the regular *Angriff* reader shaking his head in disbelief."[372]

Image 2: "A Nazi Travels to Palestine" newspaper article published on September 27, 1934, in *Der Angriff*. Picture on the left: A German Jewish emigrant to Palestine working on a tractor (evidence of the "new Jew"). Picture on the right: The orange trade in Jaffa port near Tel-Aviv. Source: Harriet Scharnberg's photo reportage, *Die »Judenfrage« im Bild* (*The "Jewish Question" in Pictures*).[370]

However, Boas cautions, "von Mildenstein was no friend of the Jews" as such. In accord nwith the official SS policy, he made a clear distinction between Zionist and assimilationist Jews. According to Boas, "[Mildenstein's] sympathy went out only to that segment of Jewry that called itself Zionist. For the so-called assimilated Jew, the Jew who claimed to be a German first and a Jew second, or denied his Jewishness altogether, and for the Jew who eschewed all racial feeling, he held no brief, his view of them being close to the official Party position."[373]

Das Schwarze Korps (*The Black Corps*) was the official weekly newspaper and propaganda agency of the SS. Every SS member was required to read it and induce others to do likewise. The newspaper was published by the Reichsführung-SS (High Command of the SS) at the NSDAP's (Nazi Party's) own publishing house in Munich.[374] On May 15, 1935, the paper published two articles that clearly outlined the contrast between the Third Reich's approach to assimilationist Jews as opposed to its approach to Zionist Jews. The feature article, titled "No Place for Jews in the Army!" (Image 4) actually started on a very positive note addressing Zionist Jews: "It will not be long before the land of Palestine gets back its sons, who have been lost for more than a thousand years. Our good wishes go with them, together with an official goodwill."[375]

Image 3: Goebbels's *Der Angriff* medal commemorating Mildenstein's six-month visit to Palestine. The Star of David side inscription: "A Nazi travels to Palestine." The Swastika side inscription: "And tells about it in the *Angriff*." Image source: Bidspirit online auctions.

However, as the article continues, it addresses assimilating Jews and completely changes tone, referring to them as "Many Jews who are still fighting with all means against their social and political distancing," and "regard Germany as their 'ancestral homeland.'" To those Jews, the article states, "When Germany became a playground for traitors to the fatherland, these organizations, which acted as guardians of inalienable rights, did nothing to stop this disgrace. ...

They always point to the fact that some of them also wore the grey uniform [of the German army in WWI]. This can only be answered, that it is not about the role played by Jews in the [First] World War. It is pointless to offset the number of Jewish front fighters with pathos. ... It does not matter with what enthusiasm the Jews went to war at that time ... a discussion about it is unnecessary. It would also miss the crucial issue: for when our German people were in danger of losing their nationality ... prominent Jews became spokesmen of everything that was politically and morally intended to ruin the German people. ... It is not considered a certificate of a certain German attitude, that Jews at that time could be German soldiers. It is a threadbare statement. ... In the future, there will no longer be any grievous incidents in the German army that regimental commanders are forced to accept Jews."[376]

The second article on that very same day, titled "The Visible Enemy," reiterated perhaps even more explicitly the position of Nazi Germany toward the Jews, aiming to rid them of any illusions they might still have with regard to the Third Reich: "After the Nazi seizure of power, our racial laws did in fact curtail considerably the immediate influence of Jews. But the Jew in his tenacity has seen this merely as a temporary restriction. The question as he sees it is still: How can we win back our old position and once again work to the detriment of Germany?"[377]

Now the article divides German Jewry again into two separate entities: "But we must separate Jewry into two categories according to the way in which they operate: those who work openly as Jews and those who hide behind international Jewish welfare agencies and the like. The Jews in Germany fall into two groups: the Zionists and those who favor being assimilated. The Zionists adhere to a strict racial position and by emigrating to Palestine they are helping to build their own Jewish state. The assimilation-minded Jews deny their race and insist on their loyalty to Germany or [implying that conversion is also unacceptable from the perspective of the SS] claim to be Christians because they have been baptized in order to overthrow National Socialist principles."[378]

Image 4: *Das Schwarze Korps* (*The Black Corps*) May 15, 1935 front page featuring the article *Für Juden ist kein Platz im Heer!* ("No Place for Jews in the Army!")[379]

Practicing Differentiation

The Nazis not only stated their distinction between Zionist and assimilationist Jews; they made it part of their law and practiced it! Item four in the notorious Nuremberg Laws, for instance, contained two sub-items. The first, which related to the Jews as a whole, stated, "Jews are forbidden to fly the Reich or national flag or display Reich colors." The second sub-item gave Zionist Jews a privilege that no other minority group in Germany was given, and even gave that privilege official state protection: "They [Jews] are, however, permitted to display the Jewish colors. The exercise of this right is protected by the state"[380] (Image 5). Those Jewish colors later became the Star of David flag that is today the flag of the State of Israel.

§ 4

(1) Juden ist das Hissen der Reichs- und Nationalflagge und das Zeigen der Reichsfarben verboten.

(2) Dagegen ist ihnen das Zeigen der jüdischen Farben gestattet. Die Ausübung dieser Befugnis steht unter staatlichem Schutz.

Image 5: Item 4 in the Nuremberg Race Laws. Source: *Reichsgesetzblatt* (Reich Law Gazette, RGBI) I, 1935, p. 1146.

But the Nazis did far more than permit Jews to "wave the Jewish flag." *Jüdische Rundschau (Jewish Review)*, the largest and most important Zionist weekly newspaper in Germany at the time, "was essentially exempt from the so-called *Gleichschaltung* or 'uniformity' demanded by the Nazi Party of all facets of German society. *Jüdische Rundschau* was free to preach Zionism as a wholly separate political philosophy—indeed, the only separate political philosophy sanctioned [endorsed/authorized] by the Third Reich. In 1933, Hebrew became an encouraged course in all Jewish schools. By 1935, uniforms for Zionist youth corps were permitted—the only non-Nazi uniform allowed in Germany," writes Prof. Black.[381]

Transfer or Boycott—That Is the Question

When the Nazis came to power, the Jews outside of Germany were just as baffled as the Jews within it. A sense of urgency and crisis engulfed the Jewish world and Jewish leaders were bewildered, unsure how to relate to the blatant anti-Semitic rhetoric coming out of Germany, or how to assess the danger its government posed to German Jewry, in particular, and to world Jewry as a whole.

After the initial shock, two clashing approaches formed: One approach maintained that world Jewry must not keep silent. It must boycott all German goods and urge governments in their respective countries—primarily the US, Great Britain, and France—to do the same. As a result of the Treaty of Versailles following WWI, which guaranteed Germany would not be able to restore its military and industrial might, advocates of the boycott hoped that a boycott would tip Germany's vulnerable economy over the edge and in the mayhem that would ensue, the Nazi government would topple.[382]

The other approach took a completely opposite course: cooperate and leverage the situation. The result of the latter approach was the Transfer Agreement—the most unlikely, unacceptable, and some would say "immoral" deal ever signed, and at the same time the only measure that Jews took in response to Nazism that actually saved Jewish lives. In fact, the Transfer Agreement saved approximately

50,000 German and Austrian Jews. The economic closure imposed on Germany with the outbreak of WWII terminated the agreement late in 1939, a few months after the war broke out. Had it not been terminated by the closure, there is no telling how many more Jews would have been saved.

But the Transfer Agreement was not only a life saver for tens of thousands of Jewish lives; it brought with it an economic boom and enriched the Yishuv [Jewish settlement in Palestine] with 14 million sterling pounds, more than 1.1 billion US dollars in 2019 value. This huge contribution to the fledgling Jewish state boosted its economy and was paramount in facilitating the Jewish military forces, infrastructure, and jobs for many more Jewish emigrants in addition to the 50,000 who came from Germany.

From May to August 1933, the Transfer Agreement went through three stages of development before reaching its final structure. Its goal was to allow German Jews to leave Germany while keeping some of their wealth and bypassing the stringent German money transfer restrictions. According to an essay on the Transfer Agreement in *The National Library of Israel*, "In 1931, following the global economic crisis [which brought the economy of the German Weimar Republic to near bankruptcy], those who emigrated from Germany were forced to pay exceedingly high taxes for the transfer of their property to points abroad; this policy remained in effect during the Nazi period."[383]

Succinctly, the Transfer Agreement was carried out in the following way: Two companies were established in order to implement it—in Germany, it was the Palästina Treuhandstelle Zur Beratung Deutscher (PALTREU), a partnership of Anglo-Palestine Bank and Max Warburg and Oscar Wasserman Bank. In Tel-Aviv, it was the Haavara (Hebrew: transfer), a daughter company of Anglo-Palestine Bank. PALTREU received the money from Jews who wanted to immigrate to Palestine and bought with it German products for export to Palestine. In Palestine, Haavara would collect the imported goods from Germany, sell them, and subsequently give the new immigrants their share.[384]

A *Jewish Telegraphic Agency* (JTA) May 25, 1936 news bulletin details the division of sums transferred to Palestine through the Transfer Agreement. Of the more than 26 million Reichsmarks transferred to Palestine "up to the end of 1935," some forty-three percent went to the new immigrants. The rest of the funds were invested in public and private infrastructure, utility, and industrial companies such as the Jewish National Fund, Nir, Ltd., and Rasco.[385] Forty-three percent may not seem like much, but considering the situation of the Jews in Germany, and considering the fact that had they emigrated by themselves, they would have been able to salvage much less of their wealth, if any, forty-three percent was a bargain! Moreover, the rest of the funds were a game changer in terms of the Yishuv's economy, and helped it establish its own military and civil industries, as well as purchase much needed arms for the coming battles. In Black's words, "Now that the world has confronted the issue of pilfered Holocaust-era assets—Jewish gold, Jewish art, Jewish insurance, and Jewish slave labor—the Transfer Agreement stands out as the sole example of a Jewish asset rescue that occurred before the genocidal period. It was the sole success—and daring in its scope."[386]

However, at that time, matters were far less evident. Germany's overt sympathy toward Zionism was viewed with suspicion by much of the Jewish world. If Germany were to make a deal with the Zionist leadership in Palestine, it would undermine the attempts of world Jewry to boycott German goods.

Yfaat Weiss, Director of the Dubnow Institute and Professor of Jewish History at Leipzig University, provides a good summary of the complexities of Jewish approaches toward the boycott vs. transfer question.[387] According to Weiss, there were several contenders in the struggle between advocates of the Transfer Agreement and advocates of the boycott. "The [boycott] movement ... began with the famous rally sponsored by the American Jewish Congress under Stephen Wise in Madison Square Garden, New York, on March 27, 1933." However, in America, the boycott "evoked greatest sympathy among small merchants and people of meager means, rather than among big business people."[388] The Germans did not miss this disunity, "as the secretary of state of the

Reich Chancellery expressed it: 'In spite of its seeming success, for the Jews in America, too, the boycott is a double-edged sword. … Moreover, on account of economic interests, leading businessmen among them who have German assets at their disposal have violated it, so that a rift has already developed within American Jewry ('white' Jews against the so-called 'kikes,' or Eastern European Jews)."[389]

By and large, continues Weiss, "The Jewish movement to boycott German goods was foremost among the efforts of international Jewish organizations on behalf of German Jewry, and Jewish communities worldwide—especially in the United States, France, and Great Britain—took part in it. The boycott movement in Poland was particularly strong and became pre-eminent in Jewish actions against Nazi Germany."[390] At the same time, the people most affected by Nazism up until that point, namely German Jewry, generally opposed the whole idea of boycott. "The boycott movement was widely perceived as a threat to the interests of German Jews, for it might cause the Germans to toughen their own anti-Jewish economic boycott. It was also considered a potential impediment to the Transfer Agreement, an arrangement that served the basic interests of German Jewry with respect to economics and emigration," argues Weiss.

Historian Yoav Gelber writes about the German Jewry opposition to the boycott and the support it received from the Jewish National Council (JNC). Gelber explains that in order to support the position of the Zionist Federation in Germany, the JNC convened on March 30, 1933, in London, and "the majority of the participants demanded that the question of immigration, as opposed to that of the boycott, be the focus of the debate and be considered the main issue of the Jewish response to the Nazi policies."[391] This, they estimated correctly, would enable them to continue Zionist activity in Germany.

Deeply Rooted Alienation

The dispute over the Transfer Agreement and the boycott was fierce and venomous. It reflected more than the disagreement over the proper way to react to Nazism, which was a grave enough issue in its own right. Underneath it were layers of contempt and enmity among the disputed communities.

There were three main camps among the Jews: 1) orthodox—which were chiefly Polish Jewry, 2) Zionists—most of whom resided in Palestine, and 3) assimilationists—mainly German and Austrian Jews. American Jewry was divided between orthodox, assimilationist, many of whom were of German descent and some even still owned assets and had interests in Germany, and Zionists, who were mostly members of Jabotinsky's Revisionist Movement.

The relationships among those three communities had been fraught with tension, hostility, and alienation since the beginning of the emancipation in the early 19th century, and the emergence of Zionism in the late 19th century only exacerbated the disunity as it went against the religious views of the Orthodox—that the return to Zion must come only after the coming of the Messiah, and of the assimilationist Jews, who viewed Germany as their fatherland. According to German historian Tobias Grill, another aspect of separation within the Jewish world was that German Jews, most of whom were secular and assimilationists patronized Polish Orthodox Jews. During World War I, they hoped "that their East European brethren would be liberated from the Tsarist yoke and be restored to a higher cultural level. About two months after the beginning of the war, Professor Ludwig Stein (1859–1930) gave a talk at the *Association for Jewish History and Literature of the Jews*, stating that ... 'If it will be of success to drive Russia where it belongs, to Asia, then it is not impossible that we will lead the Russian Jews back to German culture and civilization.'"[392]

The conceit of the German Jewry did not stay in Germany. When German Jews immigrated to America, they carried with them their attitude toward Polish Jewry. Edwin Black writes that "Both the American Jewish Committee and B'nai B'rith were founded by well-to-do German Jews with a special outlook. ... Unlike their East European counterparts, the Germans clung to their original national identity, and were economically more established. Moreover, many

German Jews believed they were so-called *Hofjuden*, or courtly Jews, and that coreligionists from Poland and Russia were 'uncivilized' and embarrassing. The bias was best summarized in a June 1894 German-American Jewish newspaper, the *Hebrew Standard*, which declared that the totally acclimated American Jew is closer to 'Christian sentiment around him than to the Judaism of these miserable darkened [black coats] Hebrews.'"[393]

At the same time, Zionists could not stand assimilationist Jews. "On January 31, 1933," writes Black, "within twenty-four hours of Hitler's appointment, the ZVfD [Zionist Federation of Germany] newspaper, *Jüdische Rundschau* [*Jewish Review*], asserted that the defense of Jewish rights could be waged only by Zionists, not mainstream Jewry. After the May 10 Nazi book burnings, *Jüdische Rundschau* mourned the loss as did all Jews, but could not resist publicly labeling many of the Jewish authors 'renegades' who had betrayed their roots. The anti-assimilationist barrage continued weekly with Zionist aspersions sounding painfully similar to the Nazi line discrediting the German citizenship of Jews."[394]

While Zionists were not keen on assimilationist Jews, they still saw some benefits in them. After all, Jews in America and Great Britain were capable of supporting Zionism both financially and politically. But when it came to Polish Orthodox Jewry, Zionists were far more acerbic in their expression and attitude. In the previous chapter, we mentioned Chaim Weizmann's appalling words during the 20th Zionist Congress in 1937 concerning the fate of Poland's Jews being "dust, economic and moral dust," that "only a remnant shall survive," and that "we have to accept it," or the hateful words of poet Uri Zvi Greenberg about Polish peddlers finally remembering Palestine now that the gates to all the countries are shut.

However, these leaders were not alone. Rather, they expressed the prevailing spirit in the Zionist Movement. Yitzhak Gruenbaum, who until 1931 was the leader of the Zionist movement in Poland, warned that Polish Jewry was in grave danger. According to previously mentioned historians Reinharz and Shavit (section "The Dawn of

Zionism"), in March 1936 Gruenbaum warned, "'We are heading toward a new catastrophe in the life of our people, a catastrophe that will be greater than that of German Jewry.' That month he reported to Nahum Goldmann, representative of the Zionist Executive to the League of Nations and founder of the World Jewish Congress, that the danger in Poland was 'great. [. . .] If we cannot overturn the situation it will reach a catastrophe similar to that of Germany, but the difference is that in Germany there were 600,000 Jews and in Poland 3 million.'"[395]

Despite Gruenbaum's morose report, that same Nahum Goldmann met with Poland's Foreign Minister Józef Beck on October 2, 1936 in order to deter him from helping Jabotinsky—the only Zionist leader to attempt to help Polish Jewry—in his plan to send a million Jews from Poland to Palestine. "The Zionist movement, Goldmann said, 'admits that Palestine by itself cannot absorb all Jewish emigrants and therefore one should still find other destination countries.' Moreover, its immigration policy was guided by the assumption that not all those wishing to emigrate were suited for Palestine, and therefore the policy was based on the principle of selective immigration."[396]

Even Gruenbaum acted against his own report. "If the Zionist movement encouraged a massive exodus of Jews from Poland ... 'We who are building the land can expect torrents that would be self-inflicted.'"[397] "This warning, that 'a torrent of immigrants' would jeopardize the Zionist project in Palestine," continue Reinharz and Shavit, "was not an isolated opinion, [and] came from someone who knew well and understood which way the winds were blowing in the Polish government and public."[398]

Three years prior, in October 1933, having returned from a trip to Poland, David Ben-Gurion wrote Weizmann, "Judaism is being destroyed and strangled. [...] I have seen the situation of the Jews in Poland, in Lithuania, in Latvia. We cannot go on like this. Germany is only a prelude. Not only the poverty, the lack of livelihood opportunities, the political pressure, the intensifying antisemitism—the terrible thing is the total lack of hope."[399] Still, Ben-Gurion "did not envisage an immigration of millions or hundreds of thousands—rather of tens of thousands ... because 'obviously Palestine does not yet offer a solution for all Polish Jews. Immigration to Palestine is necessarily limited, and therefore there is need for selective immigration.'"[400]

In conclusion, it can be said that "The heads of the Zionist movement made a distinction between the threat the war held for the Jews of Europe and the threat to the Yishuv [Jewish settlement in Palestine]... Their main concern was to preserve the Zionist project in Palestine."[401]

As detailed in Chapter 5, the enmity between Zionism and Orthodox Jewry was firmly entrenched and deeply rooted. It began in the mid-19th century when Tsar Alexander II emancipated Russian Jewry and young Orthodox Jews flocked in droves to secular universities where they became secular, socialists, communists, and often even revolutionaries. When the "Storms in the South" pogroms broke out in 1881, many socialist Jews opted out of Russia and headed for Palestine to create a homeland for the Jews. But they envisioned it as a secular, socialist state, not as an Orthodox Jewish sovereign shtetl [a Jewish town in Eastern Europe]. David Ben-Gurion, Chaim Weizmann, Berl Katznelson, and virtually all the leaders of the Zionist movement came from the shtetls of Eastern Europe and did not want to bring them over to Palestine. They would not have Orthodox Jewry become a dominant force in the new homeland they were building in Palestine. In that sense, Orthodox Jewry in Eastern Europe had no reason to hope that the Zionists would fight for its salvation. Nor, in fact, did Orthodox Jewry want to immigrate to Palestine.

Prof. Weiss explains that the Labor movement in Palestine, led by David Ben-Gurion and Berl Katznelson, "based its position [against the boycott] on the dichotomy between building up the country and the Diaspora, between action and pride. Moshe Shertok, Arlosoroff's successor as head of the Jewish Agency Political Department, minced no words: 'I opposed the boycott from the start because I considered it a Diaspora-style gesture, a balm for the wounded soul. A Jewish heart harbors such a feeling, but a political movement cannot act according to feelings only.' [Yosef Aharonowitz, in charge of finances at the Jewish Agency] called the boycott a 'bloated skin gourd.'"[402]

In fact, according to Black, even the Transfer Agreement, whose official aim was to save German Jewry, was to be exploited for the benefit of the *halutzim* [Zionist pioneers in Palestine]. "By 1933," writes Black, "more than half the Jewish Palestinian work force and about 80 percent of the *kibbutzniks* [members of kibbutzim— agrarian Jewish settlements in Palestine] were *halutzim*. The vast majority of this Zionist vanguard were steeped in European socialist thought and were active members of [Ben-Gurion's party] Mapai. But in Germany, there were fewer than 3,000 *halutzim*, and many of those were non-Germans residing in the Reich. Clearly the pauperized German Jewish masses ... would have great difficulty being selected for entry to Palestine. However, Mapai wanted the worker immigrant quota filled not so much by German *halutzim* as by *halutzim* from Poland, Czechoslovakia, Rumania, and other nations. Dr. Ruppin [one of the leaders of the Zionist Organization and among the architects of the Transfer Agreement] had in fact hinted that the great Palestinian structure to be yielded by the German crisis would have to serve the needs of Jewish communities throughout Europe, and not just Germany."[403]

Meanwhile, in Poland, Orthodox Jews were just as contemptuous toward Zionism and Palestine as the Zionists were toward them. Jabotinsky's effort to help the Jews exit Poland was not the first attempt to do so. Prof. Weiss writes that "An accord similar to the Transfer Agreement, known as the Clearing Agreement, was worked out between the Jewish Agency and the Polish Government in the second half of 1936 and signed in March 1937. Its purpose was to enable Jewish emigrants from Poland to transfer their assets to Palestine despite Polish currency laws by purchasing Polish goods."[404]

However, the agreement saw very little success which, as one might expect, "stemmed from internal struggles on the Jewish side. The Revisionists, after having formed a broad front in opposition to the Transfer Agreement when it was being drafted, evinced great interest in the Clearing Agreement and attempted to conclude separate arrangements that would circumvent the Jewish Agency, from which they had seceded by this time. The Clearing Agreement began to coalesce as the condition of Polish Jewry deteriorated and debates on 'evacuation' became more frequent. Gruenbaum led the negotiations on behalf of the Jewish Agency, thereby implementing his gloomy prophecy concerning 'flight and organized exodus.' These subsequent developments in Poland thus proved the sorrowful impotence of the boycott movement in contrast to the practicality of Zionist formula,"[405] namely the Transfer Agreement.

Reinharz and Shavit, too, describe the woeful fate of the Clearing Agreement. According to them, "The agreement was meant to enable the transfer of Jewish capital from Poland—a necessary condition for absorption of a large immigration in Palestine. ...The agreement came into force on March 1, 1937, but only very few Jewish 'capitalists' showed any interest in it, and in August 1938 it was terminated."[406] In fact, "In the second half of the 1930s," they continue, "a large number of Jews were knocking at the doors of the Palestine offices in Poland in order to receive certificates. Nevertheless," out of conceit that turned out to bear tragic consequences, "many of those who expressed interest chose to remain in Poland or sought other preferred emigration destinations."[407]

The Good High Commissioner

Of the 600,000 Jews who lived in Germany and Austria, less than ten percent took advantage of the Transfer Agreement and immigrated to Palestine. One of the more oft-heard arguments concerning Jewish immigration to Palestine is that even if Jews did want to come to Palestine, the British Mandate's restrictive immigration policy would curb it. Yet, if that were the case, then what was the point of signing the Transfer Agreement in the first place? For whatever reason, the common narrative concerning the British Mandate policy toward Jewish immigration to Palestine during the Nazi era often overlooks critical facts that, when added to the story, present the unfolding of events in a completely new light.

In 1929, the Palestinian Arabs began a series of attacks against Jews. Within a week, between August 23 and August 29, 1929, 133 Jews were murdered, and some 200 hundred were injured. Many of the victims were tortured, molested, and abused physically and sexually. During the riots, seventeen Jewish settlements, mostly small and poorly protected, were evacuated or deserted.

Israel Amikam, a lawyer and a writer who interviewed some of the victims of the riots and documented the responses of the British Mandate in Palestine at the time, published a book titled *The Attack on the Jewish Settlement in the Land of Israel, 1929* (title translated from Hebrew). In his book, Amikam describes numerous cases of torture, slaughter, rape, burning, and other acts of unspeakable cruelty against defenseless women, children, and elderly.[408]

The traumatic events of the summer of 1929 sent shockwaves not only throughout the Jewish settlement in Palestine, but also in Great Britain. Following the events, the British government appointed Sir John Hope Simpson to enquire about the riots and draw practical conclusions to remedy the situation. The result was the Hope Simpson Report, which was, as acclaimed historian Prof. Norman Rose put it, "exceedingly critical of Zionist methods in Palestine."[409]

In line with the conclusions and recommendations of the Hope Simpson Report, Colonial Secretary Lord Passfield issued a formal statement of British policy in Palestine, which became known as the Passfield White Paper. In his book *A Senseless, Squalid War*, Prof. Rose writes that the overriding tone of the Passfield White Paper "was exceedingly critical of Zionist methods in Palestine, particularly regarding immigration policy and land purchases. Only in one particular could the Zionists draw some satisfaction: the violence, it was affirmed, had resulted from attacks by Arabs upon Jews for which there was no excuse."[410] Passfield encapsulated his findings in his statement of policy, which espoused "drastic restrictions in the scale of Jewish immigration and land purchases, and far-reaching constitutional proposals inimical to the National Home. Even Beatrice Webb, Passfield's wife, herself no friend of Zionism, thought it 'Badly drafted [and] tactless.'"[411]

Not surprisingly, the White Paper did not receive a warm welcome among the Zionists. Weizmann and other leaders of the Jewish Agency resigned in protest of what they called the effort to "throttle the Jewish National Home."[412] But although he officially resigned, Weizmann did not become inactive. He and other Zionists responded to the White Paper by launching a campaign against it. As a result, "In a letter to Weizmann that was laid before the Council of the League of Nations as an official government document, dispatched to the High Commissioner as a Cabinet instruction and tabled and recorded in the proceedings of Parliament, Ramsey MacDonald, the [British] Prime Minister, partially made amends. It did not abrogate the Passfield White Paper but its style and substance modified it to a degree that rendered it virtually meaningless. ...The MacDonald letter heralded a period of unprecedented growth and expansion of the *Yishuv*. The Arabs, naturally, viewed it differently... Disparagingly, they dubbed it 'the Black Letter.'"[413]

After the general elections of October 1931 completely changed the political map in England, and the Labor Party was badly defeated, MacDonald, who had by then retired from it, was reelected as Prime Minister, but formed a completely different cabinet—one that was far warmer toward the Jewish cause. Soon after the elections, MacDonald removed the unsympathetic High Commissioner Chancellor and instead appointed General Sir Arthur Grenfell Wauchope. "For the Zionists," writes Rose, "Wauchope was perhaps the best High Commissioner Palestine had had. I'm giving you 'a good man, a fellow Scot,' Ramsey MacDonald assured Ben Gurion."[414] Wauchope immediately set out to put into practice the spirit of the MacDonald letter. The new High Commissioner's "administration witnessed a sharp rise in Jewish immigration. The years 1933-35 saw 134,540 authorized immigrants enter Palestine, a truly dramatic increase from the overall figure of 247,404 for the period 1921-35. Hitler's accession to power in January 1933 provided the impetus for this surge in Jewish immigration, that if allowed to continue threatened to change the demographic structure of the country."[415] Regrettably, as noted before, only 26,000 Jews came from Germany. The rest came mainly from Eastern Europe.

In fact, not only Wauchope was favorable toward the Jewish cause in Palestine. In preparation for the Transfer Agreement, Chaim Weizmann and Chaim Arlosoroff conducted a meeting on April 14, 1933, with High Commissioner Wauchope and Sir Phillip Cunliffe-Lister, the British colonial secretary, at an experimental agricultural station near Tel Aviv. "Cunliffe-Lister was the cabinet officer with direct purview over England's colonies and the Palestine Mandate," writes Prof. Black. "Together, Wauchope and Cunliffe-Lister possessed the power to change radically the course of Jewish nationalism in Palestine. Cunliffe-Lister had already talked to [Jewish Palestinian industrialist Pinhas] Rutenberg in London about transplanting German Jews to Palestine via a liquidation company. Essentially, the colonial secretary approved."[416]

The Arabs, in frustration, launched their first and only revolt directed explicitly against the British Mandate. On Friday, October 27, 1933, the Arab Executive Committee led several simultaneous violent demonstrations against British Mandate police officers throughout Palestine. The riots were a sequel to Arab demonstrations that took place two weeks prior in Jerusalem. According to *The Sunday Times*, twenty Arab rioters were killed in those riots.[417]

Nevertheless, Jewish immigration continued virtually undisturbed. By now the relationship between the leaders of the Zionist Organization [ZO] and the existing British government was more than cordial; it was outright supportive. In fact, many years prior, Chaim Weizmann had already met with Herbert Samuel, who was now MacDonald's Home Secretary. In that meeting, Samuel, a nominally-practicing liberal Jew, was even more enthusiastic about the idea of a Jewish homeland than was Weizmann himself. In a letter that Weizmann wrote describing his meeting with Herbert Samuel, he remarks in surprise, "He [Samuel] believed that my demands were too modest, that big things would have to be done in Palestine; he himself would move and would expect Jewry to move immediately [once?] the military situation was cleared up. He was convinced that it would be cleared up favorably."[418] But most astonishing of all were Weizmann's final words about the meeting, "[Samuel] also thinks that perhaps the Temple may be rebuilt, as a symbol of Jewish unity."[419]

The Window Gradually Closes on German Jewry

When Mildenstein founded the Jewish Department in the SD (the SS intelligence agency), his aim was to facilitate Jewish immigration to Palestine. Not only was he an enthusiast of Zionism, he infused his passion into the rest of his office. One of Mildenstein's deputies, who was, in a sense, Mildenstein's "protégé," was an anonymous fellow Austrian who joined the Nazi Party a few months after Hitler took power in Germany. His name was Adolf Eichmann. According to acclaimed novelist and publisher Anna Porter, "Eichmann had his uniform made when National Socialism was still outlawed in Austria."[420]

In 1934, Eichmann's "big break," as he later referred to it, came "when he was told to report to Second Lieutenant Leopold von Mildenstein at 102 Wilhelmstrasse in Berlin. [...] A fellow Austrian with an easy manner, von Mildenstein took an interest in teaching Eichmann the basics of his department. He told him that his first task was to read *The Jewish State* by Theodor Herzl. Eichmann loved the book. He thought it gave him insight into the Jewish mind, and it also presented a possible solution to the 'Jewish problem': emigration to Palestine. He had finally found his focus. He determined that he would become an authority on the Jews. After Herzl, he read Max Nordau and Moses Hess. He wrote a paper on Herzl's ideas and on Zionist organizations. He learned the Hebrew alphabet, and, within a few months, he could read, albeit slowly, a Yiddish newspaper. He subscribed to *Haint* (*Today*), a Jewish periodical. He wanted to see who was writing about what aspects of Jewish life in the Reich. He wanted to understand what kind of people Jews were."[421]

Yet, despite the Transfer Agreement, which offered Jews immigrating to Palestine benefits that no other country offered, and despite the British Mandate's benign policy toward Jewish immigration to Palestine, which created an influx of Jews from other countries, German Jewry occupied a very small portion of the immigrants. Evidently, these measures still did not provide sufficient impetus for German Jews to move to Palestine; most of them still stayed put.

As noted earlier in the chapter ("Two Kinds of Jews," last paragraph), to promote the immigration of Jews to Palestine, Nazi Germany supported Zionist organizations within Germany. Prof. Black elaborates on just how thorough that support really was. "The Nazi recognition of Zionism that began in April of 1933 was apparent because the Zionists enjoyed a visibly protected political status in Germany. Immediately after the Reichstag Fire of February 27 [1933], the Nazis crushed virtually all political opposition. Through emergency decrees, most non-Nazi political organizations and suspect newspapers were dissolved. In fact, about 600 newspapers were officially banned during 1933. Others were unofficially silenced by street methods. The exceptions included *Jüdische Rundschau* [*Jewish Review*], the ZVfD's weekly [Zionist Federation of Germany], and several other Jewish publications. German Zionism's weekly was hawked on street comers and displayed at newsstands. … Although many influential Aryan publications were forced to restrict their page size to conserve newsprint, *Jüdische Rundschau* was not affected until mandatory newsprint rationing in 1937."[422]

But for all their efforts, too few Jews opted out of Germany and into Palestine. Von Mildenstein—who wrote the sympathetic articles about Zionism in *Der Angriff,* established the Jewish Department in the SD (intelligence agency of the SS), and was now Eichmann's boss—was growing increasingly impatient toward Jews. Worse yet, so were his superiors.

In June 1936, Mildenstein left (or was removed from) his office, apparently the outcome of his failure to encourage the Jews to leave Germany and go to Palestine. He was still concerned with Palestine, but from the other end. In 1938, "Mildenstein ... joined the Propaganda Ministry [under Goebbels] where, as chief of the Near East division of propaganda, he worked to undermine his former policies and incited Arab violence against Jews in Palestine."[423]

Mildenstein's departure brought with it a shift in the attitude of the Jewish Department toward Jews, at the end of which Adolf Eichmann had become the head of the department. "In the early 1940s," writes Black, "Eichmann's domain would change from emigration and Zionism to deportation and genocide, as he orchestrated the shuttling of millions of Jews to the gas chambers of Europe."[424]

Plan B: Force Out the Jews

We already showed the great lengths to which the Nazis went to encourage immigration to Palestine as a means to solve the "Jewish question." They not only supported Zionist organizations, they also heavily suppressed non-Zionist and especially assimilationist Jewish organizations. Francis Nicosia and David Scrase write in *Jewish Life in Nazi Germany* that "between 1933 and 1935, the Zionist movement rapidly became the only political option for Jews in Germany as its growth soon outstripped that of the non-Zionist organizations and it came to dominate the political discourse among the German-Jewish leadership in Berlin. In November 1935, the Verband nationaldeutscher Juden (VnJ) [Association of German National Jews] was dissolved, and the CV was forced to change its name to the Centralverein der Juden in Deutschland (Central Association of Jews in Germany) and to eliminate any and all 'assimilationist' tendencies. The Jewish war veterans' organization was slowly eliminated over the next three years. With the CV and the RjF [Reich Federation of Jewish Front-Line Soldiers] rendered increasingly irrelevant, the two Zionist organizations were the only Jewish organizations of a political nature that continued to function and grow...

"The dramatic increase in the public activities of the various organizations affiliated with the Zionist movement in Germany is indicative of its increasingly dominant role in Jewish life in Germany during the 1930s. [...] At events that were almost daily occurrences ... topics under discussion included the futility of emancipation and assimilation as solutions to the Jewish Question, the correctness of Zionism, and the issues and problems involved in settlement work in Palestine... Hebrew courses were increasingly in demand as more and more youths considered emigrating from Germany to Palestine. Prominent Berlin Zionists such as Rabbi Joachim Prinz, Kurt Blumenfeld, Georg Landauer, Siegfried Moses, and others spoke often in Berlin and traveled constantly to other German cities to be featured speakers. Some, like Blumenfeld, Landauer, and others, were permitted to return to Germany from time to time after their emigration to Palestine in 1933 to speak at Zionist events. All events were registered with the authorities, and police observers were always in attendance. According to police reports, attendance, especially in Berlin, was almost always very high, ranging from one hundred to one thousand or more, and the police reports always expressed satisfaction with the course of the events, particularly with the programs' emphasis on doing everything to promote emigration to Palestine."[425]

Despite their efforts, the actual pace of Jewish emigration to Palestine did not please the Nazis. After the initial (barely) tolerable pace of more than 26,600 Jewish emigrants from Germany to Palestine between 1933 and 1935, the flow dwindled even more.

After Mildenstein left the office of Jewish affairs, Germany continued to push for Jewish emigration, though it became increasingly evident that its aim was more to force the Jews out of Germany than to endorse Zionism as such. "The fate of [the Transfer Agreement] was not settled ... and the agreement continued to function until December 1939 [two months after the beginning of WWII], the policy of promoting Jewish emigration from Germany to Palestine was maintained and even intensified in 1938," writes Francis Nicosia in *Zionism and Anti-Semitism in Nazi Germany*.[426]

However, despite Germany's efforts to impel the Jews to immigrate to Palestine, political obstacles beyond their control were beginning to mount. "The first four years of [Wauchope's] term [as High Commissioner] were the heyday of Zionist history in Palestine," writes historian Martin Connolly.[427] However, on March 3, 1938, Wauchope, who had lost the trust of his superiors in handling the Arab 1936-39 riots, was replaced by Sir Harold Alfred MacMichael. MacMichael, as historian Yehuda Bauer puts it, was "no great friend of the Jews, Zionism, or the Jewish Agency."[428] He made immigration to Palestine increasingly difficult for Jews and hampered Germany's efforts to send them there.

Faced with a virtually shut door in Palestine—apart from illegal immigration, which was a fraction of the rate that the Nazis had hoped for—Germany began to look for other alternatives. In hindsight, it is quite clear that Wauchope's departure marked the beginning of the closing of the door on the Jews in Europe.

The Evian Sham

Just nine days after Wauchope's replacement in Palestine by an unfavorable High Commissioner, another negative development unfolded. On March 12, 1938, after a series of bullying of Austrian leaders by Nazi Germany, the leaders resigned and the German army invaded Austria, declaring an *Anschluss* ["union"] of Austria with Germany.[429]

To the Austrian Jews, this clearly meant trouble and the pressure to emigrate from Austria grew substantially. In *Bystanders, Rescuers or Perpetrators?*, editors and historians at the International Holocaust Remembrance Alliance, Corry Guttstadt, Thomas Lutz, Bernd Rother, and Yessica San Román explain that "As a consequence of the growing number of refugees after the annexation of Austria, US president Franklin D. Roosevelt made a new effort to solve the refugee problem. He invited all states concerned to an international conference, which took place in July 1938 in Évian-les-Bains, France, near the Swiss border. As is well known, the representatives of 32 states failed to find the urgently needed solution to the issue that had motivated the meeting. Though most of the participants expressed regret over the refugees' tragic situation, they also announced that their countries could not, in fact, receive more newcomers. It became obvious that the US administration and several European states had expected that Latin America and Africa would be a suitable place for Jews fleeing the German domain to settle. Yet offers of help were not forthcoming from any of the Latin American participants, with the exception of Rafael Trujillo's Dominican Republic. Moreover, ...the conference's final declaration did not even criticize Germany's anti-Jewish policies that had created the crisis."[430]

In fact, "The only concrete result of the [Evian] conference was the establishment of the Intergovernmental Committee for Refugees (IGCR), which actually assumed the same tasks that the League's High Commission had already failed to accomplish: to arrange the transfer of Jewish-owned assets from Germany and finding new settlement opportunities for Jewish refugees. ...[By the time] the war began, the Intergovernmental Committee had been unable to present a list of countries willing to accept the Jews leaving Germany; this seemed to justify Joseph Goebbels's propaganda that those states criticizing Germany for its antisemitism did not want the Jews either."[431] With suave indifference, country by country excused itself from taking in Jews. The Australian delegate, T. W. White, sarcastically noted, "As we have no real racial problem, we are not desirous of importing one."[432]

Adding to the disgrace of the Evian Conference was the active participation of some of the most prominent Jews in America in discouraging the exodus of Austrian and German Jews. Sol Bloom, an Orthodox Jew who served as the chairman of the House Committee on Foreign Affairs was chosen by "the Roosevelt administration ... as a U.S. delegate to its sham refugee conference in Evian, France, in 1938, and to its equally farcical refugee conference in Bermuda five years later [discussed later in this chapter]." [433]

Following the conference, Director of the Intergovernmental Refugee Bureau George Rublee, who was appointed by the Evian

Conference delegates to negotiate with the Nazis over the conditions of emigration, was very pessimistic. Rublee "told a delegation of Jewish religious leaders ... that the bureau's task presented 'unprecedented difficulties.'"[434] Bloom, however, never expressed any dissatisfaction with the results of the Evian Conference.

One proof that the US never intended to take in refugees from Germany is a memorandum written by then Under Secretary of State Benjamin Welles on November 17, 1938, just four months after the Evian Conference and merely a week after Kristallnacht (Night of the Broken Glass), when Nazi SA paramilitary and civilians carried out a series of coordinated attacks against Jews throughout Germany and parts of Austria. The memorandum not only demonstrates the unwillingness of the US to help German and Austrian Jews, it also asserts that it does so with the support of American Jewry: "The British Ambassador called to see me this morning. ... He said that the British Government desired the Government of the United States" to permit "German refugees to enter the United States. [...] I reminded the Ambassador that the President had officially stated once more only two days ago that there was no intention on the part of this Government to increase the quota already established for German nationals. I added that it was my very strong impression that the responsible leaders among American Jews would be the first to urge that no change in the present quota for German Jews be made."[435]

Another piece of evidence that the whole conference was a fake effort to begin with came on June 12, 1939 when Secretary of State Cordell Hull wrote a telegram[436] to Joseph Kennedy Sr., the US ambassador to the United Kingdom. Hull referred to a plan proposed by Herbert William Emerson, Rublee's successor as head of the Intergovernmental Committee for Refugees. The plan suggested that destination countries to which immigrants intended to come would give one dollar for every dollar that private organizations donated in order to finance the emigration of the refugees. Hull's telegram specified in no uncertain terms that the US was unwilling to dedicate any resources whatsoever to saving refugees from Europe. "We feel it most important that you should discourage in every possible way

&&the introduction of any official plan which makes the financing of the emigration of refugees dependent upon governmental participation." Hull continues and admits that "This Government has made it clear from the time it first issued the invitation to the Evian Conference that while it desires to assist in the orderly solution of the refugee problem [he did not clarify the meaning of 'orderly'], the responsibility for financing rests with the private [namely Jewish] groups. Such discouragement on your part will undoubtedly dispose of Emerson's scheme," which was what Hull really wanted.

Sol Bloom, however, was not the only Jew who avoided any action in favor of the Jewish refugees in Germany and Austria, or praised the US government policy of inaction. Rabbi Jonah B. Wise, National Campaign Chairman of the Joint Distribution Committee, attended the Evian Conference as an unofficial observer. Following the conference all he offered was accolades to the head of the US delegation, Myron C. Taylor. According to the *Jewish Telegraphic Agency* (JTA), Wise "attributed the conference's success [as he put it] to the personal efforts of Myron C. Taylor... He praised Mr. Taylor for doing 'a marvelous job in keeping the conference to its task and from the failure freely predicted for it by cynical observers.' As a result of the leadership of the United States, which Rabbi Wise described as 'manna from the heavens to the democracies of Europe and South America,' and the personal efforts of Mr. Taylor, the conference marked 'the beginning of a new era in the rise of democracy from its humiliating deference to world tyrants,' Rabbi Wise said. 'It served principally to sound a note of humanity and protest against the problem arising out of the actions of a totalitarian government. It was remarkable that 30 nations came together and practically agreed that the problem was one of humanity and not the concern of a few groups of people.'"[437]

When reading these praises, it is easy to forget that the conference, in fact, decided not to do anything for the Jews. To cover up their inaction, they appointed George Rublee to negotiate with the Germans. And to guarantee that he would not succeed, they tied his hands in advance by deciding even before the conference began not to open their borders to refugees. In that spirit of inaction, "Rabbi Wise declared: 'There is no expectation of furthering mass emigration from Germany. Rather, the conference seemed to be resolved that Germany should be made to understand that nations of the world cannot expect to absorb a mass exodus from that country.'"[438]

Evidently, Under Secretary Wells had a good reason for his "very strong impression" that Jews would support his refusal to help German and Austrian Jews. According to the Abraham Lincoln Library and Museum, another one of those "responsible" Jewish leaders was the judge, Democratic Party activist, and presidential speechwriter Sam [Samuel] Rosenman, who "sent [President] Roosevelt a memorandum telling him that an 'increase of quotas is wholly inadvisable. It will merely produce a 'Jewish problem' in the countries increasing the quota.'"[439]

Still, probably the most unabashed display of lack of compassion of the Jews toward their coreligionists came in the midst of the discussions in Evian: According to the JTA, on July 11, 1938, in the midst of the discussions, "five leading Jewish organizations to the Evian refugee conference" sent "a joint memorandum … viewing mass emigration as no solution to Jewish troubles in central Europe."[440] Fearing that it would "produce a 'Jewish problem' in the countries increasing the quota," as Sam Rosenman put it, the Jews in the potential countries of immigration tried to employ bureaucracy to make certain that the drizzle of immigrants did not become a torrent. Their memorandum, therefore, "suggested setting up of a small executive body by the conference to direct and supervise emigration and to undertake negotiations with Germany and countries of immigration."[441] The signatories to the memorandum were the Council for German Jewry, which was clearly in denial of the fact that Jews had no future in Nazi Germany, the Jewish Colonization Association, the [American] HIAS-ICA Emigration Association, the Agudath Israel and the Joint Foreign Committee, representing both the Anglo-Jewish Association and the Board of Deputies.

To add insult to injury, *The American Hebrew* weekly magazine awarded President Roosevelt with "the 1938 American Hebrew

Medal for Outstanding Service in Promoting Better Understanding Between Christians and Jews because of his efforts to bring about a humane solution of Jewish crises."[442] According to the committee of judges who decided to give the award to the President, at least one of the reasons for choosing him was his "achievement of the Evian Conference." In the words of the committee, Roosevelt merited it "because during the past year, he took the initiative of every crisis in Jewish affairs and did everything in his power to bring about a humane solution; and because he was responsible for the Evian conference for aiding refugees of Central Europe."[443]

Clearly, faced with such a consolidated Jewish effort to hinder emigration of German and Austrian Jewry, and in light of the inherent unwillingness of countries to take Jews in, the Evian Conference had no chance of providing any real solutions. Israeli historian at UCLA Saul Friedlander writes, "No doors opened at Evian, and no hope was offered to the refugees." Instead, "An Intergovernmental Committee for Refugees was established under the chairmanship of the American [lawyer] George Rublee." Yet, as expected, "Rublee's activities ... ultimately achieved no result."[444]

We will discuss Rublee's activities later in this chapter, but to conclude the discussion on the Evian Conference debacle, Friedlander presents what is probably the most painful point of all: "Nazi sarcasm had a field day," he writes. "For the SD, Evian's net result was 'to show the whole world that the Jewish problem was in no way provoked only by Germany, but was a question of the most immediate world political significance. Despite the general rejection by the Evian states of the way in which the Jewish question has been dealt with in Germany, no country, America not excepted, declared itself ready to accept unconditionally any number of Jews. ...There was no fundamental difference between the German assessment and the biting summary of Evian by the *Newsweek* correspondent there: 'Chairman Myron C. Taylor ... opened the proceedings: 'The time has come when governments ... must act and act promptly.' Most governments represented acted promptly by slamming their doors against Jewish refugees.' The *Volkischer*

Beobachter [the Nazi Party newspaper] headlined triumphantly: 'Nobody wants them.'"[445]

Hitler, too, did not miss the opportunity to slam the nations for their duplicity. In a speech he gave on September 12, 1938, he said, "They complain in these democracies about the unfathomable cruelty that Germany ... uses in trying to get rid of their Jews. ... But it does not mean that these democratic countries have now become ready to replace their hypocritical remarks with acts of help. On the contrary, they affirm with complete coolness that over there, evidently, there is no room! Thus, they expect Germany ... to go on keeping its Jews without any problem, whereas the democratic world empires ... can in no way take such a burden upon themselves. In short, no help, but preaching, certainly!"[446]

To Nazi Germany, the nations' refusal to take in Jews was more than an indication of the world's hypocrisy. It proved to them that if they wanted to get rid of the Jews in Germany, since the world does not want them and the Jews did not want to immigrate to Palestine, they would have to cope with the "Jewish question" by themselves, even if it meant much harsher steps than thus far taken. A November 24, 1938 newspaper article on *Das Schwarze Korps* was very explicit about those measures: "After announcing the need for the total segregation of the Jews of Germany in special areas and special houses, the SS periodical went one step further: The Jews could not continue in the long run to live in Germany: 'This stage of development [of the situation of the Jews] will impose on us the vital necessity to exterminate this Jewish sub-humanity, as we exterminate all criminals in our ordered country: by the fire and the sword! The outcome will be the final catastrophe for Jewry in Germany, its total annihilation.'"[447]

The Wonderful Rublee-Wohlthat Agreement that No Country Wanted

Despite the failure of the Evian Conference, the Germans were still far from giving up on forcing out the Jews. Following the conference, Hjalmar Schacht, president of the Reichsbank (Reich's federal bank), negotiated an agreement with George Rublee, head of the Intergovernmental Committee for Refugees. However, the negotiations progressed very slowly.

Eventually, Schacht was dismissed—for reasons entirely unrelated to the negotiations with Rublee—and Rublee, too, retired from his official post. However, he remained involved in the continued negotiations. "Helmut Wohlthat, one of the highest officials of the Four-Year Plan administration, took over on the German side," writes Prof. Friedlander, and "An agreement in principle between Wohlthat and Rublee had been achieved on February 2 [1939]."[448]

Roughly, the agreement stipulated that some 150,000 Jews with their dependents would depart to countries willing to take them in (for a hefty sum of money) over the span of three years, whereas the rest, mainly the elderly Jews and those incapable of working, would stay in Germany and Austria. According to a US government memorandum titled *The Chargé in Germany (Gilbert) to the Secretary of State*[449] found in the online Office of the Historian, the Rublee-Wohlthat Agreement presented an opportunity for the Jews, which—had it been accepted—would have saved European Jewry from annihilation and the world from war. Below are some remarkable points and excerpts from the agreement:

"It has been ascertained that Germany is disposed to adopt a policy which will in every way facilitate and encourage the organized emigration of Jews. A program along the lines hereinafter outlined will be put into effect when Germany is satisfied that countries of immigration are disposed to receive currently Jews from Germany in conformity with this program.

"2. There are approximately six hundred thousand Jews remaining in Germany, including Austria and the Sudetenland, at the present time. Of this number, one hundred and fifty thousand are classed as wage-earners; approximately two hundred fifty thousand are regarded as the dependents of the wage-earners; the remainder are primarily the old and infirm who for that reason are not included in this program of emigration," and will therefore stay in Germany.

"3. The wage-earner category shall consist of all men and single women between the ages of 15 and 45 who are individually capable of earning a living and are otherwise fit for emigration.

"4. The dependent category shall consist of the immediate families of the wage-earners, excluding the old (persons over 45 years of age) and the unfit.

"5. The wage-earner category shall emigrate first, in annual contingents over a period of 3 years not to exceed a maximum of 5 years.

"6. All persons from the wage-earner category as defined above shall be admitted by the receiving governments in accordance with their established immigration laws and practices."

Germany was even willing to train Jews from the wage-earner category to make their emigration easier: "11. Facilities shall be granted for the retraining of wage-earners for emigration, notably in agricultural re-training centers but also in artisan schools. Re-training shall be encouraged."

As for the majority of Jews, those unfit for emigration and the old and sick, Germany committed to the following incredible conditions: "13. [Regarding] caring for old persons and persons unfit for emigration, who are not included in this program and who will be allowed to finish their days in Germany, it is the intention on Germany's part to assure that these persons and persons awaiting emigration may live tranquilly, unless some extraordinary circumstance should occur. There is no intention to segregate the Jews. They may circulate freely. Persons fit for work shall be given the opportunity of employment so as to earn their living; Jews employed in the same establishments as Aryans will, however, be separated from Aryan workers.

"14. The support and maintenance of the persons referred to in paragraph 13 above who are not able to earn their own living will be financed in the first instance from Jewish property in Germany... If the above resources do not suffice, there will be provided for these persons decent conditions of existence from the material standpoint in accordance with prevailing practices relating to the public relief of destitute persons generally."[450]

Despite these extraordinary concessions on the part of Germany, no government was willing to take in Jews "in accordance with their established immigration laws and practices," as mentioned in Item 6 above. As a result, the agreement was never implemented and the Holocaust ensued.

St. Louis—the Cruise Away from Hell, and Back Again

Kristallnacht, the earlier mentioned pogrom on November 9-10, 1938, was not an isolated event. It was rather the beginning of a carefully planned campaign to force the Jews out of Germany. The Rublee-Wohlthat Agreement was part of it, but certainly not the only one. Another part of it was exemplified by the sad story of the ocean liner SS St. Louis.

"On May 13, 1939, the German transatlantic liner St. Louis sailed from Hamburg, Germany, for Havana, Cuba. On the voyage were 937 passengers. Almost all were Jews fleeing from the Third Reich. ...The majority of the Jewish passengers had applied for US visas, and had planned to stay in Cuba only until they could enter the United States."[451]

The ship's German captain, Gustav Schröder—whom Yad Vashem, Israel's official remembrance center to the victims of the Holocaust, awarded after the war with the title "Righteous Among the Nations"—made certain that the passengers felt as comfortable as possible. Even though "many of the crew also displayed the Nazi emblem on their uniforms,"[452] the Jewish refugees were made to feel as guests on a cruise ship rather than as fugitives.

"On the surface," write Sarah Ogilvie and Scott Miller, directors at the United States Holocaust Memorial Museum, "the departure bore all the earmarks of normalcy. A band played. Flags flew. Friends and families of the ship's passengers waved from the pier."[453]

"'I just remember running around the ship a lot,' recalls Clark Blatteis, 'and generally having a real nice time. It was, after all, a luxury ship.' 'I loved it,' echoes Sol Messinger, who celebrated his seventh birthday during the voyage. 'I got out from under my mother's thumb'—something he had not previously been able to do as a Jewish child growing up amid the dangers of Hitler's Germany. 'Oh, we were treated so well,' remembers Alice Oster, a young lady at the time of the voyage. 'We walked about. We heard Strauss music, and we hadn't heard Strauss for a long time before that.'"[454]

Yet, the cruise was anything but normal. The majority of passengers did not intend to stay in Cuba permanently, but only until their numbers came up in the waiting list for immigration to the United States. Nevertheless, and despite the preliminary consent of the Cuban government to allow the passengers to spend their waiting time in Cuba, when the ship docked in Havana, the passengers discovered a bitter truth: "Quite suddenly, a convergence of factors—including greed, political infighting, public agitation against immigration, fascist influences, and anti-Semitism—[made] the majority of those aboard the St. Louis unwelcome on Cuban soil.

"Shortly thereafter, the German liner cruised within sight of Miami, where Captain Gustav Schröder was barred from making port. Several U.S. Coast Guard cutters surrounded the vessel to make sure that none of the would-be émigrés attempted to swim for shore. ...Appeals to [the] President and Mrs. Franklin Delano Roosevelt that referenced the persecution the refugees would encounter should they be returned to Germany went unanswered. ... Finally, on June 12, after many days of negotiations, the American Jewish Joint Distribution Committee (JDC) brokered a solution. Several European countries other than Germany agreed to take in the 908 passengers forced to return to Europe. Although 288 refugees wound up in Britain, the balance went to the Netherlands, Belgium, and France and to uncertain fates in a Europe about to be overrun by Hitler."[455]

Friedlander writes that the voyage of the St. Louis "back to Europe became a vivid illustration of the overall situation of Jewish refugees from Germany. After Belgium, France, and England finally agreed to give asylum to the passengers, the London Daily Express echoed the prevalent opinion in no uncertain terms: 'This example must not set a precedent. There is no room for any more refugees in this country.... They become a burden and a grievance.'"[456]

But probably the strongest indication of the misery and hopelessness of the passengers aboard the St. Louis was the virtually complete silence of American Jewry in regard to the crisis, and especially the silence of Rabbi Stephen Samuel Wise. Prof. Rafael Medoff, founder of the David S. Wyman Institute for Holocaust Studies, writes that Wise was "the longtime leader of the ZOA, president of the leading U.S. Jewish defense agency, the American Jewish Congress, and the most prominent Reform rabbi of his day."[457]

But as far as helping fellow members of his tribe, Wise often chose silence and inaction so as not to compromise what he believed was a warm relationship with President Roosevelt. The St. Louis ocean liner was no exception. "Rabbi Wise and other American Jewish leaders said nothing in public about the ship,"[458] writes Medoff in *The Jews Should Keep Quiet*. "This was partly in deference to the behind-the-scenes efforts by the American Jewish Joint Distribution Committee ... to negotiate the refugees' entry to Cuba or other countries." But more than attempting not to compromise the negotiations, it "reflected Wise's profound aversion to saying anything that would embarrass President Roosevelt,"[459] who did not welcome admission of Jewish refugees into America.

In defense of his inaction following Roosevelt's rebuff of the St. Louis, an unsigned editorial in the weekly publication *Congress Bulletin*—published by the American Jewish Congress, which was headed by Wise—conveniently placed the blame elsewhere. "Part of the problem, it argued, was the recently proclaimed British White Paper restricting Jewish immigration to Palestine, 'for which no Jew can be held responsible.' The other source of blame, it contended, was those Jewish groups who were trying to 'solve the problem of migration by widening the dispersion.' ... The author of the editorial seemed oblivious to the contradiction between blaming the closure of Palestine and simultaneously blaming those who sought refuge for European Jews elsewhere."[460]

Alaska—Too Cold; The Virgin Islands—Too Hot for Jews

FDR's reluctance to let the Jewish refugees aboard the St. Louis disembark on U.S. soil, and Wise's silence about the case, were not an exception. They were the norm. According to prolific journalist Matt Lebovic, "The influential General Jewish Council insisted on maintaining radio silence following Kristallnacht. Comprised of leaders from the so-called 'defense' organizations, the council issued these instructions in the pogrom's aftermath: 'There should be no parades, public demonstrations, or protests by Jews,' according to the directives. The council also reminded American Jews that it was in their interest not to advocate for admitting more Jewish refugees into the country."[461]

"When FDR asked his closest Jewish adviser, Samuel Rosenman—a prominent member of the American Jewish Committee—if more Jewish refugees should be allowed to enter the U.S. in the wake of Kristallnacht, Rosenman opposed such a move because 'it would create a Jewish problem in the US,'" continues Lebovic. Worse yet, "When news of the Holocaust started to appear on the pages of American newspapers, Rosenman ensured that FDR did not meet with what Rosenman referred to as 'the medieval horde' of 400 rabbis gathered outside the White House. During the final phase of the Holocaust, Rosenman attempted to prevent the creation of the War Refugee Board, intended to save Jewish refugees from genocide." Indeed, "The representative Jewish bodies acknowledged that 'silence' was the strategy of choice, as expressed by the American Jewish Committee in a position paper after Kristallnacht: '[The refugee resettlement] is helping to intensify the Jewish problem here,' read the position paper.

'Giving work to Jewish refugees while so many Americans are out of work has naturally made bad feelings. As heartless as it may seem, future efforts should be directed toward sending Jewish refugees to other countries instead of bringing them here.'[462]

Approximately six months before the St. Louis farce unfolded, a revolutionary idea, which became known as the King-Havenner bill[463]—was proposed as a solution to the plight of the Jews in Germany and Austria. "On Thanksgiving Day [1938], one courageous U.S. official proposed a bold rescue plan," writes Prof. Medoff. "The plan's target: Alaska. ... In 1938, the proposal did not necessarily seem like a fantasy because the secretary of the interior, Harold L. Ickes, was its most vocal proponent. [...] At a press conference on Thanksgiving eve, two weeks after Kristallnacht, Secretary Ickes proposed Alaska as 'a haven for Jewish refugees from Germany and other areas in Europe where the Jews are subjected to oppressive restrictions.' Alaska was 'the one possession of the United States that is not fully developed,' Ickes pointed out. Meanwhile, refugee advocates created a National Committee for Alaskan Development, which built an ecumenical coalition of VIPs to back the legislation. Endorsers included Academy-Award winning actors Luise Rainer and Paul Muni, theologian Paul Tillich, the American Friends Service Committee (Quakers), and the Federal Council of Churches." Nevertheless, "American Jewish leaders hesitated to support the plan. American Jewish Congress head Rabbi Stephen Wise warned that the Alaska plan 'makes a wrong and hurtful impression ... that Jews are taking over some part of the country for settlement.' He argued that 'just because small numbers of Jews might settle there' was not sufficient reason to support it. The Labor Zionists of America was the only Jewish organization to publicly endorse the King-Havenner bill."[464]

Dr. William R. Perl, a Holocaust researcher and retired Lt. Colonel in the U.S. Army who served on the war crimes prosecution team in Germany, pointedly details another woeful case of government unwillingness to help, and subsequent Jewish repression of protest: "Contrary to popular belief, the problem for Jews during the Holocaust was not how to get out, but where to go. The key figures in most governments throughout the world, instead of liberalizing their immigration laws, closed their borders to the hunted Jews, or at most admitted token numbers only. The Nazis set the house aflame, and the free world barred the doors," Perl begins his report.[465]

"Some of the measures taken by the free world that contributed to the deaths of tens of thousands remain little known," continues Perl. "Foremost among these was the thwarting by the United States Department of State of rescue plans that would have brought otherwise doomed refugees to the Caribbean, specifically to the sparsely inhabited U.S. Virgin Islands as well as the Republic of Haiti.

"As early as November 18, 1938, [even before the Alaska bill] the legislature of the Virgin Islands adopted the following resolution: Whereas world conditions have created large refugee groups, and whereas such groups eventually will migrate to places of safety, and whereas the Virgin Islands of the United States being a place of safety can offer surcease from misfortune. Now therefore, be it resolved by the Legislative Assembly of the Virgin Islands of the United States in session assembled that it be made known to Refugee peoples of the world that ... they shall find surcease from misfortune in the Virgin Islands of the United States."[466]

"The State Department immediately started action to obstruct the islanders' humanitarian efforts and to close this possible avenue of escape. ...The Secretary of State [Cordell Hull, who 'viewed the Nazis' anti-Jewish campaign 'as an internal matter of the German Government'[467]] sent a letter to all authorities possibly concerned, calling this resolution 'incompatible with existing law.'"[468]

But Hull had no reason to fear protest; he had Wise to back him up. "Rabbi Wise declined to support the Virgin Islands proposal," states an article in the above-mentioned *David S. Wyman Institute for Holocaust Studies*. Wise explained to a colleague in the autumn of 1940, shortly before the presidential election, "that admitting refugees to the Virgin Islands 'might be used effectively against [Roosevelt] in the [1940 presidential] campaign.' Therefore, Wise said, 'Cruel as I may seem, as I have said to you before, his re-election is much more important for everything that is worthwhile and that counts than the admission of a few people, however imminent be their peril."[469]

Even among members of his own tribe, the most prominent American Jewish leader was unabashed in his efforts to justify inaction when it came to helping fellow Jews in Europe. "A delegation of rabbinical students that met with Wise in 1942 received [the following] response. When the students suggested urging the U.S. to admit Jewish refugees to the Virgin Islands, Wise replied that it was 'too hot' for Jews to settle there; when they proposed Alaska, Wise said it was 'too cold.'[470]

Intrepid American historian Deborah E. Lipstadt, who never fears stating her mind, even when it means having to defend it in court, writes that "An even more piercing accusation against Wise and his colleagues has emerged. It echoes what I heard at the Atlanta Jewish Film Festival. These Americanized Jewish leaders, it is charged, were reluctant to have 'those kinds' of Jews coming here. Samuel Merlin, Peter Bergson's associate, put it quite bluntly: They were not interested in 'people who [were] behaving in embarrassing ways.'"[471]

Madagascar—the Final Destination before the Final Solution

When World War II broke out, the barred doors of the free world left European Jewry with virtually no options but to stay put and await its fate. Although the Nazis made it perfectly clear from the moment they came to power that they would not tolerate the presence of Jews among them, the Jews refused to believe that they had fallen from the zenith to the nadir and shunned the option of the Transfer Agreement. Additionally, the Zionists had their own misgivings about how many Jewish capitalists, which was how they defined German Jews, they wanted in Palestine, so as not to undercut the dominance of socialism in the nascent Jewish settlement.

Polish Jewry, too, shunned the Clearing Agreement, and did not even challenge the immigration quota set by the British Mandate.

Moreover, here, too, the Zionist leadership did not want anti-Zionist Orthodox Jews—the kind of Jewry from which most Zionists had fled—to come to Palestine in overwhelming numbers.

When the door to Palestine began to close and the Nazi pressure intensified in the late 1930s, the Jews tried other options, but the nations denied their requests, with the active support of prominent, primarily American Jewish organizations. The Evian Conference, the St. Louis ocean liner, and the Rublee-Wohlthat Agreement merely reflected the inherent reluctance of the nations to help the stranded Jews. Now they were at the mercy of the Nazis.

Still, the Nazis had not given up on deporting the Jews, not just yet. Since the late 19th century, plans to resettle European Jewry on the island of Madagascar had surfaced occasionally. In 1937, the "Polish government sent a three man commission to Madagascar to explore the possibilities of settling Jews there."[472] The commission returned from the East African island with a pessimistic view that Madagascar could not sustain more than a few thousand families.

Yet, "On March 5, 1938, the SS officer in charge of forced Jewish emigration, Adolf Eichmann, was commissioned to assemble material to provide the chief of the Security Police (SIPO) Reinhard Heydrich with 'a foreign policy solution as it had been negotiated between Poland and France,' i.e., the Madagascar Plan."[473] Diligent and meticulous, Eichmann went straight to work. At the conclusion of his research, he presented a preliminary work carried out by the security police (SD) on the project of accommodating roughly 4,000,000 Jews in Madagascar. Subsequently, "On May 29, 1940, Himmler presented his plan to Hitler and proposed 'the emigration of all Jews to Africa or otherwise to a colony.'"[474]

At the time, the Nazis intended for the Madagascar plan to be "the Final Solution." They did not want to physically annihilate the Jews since, as Himmler put it, "One is repelled by the Bolshevik method of physical extermination of a people out of conviction [and regards it] as 'not German-like' and unfeasible."[475] "Hitler agreed to the elaboration of the Madagascar Plan."[476]

Yet, the Madagascar Plan was far-fetched. The Germans intended to dedicate Madagascar to Jewish resettlement once they completed their conquest of France and seized its colonies. They conquered France and took over the island, but it still left open the question of transporting 4,000,000 European Jews to Africa, for which Germany did not have a big enough fleet. The transportation of the Jews was therefore to be carried out on English merchant ships that would be seized once the Nazis had decimated the British Royal Air Force (RAF).

Throughout the summer of 1940 and into the fall, the air battle between the RAF and the Luftwaffe (Nazi Air Force) raged in all its might. Thousands of planes were downed on each side, but no side capitulated. In the end, the RAF came out triumphant in what became known as the Battle of Britain, the Nazis could not seize the British merchant ships, and the Madagascar Plan was shelved indefinitely.

Although completely inconsequential to the final outcome, here, too, a Jewish organization meddled, and not in favor of the Jews. According to the *Jewish Virtual Library*, "Alarmed by the [news of the Madagascar] plan, the American Jewish Committee [headed by Sam Rosenman] commissioned a special report, published in May 1941, that sought to demonstrate that Jews could not survive the conditions on the island. By that time, however, the Nazis were already well underway with a different 'Final Solution.'"[477]

The Villa on Wannsee 56/58

On January 20, 1942, the senior government officials of Nazi Germany gathered for what became known as the Wannsee Conference, where the *Endlösung der Judenfrage* (Final Solution to the Jewish question) became Germany's formal policy—to exterminate all 11,000,000 Jews living in Europe and the Soviet Union.[478] The plans were laid out, the censuses completed, problems discussed and solved, and all that was left was to execute the plan country by country as the Germans were hoping to advance into Europe and beyond. Everything was methodical and calculated.

L a n d	Zahl
A. Altreich	131.800
Ostmark	43.700
Ostgebiete	420.000
Generalgouvernement	2.284.000
Bialystok	400.000
Protektorat Böhmen und Mähren	74.200
Estland — judenfrei —	
Lettland	3.500
Litauen	34.000
Belgien	43.000
Dänemark	5.600
Frankreich / Besetztes Gebiet	165.000
Unbesetztes Gebiet	700.000
Griechenland	69.600
Niederlande	160.800
Norwegen	1.300
B. Bulgarien	48.000
England	330.000
Finnland	2.300
Irland	4.000
Italien einschl. Sardinien	58.000
Albanien	200
Kroatien	40.000
Portugal	3.000
Rumänien einschl. Bessarabien	342.000
Schweden	8.000
Schweiz	18.000
Serbien	10.000
Slowakei	88.000
Spanien	6.000
Türkei (europ. Teil)	55.500
Ungarn	742.800
UdSSR	5.000.000
Ukraine 2.994.684	
Weißrußland aus-	
schl. Bialystok 446.484	
Zusammen: über	11.000.000

Image 6: Page 6 of the Wannsee Conference concluding document.[481]

Reminiscent of the Alhambra Decree, the edict of expulsion of the Jews of Spain, there was no drama in the Wannsee document, no expressions of odium, only facts and details. Even words such as extermination or killing were absent in the minutes of the conference. The document simply stated, "Approximately 11 million Jews will be involved in the final solution of the European Jewish question."[479] It is the euphemism and prosaic tone that make the final document of the Wannsee Conference so chilling.

Page 6 in the document, for example, presents Eichmann's list, which details how many Jews live in each country (Image 6 [in previous page]). The countries are divided into two groups: A) under direct (or partial, in the case of Vichy France) Reich control or occupation, and B) allied or client countries, neutral, or at war with Germany. In total, Eichmann counted over 11,000,000 Jews. On page 7, however, the document explains that it counts "only those Jews who still adhere to the Jewish faith, since some countries still do not have a definition of the term 'Jew' according to racial principles."[480]

Following the statistics comes a distressingly staid elaboration on the "levels of Jewishness" and how each level should be treated since "a prerequisite for the absolute solution of the [Jewish] problem is also the solution to the problem of mixed marriages and persons of mixed blood."[482] The statistics pertained only to *Mischling* (mixed-blood) Jews since the table on page 6 refers to full Jews, who were to be exterminated.

- *Mischlinge* (pl. of *Mischling*) of the first degree (having two Jewish grandparents) were to be treated as full Jews, namely exterminated. But if, for any reason, a first degree *Mischling* were allowed to stay (live), he or she "will be sterilized in order to prevent any offspring and to eliminate the problem of persons of mixed blood once and for all."

- *Mischlinge* of the second degree (having only one Jewish grandparent) were to be treated as Germans unless "both parents are persons of mixed blood," or "the person … has a racially especially undesirable appearance that marks him outwardly as a Jew," or has "a particularly bad police and political record that shows that he feels and behaves like a Jew."

- Mixed families of full Jews and Germans will be examined individually. If they have implications on the German relatives, they will be "evacuated" to ghettos.

- Mixed families of *Mischlinge* of the first degree and Germans: 1) Without children, only the *Mischling* is "evacuated." 2) With children, if the children are considered Jewish, they will be evacuated along with the parents. Otherwise, only the Jewish parent will be sent away.

- Families where both parents are *Mischlinge* of the first degree: The entire family is to be sent away. This also applies when both parents are *Mischlinge*, one of the first degree and one of the second degree.

Subsequently, the participants discussed the challenges that sterilization would pose and determined instead to propose the government to declare a law that "These marriages have been dissolved."[483]

Collusion to Keep Mum

Following the Wannsee Conference, the Nazis went straight to work, building extermination camps throughout German-occupied Poland and launching Operation Reinhard: the plan to exterminate Polish Jewry. Operation Reinhard went into full force that summer, and within four months, from August to November 1942, more than one million Jews were killed.[4846]

Despite Nazi efforts to conceal their atrocities, news of the genocide leaked out and the Allies learned about the atrocities unfolding in Nazi occupied territories. According to acclaimed historian Walter Laqueur, "One might expect that the Jews in Roosevelt's inner circle … would have appealed directly to Roosevelt on behalf of Jewish causes. But with the exception of Treasury Secretary Morgenthau, none lobbied the president to support rescue operations. These officials considered themselves Americans who happened to be Jews— sometimes unhappily so. For different reasons, the 10 members of the

Jewish congressional delegation, three of whom chaired committees that were in a position to aid in rescue—Foreign Affairs (Rep. Sol Bloom), Immigration and Naturalization (Rep. Samuel Dickstein), and Judiciary (Rep. Emanuel Celler)—were also loath to press the issue of liberalizing the immigration laws."[485]

Had it not been for the coordinated efforts of the US government, the aforementioned Stephen Wise, and other Jewish organizations, the world would have learned about the Holocaust much sooner than it did. In his book *Shake Heaven & Earth*, journalist Louis Rapoport mentions a letter from Wise to President Roosevelt asking for a meeting with Jewish American organizations so the president would offer his "heartening and consoling reply."[486]

It is with good reason that Wise did not ask for anything more than consoling words. In the letter (Image 7), which was sent on December 2, 1942, Wise admits that he had known about the genocide for months but kept mum about it and maneuvered other Jewish organizations to do the same. In Wise's words, "Hitler's decision was to exterminate the Jewish people in all Hitler-ruled lands, and it is indisputable that as many as two million civilian Jews have been slain." Despite knowing this, Wise continues, "I succeeded, together with the heads of other Jewish organizations, in keeping these out of the press and have been in constant communication with the State Department" (see in Image 7, end of 1st para. and then from the 2nd line in the 2nd para.).

Even after the news of the Holocaust broke out, Wise tried to stifle Jewish demands from the American government to act in favor of European Jewry and to stymie protests against the government's inaction. "As further details of the genocide reached the West," writes Medoff in *Militant Zionism in America*, Zionist organizations "...organized a pageant, *We Will Never Die*, to publicize European Jewry's plight. ... In three acts ... *We Will Never Die* dramatized the major events of Jewish history, Jewry's contributions to civilization, and the Nazi massacres. Its two opening performances at Madison Square Garden on March 9 were viewed by audiences of more

AMERICAN JEWISH CONGRESS
330 WEST 42nd STREET   NEW YORK CITY

STEPHEN S. WISE, PRESIDENT
CARL SHERMAN, CHAIRMAN, EXECUTIVE COMMITTEE
NATHAN D. PERLMAN } VICE-PRESIDENTS
LEO H. LOWITZ
LOUIS LIPSKY, CHAIRMAN, GOVERNING COUNCIL
M. MALDWIN FERTIG, CHAIRMAN, ADMINISTRATIVE COMMITTEE
JACOB LEICHTMAN, TREASURER

CABLE ADDRESS 'CONGRESS'
TELEPHONE LONGACRE 5-2600

Office of Dr. Wise
40 West 68 Street,
December 2, 1942.

The President
The White House
Washington, D. C.

Dear Boss:

I do not wish to add an atom to the awful burden which you are bearing, with magic and, as I believe, heaven-inspired strength at this time. But you do know that the most overwhelming disaster of Jewish history has befallen Jews in the form of the Hitler mass-massacres. Hitler's decision was to exterminate the Jewish people in all Hitler-ruled lands, and it is indisputable that as many as two million civilian Jews have been slain.

I have had cables and underground advices for some months, telling of these things. I succeeded, together with the heads of other Jewish organizations, in keeping these out of the press and have been in constant communication with the State Department, particularly Under Secretary Welles. The State Department has now received what it believes to be confirmation of these unspeakable horrors and has approved of my giving the facts to the press. The organizations banded together in the Conference of which I am Chairman, feel that they wish to present to you a memorandum on this situation, so terrible that this day is being observed as a day of mourning and fasting throughout the Jewish world. We hope above all that you will speak a word which may bring solace and hope to millions of Jews who mourn, and be an expression of the conscience of the American people.

I had gathered from the State Department that you were prepared to receive a small delegation, which would include representatives of the american Jewish Committee, the American Jewish Congress, the B'nai B'rith. It would be gravely misunderstood if, despite your overwhelming preoccupation, you did not make it possible to receive our delegation and to utter what I am sure will be your heartening and consoling reply.

As your old friend, I beg you will somehow arrange to do this.

Ever yours,

[signature]
PRESIDENT

Image 7: Letter from Wise to President Roosevelt admitting knowing about the genocide and concealing the information from the public, in collusion with the State Dept. and other Jewish organizations. Note the end of paragraph 1 and then from the 2nd line in paragraph 2.[489]

than forty thousand. When it was staged the following month in Washington, D.C.'s Constitution Hall, the audience included First Lady Eleanor Roosevelt, hundreds of members of Congress, cabinet members, Supreme Court justices, and members of the international diplomatic corps. *We Will Never Die* struck the first major blow at the wall of silence surrounding the Nazi genocide."[487] "At the same time," continues Medoff, "Sponsors of the show in upstate New York, Baltimore, and Gary, Indiana, reported pressure by local mainstream Jewish organizations to cancel their showings. Some media reports alleged that Stephen Wise had even urged New York Governor Thomas Dewey to cancel plans to declare March 9, the date of the show's Madison Square Garden debut, an official day of mourning for European Jewry."[488]

The Publisher of *The New York Times* "Doesn't Relate to 'Those People'"

Jewish organizations were not the only ones who kept mum about the genocide unfolding in Europe. *The New York Times*, the leading newspaper in America, was diligent and creative in its efforts to play down, if not conceal the tragedy.

In her damning book *Buried by the Times*, Professor of Journalism at Northeastern University Laurel Leff described the manipulations and evasions that *The New York Times*, whose Jewish owner and publisher, Arthur Hays Sulzberger, used in order to smother, mute, or altogether silence the reports from Europe. Leff describes March 2, 1944 as a typical day in *The Times* during the war: "On page four, amid 13 other stories, appeared a five-paragraph item with a London dateline. The first two paragraphs described the House of Commons's decision to appropriate 50,000 pounds to help fund the Inter-Governmental Committee on Refugees. Then came these paragraphs: '[Labor member Silverman] read a report from the Jewish National Committee operating somewhere in Poland: 'Last month we still reckoned the number of Jews in the whole territory of Poland as from 250,000 to 300,000 [out of three million who lived there before the Holocaust]. In a few weeks, no more than 50,000 of us will remain. In our last moment before death, the remnants of Polish Jewry appeal for help to the whole world. May this, perhaps our last voice from the abyss, reach the ears of the world." Without skipping a beat, the story continued: 'The Commons also approved an installment of 3,863 pounds to help the International Red Cross open an office in Shanghai…'"[490]

According to Leff, "*The Times* never acknowledged that the mass murder of Jews, because they were Jews, was something its readers needed to know."[491]

The Daily Beast writer Marlow Stern offers some statistics that demonstrate how *The Times* ignored the Holocaust: "Between 1939 and 1945, *The New York Times* published more than 23,000 front-page stories. Of those, 11,500 were about World War II. Twenty-six were about the Holocaust."[492]

Sulzberger, the publisher of *The Times*, admitted that the policy of downplaying the Holocaust was intentional. He explained that "While he is Jewish and identifies as a Jew, he doesn't think Judaism is anything more than a religious category, and therefore [he] doesn't relate to 'those people' because he does not view them as part of the same 'people' or 'race.'"[493]

Sulzberger had no sympathy for anyone or any goal that was not part of his Reform anti-Zionist agenda. He was one of the founders of the anti-Zionist American Council for Judaism, which to this day maintains its view of Judaism "as a universal religious faith, rather than an ethnic or nationalist identity."[494]

In a 2014 op-ed newspaper article on *Algemeiner*,[495] Rafael Medoff writes, "Even a visit to former Nazi concentration camps in 1945 did not alter Sulzberger's anti-Zionist convictions. In a speech the following year, Sulzberger said that while he felt sorry for the Jewish survivors living in Displaced Persons camps in Europe, they were 'but a minor percentage of the total of displaced persons' and therefore should not be receiving so much attention."

Moreover, continues Medoff: "*The Times* publisher even went so far as to claim that Zionism was to blame for some of the Jewish deaths in the Holocaust. In that 1946 speech, he alleged that the refugee crisis during the war had been 'a manageable, social and economic problem' until 'the clamor for statehood introduced an insoluable [sic] political element' into the issue. 'It is my judgment that thousands dead might now be alive' if 'the Zionists' had put 'less emphasis on statehood,' asserted Sulzberger."[496]

Bermuda—the Final Sham

Facing growing criticism of government inaction, the US government realized it had to at least pretend to be doing something. Fittingly, the United States and Britain sent representatives to a bilateral conference on refugee problems, to be held on the island of Bermuda in April 1943. In a closed session, both sides in effect agreed not to tread on sensitive areas: The British did not want to take actions that might inflame Arab riots in the Middle East or involve negotiations with Germany for the release of Jews, or require shipping food through the Allied blockade of Nazi-occupied Europe. The United States, for its part, did not want to commit to any plan that would compromise its tight immigration policy. The restrictions left very limited options, such as establishing small refugee camps in North Africa and, mainly, informing neutral countries of the American and British concern for refugees. In such circumstances, it is no surprise that the results of the deliberations were so meager that they were kept confidential.[497]

Additionally, the British government insisted that "The refugee problem cannot be treated as though it were a wholly Jewish problem" because "There is a possibility that the Germans or their satellites may change over from the policy of extermination to one of extrusion, and aim as they did before the war at embarrassing other countries by flooding them with alien immigrants."[498] In other words, in the eyes of the British government, exterminating Europe's Jews was the preferred solution to the Jewish Question and having Jewish refugees flee to England would expose this and embarrass the British government.

In line with the British approach, a May 22, 1943 letter from Secretary of State Cordell Hull to President Roosevelt revealed that the US government had no intention of taking any meaningful steps to help the stranded Jews to begin with. Hull wrote about the conference that "A meeting of that character would attract world-wide attention." Therefore, "Unless the American and British Governments were determined in advance as to the purposes which they would pursue and as to the extent to which they would commit themselves on financial accounts, the Conference could not come to any satisfactory conclusions,"[499] which were, as said above, primarily "informing neutral countries of the American and British concern for refugees."

To secure the achievement of disguised inaction, the US government had to appoint a delegate who would be both obedient and publicly acceptable. The immediate candidate was Jewish Congressman Sol Bloom, chairman of the House Committee on Foreign Affairs. And indeed, "The Roosevelt administration chose him as a U.S. delegate to its ... farcical refugee conference in Bermuda... Afterward, Bloom declared, 'I as a Jew am perfectly satisfied with the results,' prompting one Jewish periodical to charge that Bloom had been 'used as a stooge to impede Jewish protests against the nothing-doers of the Bermuda conference.'"[500]

Bloom was a natural choice. After all, he "worked closely with the administration to block congressional resolutions supporting rescue and Jewish statehood. He even backed the State Department's proposal to ban all public discussion of the Palestine issue for the duration of World War II."[501]

For this reason, "When Bloom was chosen as a member of the American delegation to the Bermuda conference, many in the Jewish community saw the choice as a ploy to deflect criticism of U.S. refugee policy. Assistant Secretary of State Breckinridge Long privately wrote in his diary that he chose Bloom because the congressman was known to be 'easy to handle' and 'terribly ambitious for publicity.'"[502]

Again, to no one's surprise, neither the U.S. nor the British delegation came up with any serious solutions to save what was left of European Jewry. The U.S. administration refused to use any trans-Atlantic ships to transport refugees or increase the quota of refugees admitted to the

United States. The British, for their part, refused to discuss Palestine as a possible refuge.

And despite the dismal results, "Congressman Bloom announced that 'as a Jew,' he was 'perfectly satisfied' with the results. In his autobiography, published after the war, Bloom continues to defend the outcome of the Bermuda conference, arguing that any announcement of aid to the Jews would have led 'to intensified persecutions.' [Fellow member of the Democratic Party] Congressman Emanuel Celler, characterized Bloom as 'a sycophant of the State Department.'"[503]

A Short Summary of Deadly Alienation

Sol Bloom's demeanor at the Bermuda Conference was not exclusive to the conference. It was indicative of the way he and most American Jewish persons in positions of influence conducted themselves before, during, and even after World War II. According to Prof. Kurt Stone, at the 1945 United Nations Conference on International Organization in San Francisco, where the United Nations was established, "Bloom was the only Jew selected for the eight-man American delegation that went to San Francisco ... to write the United Nations Charter. At the sessions of the nascent world body, Bloom, viewed by more than one prominent historian as a 'perennial court Jew,' argued vociferously on behalf of refugees. It was too little, too late. In 1943, Bloom had been the sole Jew on the American delegation to the Bermuda Conference, convened to discuss the single issue of wartime immigration. No aid was forthcoming for the Jews of Europe; Bloom's presence on the delegation was mere window dressing. Additionally, during the innumerable congressional battles over increased immigration quotas, Sol Bloom, House Foreign Relations Committee chair, did virtually nothing to help the Jews of Europe to escape Hitler's ovens. It was Bloom, acting at the behest of the State Department, who buried a 1943 House resolution to create a U.S. Government agency to rescue Jews from Hitler. ... One wonders how in the world Congress could again and again have barred increases in the number of European refugees allowed into America, especially when the three committees most directly responsible for this type of legislation (Foreign Relations, Immigration, and Judiciary) were chaired by Jews: Bloom, Samuel Dickstein and Emanuel Celler."[504]

In conclusion, as historian Katherine Culbertson writes, "It is clear what happened to the Jews. Six million of them perished in the most shocking way. Not so plain is the epitaph for the bystanders. After the [crushing of the] revolt in the Warsaw ghetto, the suicide of Szmul Zygielbojm [a Polish Jewish leader who killed himself in protest of the Allies' inaction], and the [fiasco of the] Bermuda Conference, a writer for a small Jewish periodical called *Jewish Frontier* seemed to know: 'The Warsaw ghetto has been 'liquidated,' leaders of Polish Jewry are dead by their own hand, and the whole world which looks on passively, in its way, is dead too.'"[505]

Chapter 8: The Peculiar Case of Italy

From among all of Europe's Jewish communities, one community stands out in particular: Italian Jewry. Despite Italy's alliance with Nazi Germany, there was very little anti-Semitism in Italy before or during the war, Italy consistently refused to send Italian Jews to death camps in Eastern Europe, and the Italian Jews that did perish in the Holocaust, perished at the hands of Nazi Germany after it conquered Northern and Central Italy in 1943.

Why was there so little anti-Semitism in Italy? On the surface, Italian Jewry went through very similar processes that the rest of European Jewry experienced. Like the Jews in the rest of Europe, they assimilated, intermarried with non-Jews, some became Zionists, and some remained Orthodox. Additionally, as in other countries where Jews were emancipated, many became influential in Italian politics and economy. Still, unlike any other country in Europe where there was a significant Jewish population, their integration into the general society in Italy did not intensify Jew-hatred.

However, when you examine the similarities and dissimilarities between Italian Jewry and the rest of the sizable Jewish communities in Europe, it is hard to ignore one conspicuous difference: Despite their disagreements and different levels of Jewish observance, by and large, the various factions of Italian Jewry did not disparage or deride one another. This was markedly different from German Jewry, Austrian Jewry, Russian Jewry, or Polish Jewry, where slander, libel, and mutual banning of one faction of the Jewish community against another were the norm.

"Benign" Fascism and "Mild" Anti-Semitism

Italian Fascism was largely benign. According to British historian Jeremy Black, "The incoherent diversity of Italian Fascism ensured an extremely varied response to Jews, both Italian and foreign. It was acceptable in Italy in 1938 to ban Jewish teachers from teaching and to forbid marriage between Jews and non-Jews. ...However, compared to Germany and Austria, there was less anti-Semitic feeling among the population and less support for deportation and mass murder."[5068] Also, "Italian Fascism sought a stronger state: there was not the commitment to race seen with Germany. Indeed, Italy and Italian-occupied territory, such as Dalmatia, Nice, and parts of Greece, were safer for Jews than other German-allied states—for example Vichy France and Croatia—and, as a result, many Jews took refuge there."[507]

Indeed, the "mild" anti-Semitism that Italy implemented in its occupied territories made them "safe-havens" for Jews fleeing German-occupied territories. "Italian forces on the Eastern Front ... did not match the Germans in the habitual deliberate brutality of their treatment of Jews but did nothing to stop it," says Black. At the same time, "issues of control and status vis à vis Germany played a role in the unwillingness to deport Jews from the Balkans while, notably in response to Croat atrocities, the Italians eventually devoted special attention to the rescue of the Jews." In fact, "Quite a number of French Jews found refuge in the Italian-occupied zone of South-East France. The Italian authorities were aware of the arrival and location of Jews, but not terribly interested. The Italians also refused to deport foreign Jews from Italy. The forced labor of Roman Jews was not lethal, and there were [Jewish] army and naval officers who remained hidden 'behind desks' for years after 1938."[508]

According to the United States Holocaust Memorial Museum (USHMM), "Despite its alliance with Germany, the Fascist regime responded equivocally to German demands first to concentrate and then to deport Jews residing in Italian occupation zones in Yugoslavia, Greece, and France to killing centers in the German-occupied Poland. Italian military authorities generally refused to participate in mass murder of Jews or to permit deportations from Italy or Italian-occupied territory; and the Fascist leadership was both unable and unwilling to force the issue. Italian-occupied areas were therefore relatively safe for Jews. Between 1941 and 1943, thousands of Jews escaped from German-occupied territory to the Italian-occupied zones of France, Greece, and Yugoslavia. The Italian authorities even evacuated some 4,000 Jewish refugees to the Italian mainland,"[509] where they were kept in internment camps until the end of the war.

In fact, the Italians were so uncooperative in response to Germany's demands to round up the Jews and transfer them to forced-labor or extermination camps that "Nazi propaganda minister Joseph Goebbels [expressed] in his journal his contempt for the Italians' treatment of Jews in Italian-occupied territories."[5102] In his words, "The Italians are extremely lax in their treatment of Jews. They protect Italian Jews both in Tunis and in occupied France and won't permit their being drafted for work or compelled to wear the Star of David."[5113]

Grapes of Solace

The Jeff and Toby Herr Oral History Archive contains numerous heart-wrenching testimonials of Jews from before, during, and after the Holocaust. But the story of Flory Jagoda,[512] a Bosnian born American Jewish singer and composer of Sephardic songs in Ladino (or Judeo-Español), is quite different. When we "arrived to mainland Italy," she recalls, "it was like arriving to the Promised Land, I mean it! And there were [other refugee] boats all over the place, people coming from all over the place to Italy. And the scene that I will never forget was Italian women, dressed in black, with big, big, big! baskets of grapes, black grapes. And we were hungry; that was great! Anyway, all the refugees came to the piazza ... and a couple of the humanitarian organizations had big tables full of clothes, and they took care of our daily needs of bread. But they couldn't find places for you to live. ...So I would go from house to house, from door to door and see if we can find a place to stay. After walking for about six hours ... I knock on a door and a big heavyset lady, dressed up pretty [opens the door] and I explain to her my situation ... that I need a room for just my mother and I, and she says 'Si signora come in, I have a room for you, bring your mother.' ...This was the start of a new life."

Despite Everything—Maintaining Jewish Group Consciousness

In the book *Paths of Emancipation*, Pierre Birnbaum and Ira Katznelson explore various Jewish communities and their process of emancipation. In relation to Italian Jewry, they write, "The question this [chapter] tries to answer concerns the uniqueness of this very ancient Jewish tribe, and whether its emancipation has followed a different course from that of other Jewish communities in Europe. [The chapter asks] To what degree and in what period is it legitimate to speak of the transformation of the Jews of Italy into Italians of the Jewish faith? Why has their political and economic role in the making of a unified Italy been so great? Why have they reacted in such a singular way to the great internal conflicts of modern Judaism—orthodoxy and reform, tradition and assimilation, Italian nationalism and Zionism?"[513]

Chaim Weizmann, too, had for the Italian Jews "'the fascination of mystery' insofar as 'none of the motivations which justify the development of Zionism in other countries apply to the Italian case,' so different from that of 'those people of the Mosaic persuasion' whom Weizmann was accustomed to meeting in France and Germany. What baffled him was the fact that the Italian Jews were at one and the same time completely assimilated and so proud of their Judaism."[514]

Indeed, "it is true that the emancipation of the Italian Jews has been in many respects similar to that of Jews elsewhere in Europe: economic development, rapid assimilation to the Gentile society, renunciation of Jewish tradition through conversion and mixed marriages, adhesion to liberal and Marxist movements," write Birnbaum and Katznelson. "Yet it is equally true ... that in the period between 1830 and 1870 ...the emancipation process assumed political, psychological, economic, and cultural characteristics unique in the contemporary history of European Jewry. As a result, the Italian Jewish community, despite its small size, developed a group consciousness."[515]

Similarly, "Contrary to what was happening in France (where the Jews turned themselves in many cases into theoreticians of the secular republican state) or in England (where the Jews as a collective remained politically passive), in Italy, and especially in Piedmont, the Jews operated as a politically conscious community."[516]

Also, Italian Jews were less drawn to disputes regarding assimilation. Many of them expressed their Judaism through family ties rather than religious particularism. "The Italian Jews," continue the two researchers, "like other Jews in the nineteenth century, had to face the great internal problems of their time, including assimilation, reform, anti-Semitism, Zionism, Marxism, and secularism."[517] However, by and large, they did not take any of the trends to the extreme. Rather, "traditional Italian Jews expressed their Judaism ... through family attachment that was often more a demonstration of elitism [pride of being Jewish] than of religious particularism."[518]

Even after Italian Jewry was somewhat influenced by the various trends just mentioned and opened separate institutions for their communities, in 1917, "The Jewish institutions were ... reunited under a central roof, the Unione delle Communita Israelitiche, a decision that put an end to the confusion."

The Jewish press, too, tried its best to avoid internal confrontations. The only Jewish periodical, *II Vessillo Israelitico*, "was 'a banner [vessillo] to all winds,' without any clear ideological direction."[519] The paper did write about such Jewish problems as mixed marriages, the decline of Jewish culture and detachment from Jewish tradition, and the issues that Zionism presented. However, as a whole, the paper was "chiefly preoccupied with avoiding polemics, particularly political ones."[520]

To be sure, thousands of Italian Jews perished in the Holocaust. On September 8, 1943, Italy submitted its unconditional surrender to the Allies. As a result, the Germans occupied northern and central Italy, as well as the Italian zones in Yugoslavia, Greece, and France. According to the USHMM, "The German occupation of Italy radically altered the situation for the remaining 43,000 Italian Jews living in the northern half of the country. The Germans quickly established an SS and police apparatus, in part to deport the Italian Jews to Auschwitz-Birkenau."[521]

The Germans took great efforts to round up the Jews in Rome, Milan, Genoa, Florence, Trieste, and other major cities in northern Italy. Yet, now, too, the Italians would not cooperate. As a result, "these operations had limited success, due in part to advance warning given to the Jews by Italian authorities and the Vatican, and in part to the unwillingness of many non-Jewish Italians, including Salò police authorities, to participate in or facilitate the roundups."[522]

"In all," concludes the USHMM report, "the Germans deported 8,564 Jews from Italy, Italian-occupied France, and the islands of Rhodes and Kos, most of them to Auschwitz-Birkenau. 1,009 returned," and some 300 more died by shooting or in transit camps.[523] As devastating as it was for the victims, compared to other Jewish communities under Nazi occupation, which were all but decimated, the roughly 15% of Italian Jewry that perished in the Holocaust hardly count as a success story for the Nazi killing machine.

When reflecting on why the Germans failed, it is evident that the reluctance of the Italian people to contribute to the Nazi efforts was crucial in saving the Jewish community. The "considerable hiatus between the image [the Italians] had of the Jews in general [who displayed divergence] and the image they held of the Italian Jews [who remained united]," as Birnbaum and Katznelson describe it,[524] is clearly the reason why they treated Jews so much better than in other Nazi occupied countries. As said in the beginning of the chapter, if we compare the Italian Jewry to the Jewish communities in countries such as Poland, Germany, or Austria, clearly, the most striking difference between them and Italian Jewry is the commitment of the latter to stay as a single "politically conscious community," with "group consciousness" and an emphasis on "family attachment" above all differences.

Chapter 9: Toward a
Conscious Jewish People(?)

Foiled by Their Own Disunity

In *The Transfer Agreement*, Edwin Black points to the heart of the problem in facing the threat of Nazi Germany: Jewish disunity. However, he makes an allowance to the Jews when he says that they were "in good company," that the whole world was bewildered in the face of Nazism. In Black's words, "The Jews were the first to recognize the Hitler threat, and the first to react to that threat. The fact they were foiled by their own disunity merely puts them in the company of all mankind. Who did not confront the Hitler menace with indecision? Who did not seal pacts of expediency with the Third Reich? The Catholic Church, the Lutheran Church, and the Supreme Moslem Council all endorsed the Hitler regime. The United States, England, France, Italy, Russia, Argentina, Japan, Ireland, Poland, and dozens of other nations all signed friendship and trade treaties and knowingly contributed to German economic and military recovery. The international banking and commercial community ... [also] saw Germany as indispensable to its salvation."[525] But while everyone benefitted from Nazi Germany, the Jews were in a different situation: They were "the only ones with a gun to their heads."[526]

But since the end of WWII and until today, many good things have happened to the Jewish people. The State of Israel was established, American Jewry has acquired an unprecedented status in American culture, politics, finance, and economy, and the remnants of European Jewry seem to have found peace and prosperity once more in France, Germany, and other West European countries. At the same time, Russian Jewry has been liberated, and today Jews are free to live wherever they choose in the non-Muslim world.

Our memory is short. We tend to relate to the Holocaust as a chapter in our past which, however tragic, will not return. But history is not on our side. It has shown time and again that our disunity yields disaster, and the greater our disunity, the greater is our calamity.

In today's globalized world, we cannot speak of American Jewry, the State of Israel, German Jewry, or French Jewry as separate entities. Just as the world has become a global village, so Jewry has become world Jewry, and the fate of our entire nation is irreversibly linked to the conduct of each of our communities, just as the fate of each Jewish community is irreversibly linked to our conduct as an entire nation.

Notwithstanding, if only by their sheer size and predominance, today's two major Jewish communities—the one in America and the one in the State of Israel—have a much greater impact on the fate of world Jewry, and therefore bear a much heavier responsibility for the future of our nation.

But now that we have seen the consequences of our separation, we can make a conscious choice. In this final chapter, we will examine our options for the coming years in light of everything that we have seen happen to us from the inception of our people to the present.

A Warm Welcome

"On November 29, 1947, the UN General Assembly voted in favor of a resolution which adopted the plan for the partition of Palestine, recommended by the majority of the UN Special Committee on

Palestine. 33 states voted in favor of the resolution and 13 against. 10 states abstained. ...The UN Committee reached the conclusion that the Mandate for Palestine should be terminated, and most of its members recommended the establishment in the territory of Mandatory Palestine of an Arab state and a Jewish state."[527] That UN resolution, which became known as "Resolution 181," set off Israel's War of Independence. In the midst of the battles, "On the day the British Mandate over Palestine expired—Friday, May 14, 1948—the Jewish People's Council gathered at the Tel Aviv Museum to declare the establishment of the State of Israel."[528]

At the time of the declaration, the fledgling state was under attack from every direction, surrounded by the armies of seven Arab nations and enemies within its own territory. Yet, the Jews had two things going for them: 1) They put aside their differences and united their paramilitary organizations into the Israel Defense Force (IDF). 2) They had no choice. The Holocaust was the proof that if they did not win this war, they would not only lose the land, but their very lives.

Also, in the short burst of sympathy toward Jews after the horrors of the Holocaust became known, the world was shortly with them: "The new state was recognized that night [May 14, 1948] by the United States and three days later by the USSR."[529]

The support for the tiny Jewish state came from many countries and lasted roughly nineteen years until after the Six Day War in June 1967. In fact, probably one of the most supportive countries of the State of Israel was Germany. Officially, West Germany maintained a policy of neutrality so as not to risk its political and commercial relationship with the oil-rich Arab countries. But when Israel launched a surprise attack that freed it from the chokehold of the Egyptian army, and began the Six Day War, Germany was so thrilled it could not hide it.

"When war erupted," writes historian Carole Fink, "...the SPD [Social Democratic Party] faction leader, Helmut Schmidt, who a year earlier had made an extended visit to Israel, insisted: 'Much as we value the traditional friendship of our people with the Arab peoples, we must protest the intention of their leaders to destroy Israel.'[530] ...When it came his time to speak, Brandt [leader of the Social Democratic Party], although reiterating his government's official policy of non-intervention, stated that this did not mean 'moral indifference' or 'neutrality of the heart.'"[531,532]

"There were strong expressions of popular support for Israel," continues Fink. "Three hundred West Berlin youths volunteered for civilian service in Israel. In Frankfurt, the Bank für Gemeinwirtschaft purchased Israeli bonds valued at [Deutsche Mark] DM 3 million and the city donated an additional DM 30,000 from its budget. In Hamburg and Stuttgart, doctors donated some DM 65,000 in medical and pharmaceutical supplies. In Bonn [then capital of West Germany], some one thousand doctors, nurses, workers, soldiers, and young people offered their services to the Israeli Embassy, which also received several thousand letters, including financial donations."[533]

Prof. Fink also writes that Israel's unanticipated and overwhelming military victory created a wave of relief in Germany. Acclaimed novelist and playwright Gunter Grass joyfully announced, "A new situation has emerged . . . to express our solidarity for Israel and the fate of the Jews without our feelings being hindered by the past."[534] Likewise, in his passionate editorial on June 10, Rudolf Augstein, editor of *Der Spiegel*, rejoiced that the Arab attempt to wipe out Israel had failed: "They rolled like Rommel, won as Patton, and sang at that. 'This is a singing army. Your warriors sing like the hero of Hemingway,' marveled war correspondent James Reston. In 60 hours the armored sons of Zion smashed the Arab encirclement of Israel. They shooed the pan-Arab prophets from their dreams of dominance, and overthrew Egypt's Nasser into the depths of the Nile. Pharaoh took responsibility for the lost war and submitted his resignation."[535]

Pride and Punishment

A year after the Six Day War, Menachem Begin, founder of Likud Party and the sixth Prime Minister of Israel, gave a passionate speech about the cause for the great victory. The speech was published on

August 15, 1969 in the daily newspaper *Hayom* [today]: "Citizens of Israel," his speech began. "A year ago, one of the gravest dangers fell upon us, not only to our independence, but to our very existence... There has never been a danger like that one since the establishment of our independence. ...In the face of this peril, we, first and foremost, united. We learned the lesson from the civil war in antiquity ... we learned the lesson from the surrounded [Warsaw] ghetto where even the groups of fighters ... could not unite in the face of the murderous enemy. This time, we had resolved to unify the nation, unite it, and make longtime rivals stretch out their hands to one another and stand together—not shoulder to shoulder, but mind to mind, and mainly heart to heart—in facing the enemy. This is a lesson not only to our generation, but to posterity..."[536]

But the lesson was not learned. Israel's unequivocal victory in the Six Day War secured Israel's existence and gave it a strategic "breathing space" that it did not have before. Prior to the war, the distance in some places between the eastern border with Jordan and the Mediterranean Sea was six miles. In Northern Israel, the Syrians controlled the strategically dominating Golan Heights all the way down to the Sea of Galilee. This enabled them, should they choose, to simply drive their tanks through the narrow strip that is northern Israel and within an hour reach the Lebanese border, thereby disconnecting northern Israel from the rest of the country. In the south, the conquest of Sinai moved the Egyptian army farther away from the Tel-Aviv metropolis, the hub of Israel's business life and economy. The expansion of the country brought with it a tactical relief and room to maneuver in the case of war.

However, the military victory also engendered two major negative consequences whose impact is only worsening over time. The first consequence was a shift in the way the world perceives Israel: from being perceived as the victim to being perceived as the villain. The second, and perhaps worst consequence of all, was pride and division.

In the war, Israel suddenly became the conqueror of territories filled with civilian population, and the governing power of holy sites such as the Temple Mount in Jerusalem and the Cave of Machpelah in Hebron. Israelis were amazed at their own military might, of which they had no idea, and became overconfident and arrogant. Worse yet, the false sense of omnipotence soon spilled over from the military into civilian life, and deepening social rifts began to emerge in the Israeli society, which was still very much a nation of immigrants from numerous countries and cultures. It is not as though the rifts between immigrants from different countries did not exist prior to the Six Day War, but the sense of complacency and confidence in Israel's military might allowed Israelis to emphasize these differences, and not in order to unite above them but rather to patronize other factions in the population.

The October 1973 surprise attack of the Egyptian and Syrian armies in what became known as the Yom Kippur War [or The October War] found Israel completely unprepared. The intelligence misread the intentions of Israel's enemies, and the hubris of the political establishment resulted in a hard and painful awakening. It reminded Israelis that a strong army was not a guarantee for peace. However, the turmoil of the war did not mend the growing chasms in Israeli society. If anything, it deepened them.

As always, when Israel are divided, the world turns against them. As the rifts that began to appear after the Six Day War continued to deepen, the tone toward Israel became increasingly critical and angry. Today, with the Israeli society being more fractured than ever, the situation of the State of Israel in the international arena is so dire that if the vote on the establishment of the Jewish state were to be taken these days, very few countries, if any, would vote in favor of it.

Still, the struggles within Israel's political parties and the alienation between the various factions of society keep growing. And the more they do, the more the nations despise and loathe Israel, regardless of its efforts to please and appease the world.

As has always happened, when Israel fight among themselves, the nations fight against them. Continued deterioration of the disunity and strife within the Israeli society, therefore, will inevitably lead to a disaster that will come to Israel at the hands of the nations. Each tragedy in human history has its own characteristics and phases of development, but the one gauge that determines the intensity of a tragedy to the Jewish people in specific is the level of animosity within the tribe, and in the case of Israel, within the Israeli society. Add to this the abyss that has grown between American Jewry and the State of Israel, and you have a looming perfect storm whose outcome is anyone's guess, but which will no doubt be inconceivably horrific.

The (Jewish) American Dream

Much like 15th century Spain and 20th century Germany, American Jewry has abandoned the aspiration to return to Zion. Moreover, young American Jews are turning their backs on the Jewish state altogether, and in many cases on their own Jewishness. Like the German Jews before them, they have made New York City their New Jerusalem. Much like the mutual odium between *conversos* and Jews in Spain, and between Orthodox Jews and assimilationist Jews in Germany, or between both groups and the Zionist Jews, today's American Jewry is divided within itself into factions and groups that simply cannot stand one another.

Until relatively recently, the mutual disdain was mainly between Orthodox Jews and most other Jewish denominations. But especially since the 2016 elections campaign, the rift between supporters of the Democratic Party and supporters of the Republican Party has also deepened to the point that politically conscious Jews—and most Jews are politically conscious—often hate their fellow tribe's members who support the other party, merely for their political views.[537,538]

Additionally, if previously, there were tensions between American Jewry and the Jewish state (Israel), today the schism has grown to a point where it seems it can no longer be bridged. As leading Jewish organizations are adopting increasingly pro-Palestinian and anti-Zionist agendas, the gulf keeps growing and is already threatening the very fabric of our nation.

No One Is Right; Everyone Is Wrong

In the struggle to prove agendas and approaches, the factions of our nation forget that it is not because we are Republicans or Democrats, religious, secular, or anything in between that the nations torment us every so often. It is because we are Jews. More accurately, it is because we are *disunited* Jews.

Our division as a nation brings upon us calamity after calamity, and today's level of internal antipathy is at such levels that the next cataclysm in the sad, painful, and bloody annals of our people is well within sight. When it comes to disunity, we are all sinners, none excluded. As long as there is hatred among us, we are all wrong, no one is right, and we will all pay the price.

Throughout the ages, the spiritual leaders of our people warned us time and again that unless we united, we would suffer. Throughout the ages, we would not listen. Today, the price for not listening will, in all likelihood, be too heavy to bear.

"The prime defense against calamity is love and unity. When there are love, unity, and friendship between each other in Israel, no calamity can come over them. … [If] there is bonding among them, and no separation of hearts, they have peace and quiet … and all the curses and suffering are removed by that [unity]."[539] These words of wisdom that the author of *Maor VaShemesh* [*Light and Sun*] wrote centuries ago are just as true today, if not more so. Similarly, the book *Maor Eynaim* [*Light of the Eyes*] stresses, "When one includes oneself with all of Israel and unity is made … at that time, no harm shall come to you,"[540] and the book *Shem MiShmuel* [*A Name Out of Samuel*] adds, "When [Israel] are as one man with one heart, they are as a fortified wall against the forces of evil."[541]

Unity: A Tool to Accomplish a Mission

At the end of Chapter 1, we mentioned historian Paul Johnson, who wrote that the early Jews had "detected a divine scheme for the human race, of which their own society was to be a pilot." That scheme was never a secret, nor was it its nature. Our forefathers knew that their success depended on their unity, although they often failed to maintain it. Nevertheless, when strife among them struck, they knew its cause was the intensification of the ego, and they knew what they had to do in order to correct it. Moses demanded that the people unite "as one man with one heart"[542] if they were to merit receiving the Torah—the law of unity by which they became a nation worthy of being a role model people, "a light unto nations" (Isaiah 42:5, Isaiah 49:6). Likewise, King Solomon stated very clearly how people should relate to the hatred that erupts among them despite their efforts to unite: "Hate stirs strife, and love will cover all crimes" (Proverbs 10:12).

This strategy of uniting above revealed hatred was so novel and so unlike the natural tendency to stifle hatred and pretend that it does not exist until the next time it erupts, and usually more forcefully, that since the inception of the nation, its leaders and educational texts repeatedly reiterated the importance of doing so. Perhaps this need to reiterate the importance of rising above conflicts rather than repressing them can explain the existence of such enigmatic statements in *The Book of Zohar*—the seminal book in Kabbalah—as this one: "All the wars in the Torah are peace and love,"[543] or this poetic excerpt (see also Chapter 2): "'Behold, how good and how pleasant it is for brothers to also sit together.' These are the friends as they sit together, and are not separated from one another. At first, they seem like people at war, wishing to kill one another ... then they return to being in brotherly love. ...And you, the friends who are here, as you were in fondness and love before, henceforth you will also not part from one another ... and by your merit, there will be peace in the world."[544]

From the very beginning, unity was not an end in itself, but a means to a much greater goal. When Abraham first introduced the method of uniting above hatred and separation to his Babylonian countryfolk, they rejected him and ejected him from their land. But the people who followed him precisely because of this social doctrine grew and strengthened, as elaborated in Chapter 1, and their cohesion made them increasingly more potent until they became a nation: the Israeli people.[545]

The official "inauguration" of the Jewish people happened at the foot of Mt. Sinai when the people united "as one man with one heart" and subsequently received the law, the Torah, of which the fundamental rule is "Love your neighbor as yourself." Only then could the people be told, "This day you have become a nation" (Deuteronomy 27:9).

Since then, as we have seen throughout this book, the annals of the Jewish people have been a procession of periods of internal strife, disunity, and subsequent affliction, followed by temporary, and mostly partial, reestablishment of unity and subsequent relative peace and prosperity.

Until the 20th century. The previous century saw meteoric developments in technology, industry, and economy. Aviation became accessible to everyone; space became the final frontier, and even the moon was no longer out of reach. Cars, phones, everything became accessible and even personal.

Yet, in the 20th century, homicides became easy, too, as weapons of mass destruction and ideologies of mass extinction were not only conceived, but also implemented. The intensification of the ego that unfolded in Babylon and prompted Abraham to develop his technique of uniting above it reappeared in the 20th century, but thousands of times more potently.

Worse yet, the worldwide intensification of the ego caused every major crisis to become a global crisis. This was true especially of wars and genocides. Of the latter, two episodes stand out as particularly demonic: that of Stalin and that of Hitler. "Between the early 1930s and his death in 1953, [ruler of the Soviet Union] Joseph Stalin had more than a million of his own citizens executed. Millions more fell victim to forced labor, deportation, famine, bloody massacres, and detention and interrogation by Stalin's henchmen," writes historian Norman M. Naimark in the description of his book, Stalin's Genocides.[546]

Still, nothing compares to the Holocaust. As described in the previous chapters, and in thousands of books depicting the evolution of the Nazi ideology of superiority of the Aryan race and the incorrigibly vile nature of the Jew, WWII and the Holocaust as part of it set a precedent. This was the first time that a leader and a nation resolved to exterminate the entirety of the Jewish people, at least in Europe, but eventually the world over.

Worse yet, as we saw above, for the most part, the Germans' efforts met with no resistance on the part of the nations under their control. In fact, in many cases, the Nazis even relied on the active assistance of local people in their efforts to eliminate the Jewish people. Clearly, the 20th century marked a new level in the cruelty of humankind, especially toward Jews.

Having experienced the Holocaust, we cannot be certain that it will not happen again. If it happened once, it can happen twice, or thrice, and the globally mounting hatred toward Jews and toward the State of Israel proves that the fear of a second Holocaust is well-founded.

This, once again, reminds us of the necessity to return to Abraham's method of uniting above our differences, and of our duty to set an example to the world by so doing. Interestingly, in the face of growing anti-Semitism in Germany, even before the Nazis came to power, some leading Jews already linked the hatred toward them with the disunity among them. Dr. Kurt Fleischer, the leader of the Liberals in the Berlin Jewish Community Assembly, argued in 1929, "Anti-Semitism is the scourge that God has sent us in order to lead us together and weld us together."[547] Regrettably, the awareness of the linkage between anti-Semitism and internal disunity did not penetrate deep enough and in 1933, when the Nazis came to power, the Jews did not see what was coming and what they ought to do about it.

Today we know where things will go. We have seen the precedent, and we know what we must do in order to reroute them.

Dr. Fleischer was not the first, and certainly not the most vociferous voice warning about anti-Semitism. Before WWII, and in fact, even before WWI, there were Jewish leaders, both secular and religious, who predicted a calamity more horrific than ever before. In the early 1900s, Rav Kook, who later became the first Chief Rabbi in Palestine, wrote, "In Israel is the secret to the unity of the world."[548] Moreover, he stressed the role of Israel in achieving this unity: "Humanity deserves to be united into a single family. At that time all the quarrels and the ill will that stem from divisions of nations and their boundaries shall cease. However, the world requires mitigation, whereby humanity will be perfected through each nation's unique characteristics. This lack is what the Assembly of Israel will complement."[549]

During World War I, Rav Kook felt compelled to outline the connection he saw between the world's troubles and Israel's unity. In his book, *Orot* (*Lights*), he wrote, "The construction of the world, which is currently crumpled by the dreadful storms of a blood-filled sword, requires the construction of the Israeli nation. The construction of the nation and the revealing of its spirit are one and the same, and it is one with the construction of the world, which is crumbling in anticipation for a force full of unity and sublimity, and all that is in the soul of Israel."[550]

Yet, Rav Kook also saw the perils that the world's growing anti-Semitism posed to the Jews. In his latter years he wrote, "Amalek, Petlura [anti-Semitic Ukrainian leader], Hitler, and so forth, awaken for redemption. One who did not hear the voice of the first *Shofar* [a call to unite], or the voice of the second ... for his ears were blocked, will hear the voice of the impure *Shofar*, the foul one. He will hear against his will."[551]

Completely unrelated, but at approximately the same time, Zeev Jabotinsky, leader of the Revisionist movement, "began to warn that the near future for Polish Jews was black and that a great disaster was about to befall them: 'The volcano will soon start to emit its annihilating flames. ... I see a terrible picture. The time to save you is running out. I know that you cannot see this because you are occupied with day-to-day concerns. Listen to me at this hour, the midnight hour, for God's sake. Let each person save himself as long as there is time because time is running out.'"[552]

As we mentioned in Chapter 7, Ben-Gurion, head of the Zionist Organization in Palestine, was also very worried about the future of the Jews in Europe, particularly in Poland. In 1933, when he returned from Poland, he wrote, "Judaism is being destroyed and strangled. ... Germany is only a prelude."[553]

But the most vociferous among the leaders who warned about the impending calamity was Rav Yehuda Ashlag. Back in Poland, he was a *dayan* [an Orthodox judge] in Warsaw—at the time the largest and most prominent Jewish community in Europe. After he immigrated to Palestine, he became a prolific author of commentaries on kabbalistic texts, as well as books and essays in political science, politics, international relations, global affairs and trends, and the role of the Jewish people in the world. Ashlag did not settle for publicly announcing that all Jews must flee Europe. While still in Poland, he arranged for the purchase of 300 wooden shacks from Sweden and a place for them to be erected in Palestine. Regrettably, his plan was thwarted by opposition from leaders of the Orthodox Jewish community in Poland, and he and his family were excommunicated. The tragic result of this affair was that of all the Jews who contemplated immigrating to Palestine with Ashlag, only he and his family did so while the rest of the families remained in Poland and perished in the Holocaust.[554]

The Memory of the Dead and a Lesson for the Future

After the war, Yehuda Ashlag did not forget his lost family and tribe's members who perished in the Holocaust. He also did not mourn them passively. Instead, he continued his proactive attitude of illustrating the role of the Jewish people in the world and what happens when we do not do our part.

Ashlag wrote about the need to unite in both secular texts and kabbalistic texts. In "The Writings of the Last Generation," he asserts, "I have already screamed like a crane about it back in 1933, in my pamphlet 'The Peace,' warning that wars today have reached such proportions that they endanger the life of the entire world. ... Needless to say, today, after the discovery and use of atom bombs, and the discovery of hydrogen bombs, there is no longer a doubt that after one, two, or three wars, the entire human civilization will be totally ruined, leaving no relics."[555]

Similarly, but from a kabbalistic angle, Ashlag dedicated several pages at the end of his introduction to his commentary on *The Book of Zohar* to the role of the Jewish people and the consequences of not carrying it out.[556] He begins by saying that according to the wisdom of Kabbalah, humanity is divided into concentric circles that expand from within outwards. From the perspective of the correction of the world from disunity to unity, writes Ashlag, the people of Israel are regarded as the innermost circle. This means that the correction begins with them and spreads from them to the rest of humanity. In other words, as long as the people of Israel do not begin to shift from separation to connection, neither can the rest of the world. This, in itself, explains why so many people in the world blame Jews for everything that is wrong with the world and with their lives.

Ashlag mentions Israel's duty toward the world in several of his writings. In the essay "A Handmaid Who Is Heir to Her Mistress," for example, he writes, "Know that a branch that extends from the internality are the people of Israel, who have been chosen as the operators of the correction."[557]

Returning to the introduction to *The Zohar*, after he describes the concentric circles of humanity as Kabbalah explains them, Ashlag elaborates that since the correction spreads from the inside out, anyone who joins the correction process and helps shift the world from division to cohesion is regarded as being in a more internal circle and makes a greater impact on the correction of the world. To emphasize this point, he writes, "Do not be surprised that one person's actions bring elevation or decline to the whole world."[558] This means, according to Ashlag, that one who works on increasing unity in the world affects the entire world and not just one's close environment. In the early 1950s, when Ashlag first published this introduction, most people could not understand him. Today, when globalization and interdependence are a recognized fact of life, the validity of his words is in plain sight.

Nevertheless, it should be noted that when Ashlag speaks of unity, he is not referring to being well-mannered. Quite the contrary, he speaks of revealed hatred—just as we see appearing today throughout the world—yet covering it with love, in line with the principles by which the ancient Hebrews aspired to live. In this regard, we should reiterate the astounding recommendation of Henry Ford in his anti-Semitic composition *The International Jew*: "Modern reformers, who are constructing model social systems ... would do well to look into the social system under which the early Jews were organized."[559] Returning to this principle, Ashlag explains, is the only way to maintain sustainable unity and establish a prosperous society.

After he explains the structure of humanity according to the wisdom of Kabbalah, Ashlag details what would happen if Israel do not do what they must, namely initiate the correction of the world through unity above hatred. To do this, Ashlag references a special part in *The Book of Zohar* known as *Tikkuney Zohar* [lit. corrections of *The Zohar*]. He refers particularly to *Tikkun* [correction] number thirty, which states that if Israel do not carry out their task "then they [Israel] make all the ruin and the heinous slaughter that our generation had witnessed [a reference to the Holocaust]."[560]

Later, Ashlag continues to reference *Tikkun* number thirty, which says about Israel that when they are immersed in selfishness, they cannot even do good deeds with the right intention. In the words of *The Zohar*, "All their mercies are as the flower of the field; every mercy that they do, they do for themselves."[561] "At that time," concludes *The Zohar*, "the spirit leaves and will not return to the world."[562]

Later, Ashlag concludes his quoting of *The Zohar*, "Woe unto them who cause [the spirit] to leave the world and not return to the world... Woe unto them, for they cause poverty and ruin, looting and killing, and destruction in the world. Woe unto them, for with these actions they bring about the existence of poverty, ruin, and robbery, looting, killing, and destructions in the world."[563]

Continuing to explain that the well-being of the entire world depends on Israel's willingness to unite and allow the spirit of unity to flow to the rest of the world, Ashlag stresses even more the outcome of not doing so. Again, he does this using our own Jewish sources, in this case the Talmud: "In such a generation," when Israel do not correct themselves through unity, "all the destructors among the nations of the world raise their heads and wish primarily to destroy and to kill the children of Israel, as it is written, 'No calamity comes to the world but for Israel.'[564] This means, as it is written in the above *Tikkunim* [corrections], that they [Israel] cause poverty, ruin, robbery, killing, and destructions in the whole world."[565]

But Ashlag does not end the introduction in despondency or dejection. Rather, he ends it with hope and a proactive approach. "After we have witnessed, through our many faults, all that is said in the above-mentioned *Tikkunim*, and moreover, the judgment struck the very best of us," he writes, "and of all the glory that Israel had had in the countries of Poland and Lithuania, etc., there remains but the relics. ... Now it is upon us, relics, to correct that dreadful wrong. Each of us remainders should take upon himself, heart and soul, to intensify [our unity] and give it its rightful place."[566]

And latterly, Ashlag quotes Prophet Isaiah in order to describe what will happen if Israel do carry out their task, unite, and stream unity through the rest of the circles of humanity: "Then, all the nations of the world will recognize and acknowledge Israel's merit ... and they will follow the words (Isaiah 14), 'And the peoples will take them and bring them to their place...' And also (Isaiah 49), 'And they will bring your sons in their arms, and your daughters will be carried on their shoulders.'"[567]

This will be the end of anti-Semitism, the end of war, all wars, and the dawn of a new and blissful era. At that time, so the leaders of our nation have stressed throughout the ages, we will be as we were meant to be, and the nations will say once more what they had said in the days of the Second Temple (see Chapter 2) as they would "go up to Jerusalem and see Israel ... and say, 'It is becoming to cling only to this nation.'"[568]

Appendices

Who Are You, People of Israel?

Published in *The New York Times* on September 20, 2014

Time and again, Jews are persecuted and terrorized. Being Jewish myself, I often ponder the purpose of this relentless agony. Some believe that the atrocities of WWII are unimaginable today. And yet, we see how easily and abruptly the state of mind preceding the Holocaust is re-emerging, and "Hitler was right" shouts are sounded all too often and all too openly.

But there is hope. We can reverse this trend, and all it requires is that we become aware of the bigger picture.

Where We Are and Where We Come From

Humanity is at a crossroads. Globalization has made us interdependent while people are growing increasingly hateful and alienated. This unsustainable, highly flammable situation requires making a decision about humanity's future direction. Yet to understand how we, the Jewish people, are involved in this scenario, we need to go back to where it all began.

The people of Israel emerged some 4,000 years ago in ancient Babylon. Babylon was a thriving civilization whose people felt connected and united. In the words of the Torah, "The whole earth was of one language and of one speech" (Genesis 11:1).

But as their ties grew stronger, so did their egos. They began to exploit, and finally hate one another. So while the Babylonians felt connected, their intensifying egos made them increasingly alienated from each other. Caught between a rock and a hard place, the people of Babylon began to seek out a solution to their plight.

Two Solutions to the Crisis

The search for a solution led to forming two conflicting views. The first, suggested by Nimrod, king of Babylon, was natural and instinctive: dispersion. The king argued that when people are far from one another, they do not quarrel.

The second solution was suggested by Abraham, then a renowned Babylonian sage. He argued that according to Nature's law, human society is *destined* to become united, and therefore strove to unite the Babylonians despite, and *atop* their growing egos.

Succinctly, Abraham's method was a way to connect people above their egos. When he began to advocate his method among his countryfolk, "thousands and tens of thousands assembled around him, and ... He planted this tenet in their hearts," writes Maimonides (*Mishneh Torah*, Part 1). The rest of the people chose Nimrod's way: dispersion, as do quarrelsome neighbors when they try to stay out of each other's way. These dispersed people gradually became what we now know as "human society."

Only today, some 4,000 years down the line, we can begin to assess whose way was right.

The Basis of the People of Israel

Nimrod forced Abraham and his disciples out of Babylon, and they moved to what later became known as "the land of Israel." They worked on unity and cohesion in accord with the tenet "Love your neighbor as yourself," connected above their egos, and thus discovered "the force of unity," Nature's hidden power.

Every substance consists of two opposite forces, connection and separation, which balance themselves out. But human society is evolving using only the negative force—the ego. According to Nature's plan, we are required to *consciously* balance the negative force with the positive one—unity. Abraham discovered the wisdom that enables balance, and today we refer to his wisdom as "the wisdom of Kabbalah."

Israel Means Straight to the Creator

Abraham's disciples called themselves *Ysrael* (Israel) after their desire to go *Yashar El* (straight to God, the Creator). That is, they wished to discover Nature's force of unity so as to balance the ego that stood between them. Through their unity, they found themselves immersed in the force of unity, the force that is the upper root of reality.

In addition to their discovery, Israel also learned that in the process of human development, the rest of the Babylonians—who followed Nimrod's advice, dispersed throughout the world and have become today's humanity—would also have to achieve unity. That contradiction between the people of Israel, which formed through unity, and the rest of humanity, which formed as a result of separation, is felt even today.

Exile

Abraham's disciples, the people of Israel, experienced many internal struggles. But for 2,000 years their unity prevailed and was the key element that held them together. Indeed, their conflicts were meant only to intensify the love among them.

However, approximately 2,000 years ago, their egos reached such intensity that they could not maintain their unity. Unfounded hatred and egotism erupted among them and inflicted exile on them.

Indeed, Israel's exile, more than it is exile from the physical land of Israel, it is exile from unity. The alienation within the Israeli nation caused them to disperse among the nations.

Back to the Present

Today humanity is in a similar state to the one the ancient Babylonians experienced: interdependence alongside alienation. Because we are completely interdependent in our global village, Nimrod's solution of parting ways is no longer practical. Now we are required to use Abraham's method. This is why the Jewish people, who previously implemented Abraham's method and connected, must rekindle their unity and teach the method of connection to the whole of humanity. And unless we do it of our own accord, the nations of the world will compel us to do it, by force.

On that note, it is interesting to read the words of Henry Ford, founder of Ford Motor Company, and a notorious anti-Semite, in his book *The International Jew — The World's Foremost Problem*: "Society has a large claim against him [the Jew] that he ... begin to fulfill ... the ancient prophecy that through him all the nations of the earth should be blessed."

The Roots of Anti-Semitism

After thousands of years of exerting to build a successful human society using Nimrod's method, the nations of the world are beginning to understand that the solution to their problems is neither technological, nor economic or military. Subconsciously, they feel that the solution lies in unity, that the method of connection exists in the people of Israel, and therefore recognize that they are dependent on the Jews. This makes them blame the Jews for every problem in the world, believing that the Jews possess the key to the world's happiness.

Indeed, when the Israeli nation fell from its moral apex of love of others, hatred of Israel among the nations commenced. And thus, through anti-Semitism, the nations of the world prod us to disclose the method of connection. Rav Kook, the first Chief Rabbi of Israel, pointed to that fact with his words, "Amalek, Hitler, and so forth, awaken us toward redemption" (*Essays of the Raiah*, Vol. 1).

But the people of Israel are unaware that they are holding the key to the world's happiness, and that the very source of anti-Semitism is that the Jews are carrying within them the method of connection, the key to happiness, the wisdom of Kabbalah, but are not revealing it to all.

Mandatory Disclosure of the Wisdom

As the world groans under the pressure of two conflicting forces— the global force of connection and the separating power of the ego, we are falling into the state that existed in ancient Babylon prior to its collapse. But today we cannot pull away from one another in order to calm our egos down. Our only option is to work on our connection, on our unity. We are required to add to our world the positive force that balances the negative power of our ego.

The people of Israel, descendants of the ancient Babylonians who followed Abraham, must implement the wisdom of connection, namely the wisdom of Kabbalah. They are required to set an example to the whole of humanity, and thus become a "light for the nations."

The laws of Nature dictate that we will all achieve a state of unity. But there are two ways to get there: 1) a path of world suffering wars, catastrophes, plagues, and natural disasters, or 2) a path of gradual balancing of the ego, the path that Abraham planted in his disciples. The latter is the one we suggest.

Unity Is the Solution

It is written in *The Book of Zohar*, "Everything stands on love" (Portion, *VaEtchanan*). "Love your neighbor as yourself" is the great tenet of the Torah; it is also the essence of the change that the wisdom of Kabbalah is offering humanity. It is the obligation of the Jewish

People to unite *in order to share* the method of Abraham with the entire human race.

According to Rav Yehuda Ashlag, author of the *Sulam* (Ladder) commentary on *The Book of Zohar*, "It is upon the Israeli nation to qualify itself and all the people of the world ... to develop until they take upon themselves that sublime work of the love of others, which is the ladder to the purpose of Creation." If we accomplish this, we will find solutions to all the world's problems including the eradication of anti-Semitism.

What We Jews Owe the World

Published in *The New York Times* after *Yom Kippur*, October 11, 2014

Buying Our Way to Heaven

The holiest day of the year for Jews is *Yom Kippur* (Day of Atonement), when they fast and pray. A key part of the prayer is reading the book of Jonah the Prophet. Interestingly, many observant Jews believe that buying the privilege to read the book will make them successful for the rest of the year.

Naturally, only the wealthiest in the community can afford to compete for it. The sums vary according to the affluence of the community, and in some cases the privilege is sold for well over half a million dollars.

Cracking the Code

What people are not aware of, however, is the real reason why the book of Jonah is so important. Kabbalists determined that this reading is the most important in the year because it details the code for saving humanity, and this, in the eyes of Kabbalists, is more important than anything.

Jonah's story is special because it speaks of a prophet who first tried to dodge his mission, but finally repented. Another special aspect of Jonah's story is that his mission was not to admonish the people of Israel, but to save the city of Nineveh, whose residents were not Jewish. In light of today's precarious state of the world, we should take a closer look at this story and its meaning for each of us.

Shape Up or Ship Out

God orders Jonah to tell the people of Nineveh, who became very mean to one another, to correct the relationships among them if they want to survive. However, Jonah bailed out of his mission and took to the sea in an effort to escape God's command.

Like Jonah, we Jews have been evading our mission for the past 2,000 years. And yet, we cannot afford to keep evading it. We have a task that was passed on to us when Abraham united us into a nation based on love of others, and it is our duty to set an example of unity for the rest of the world. Abraham wanted to unite all of humanity, but back then he only managed to establish a small group.

That group, namely the people of Israel, must still become a role model to the world. Rav Avraham Itzhak HaCohen Kook (The Raiah), the first Chief Rabbi of Israel, put it poetically in his book, *Orot Kodesh* (Sacred Lights), "Since we were ruined by unfounded hatred, and the world was ruined with us, we will be rebuilt by unfounded love, and the world will be rebuilt with us."

Sleeping through the Storm

In the story, Jonah's escape from his mission by ship caused the sea to roar and nearly sank the vessel. At the height of the storm Jonah went to sleep detaching himself from the turmoil and leaving the sailors to fend for themselves. Gradually, they began to suspect that someone among them was the cause of the storm. They cast a lot and discovered that it was Jonah, the only Jew on board.

In many ways, today's world is similar to Jonah's ship: It has become a global village, as though we're all in one boat, and the sea around us is raging. And the sailors—all of humanity—are blaming the Jew on board for all their troubles.

Like Jonah, we are sound asleep. Though we are beginning to wake up to the existence of hatred toward us, we have yet to realize that not carrying out our mission, just like Jonah, is the reason for the hatred. If we do not wake up soon, the sailors will throw us overboard, as they did with Jonah. In the words of Rav Yehuda Ashlag, author of the *Sulam* (Ladder) commentary on *The Book of Zohar*: "It is incumbent upon the Israeli nation to qualify itself and the rest of the people in the world ... to evolve into assuming this sublime work of love of others" ("The Arvut" (Mutual Guarantee)).

The Wake Up Call

The sailors on Jonah's boat make a desperate attempt to calm the sea, and by Jonah's order they throw him overboard. Once he is in the water, the storm calms, but a whale comes along and swallows Jonah. For three days and three nights he introspects in its abdomen. He begs for his life and promises to carry out his mission.

Like Jonah, each of us carries within something that is stirring up the world. We, the people of Israel, carry a method for achieving peace through connection. Unity is the very root of our being. This DNA is what makes us a people, and today we must rekindle it because wherever we go, this untapped power is destabilizing the world around us in order to compel us to unite.

The unity between us will inspire, even compel, the rest of the nations to follow suit, just as the current separation among us projects separation to the whole of humanity. This is the reason for all our troubles, including anti-Semitism. When we unite, it will endow humanity with the energy required to achieve world-wide unity, where all people live "as one man with one heart." So the only question is whether we assume our responsibility, or prefer to be thrown overboard, only to subsequently agree to carry out our task.

Indeed, if we want to end our troubles and be rid of anti-Semitism, if we desire to turn judgment into mercy and have a safe and happy life, we must unite and thus set an example of unity for all the nations. This is how we will bring peace and quiet to the world. Otherwise the nations' hatred toward us will keep growing. Now we can see why people are willing to pay so much for the privilege of reading the book of Jonah on *Yom Kippur*.

I'd like to conclude this essay with another quote from Rav Kook: "Any turmoil in the world comes only for Israel. Now we are called upon to carry out a great task willingly and mindfully: to build ourselves and the entire ruined world along with us" (*Igrot* [Letters]).

Bibliography

Books

Amikam, Israel. *The Attack on the Jewish Settlement in the Land of Israel, 1929.* Excerpt translated by Chaim Ratz http://www.daat.ac.il/daat/vl/tohen.asp?id=36.

Ashlag, Rav Yehuda (Baal HaSulam). *Ohr HaBahir: Entries in Kabbalah, Judaism, and Jewish Philosophy.* Jerusalem, 1991.

Ashlag, Rav Yehuda (Baal HaSulam). "The Peace." *The Writings of Baal HaSulam.* Vol. 1. Translated by Chaim Ratz. USA: Laitman Kabbalah Publishers, 2019.

Avot de Rabbi Natan

Azulai, Rav Chaim Yosef David. HaCHIDA. *Pnei David.*

Babylonian Talmud, *Masechet Yoma*

Babylonian Talmud, *Megillah*

Baer, Yitzhak. *A History of the Jews in Christian Spain.* Vol. 1. Translated by Louis Schoffman. Illinois, USA: Varda Books, 1961.

Bartal, Israel. *The Jews of Eastern Europe, 1772-1881.* Translated by Chaya Naor. US: University of Pennsylvania Press, 7 June, 2011.

Bauer, Yehuda. *Jews for Sale? Nazi-Jewish Negotiations, 1933-1945.* US: Yale University Press, 1994.

Ben Maimon, Rav Moshe (Maimonides). *Mishneh Torah.* Part 1, "The Book of Science."

Ben Yetzhak, Rabbi Shlomo (RASHI). *The RASHI Interpretation on the Torah.*

Birnbaum, Pierre and Ira Katznelson, eds. *Paths of Emancipation: Jews, States, and Citizenship.* Princeton, NJ: Princeton University Press, 1995.

Black, Edwin. *The Transfer Agreement: The Dramatic Story of the Pact Between the Third Reich and Jewish Palestine.* US: Dialog Press, August 16, 2009.

Black, Jeremy. *The Holocaust: History and Memory.* US: Indiana University Press, 2016.

Bond, Helen K. *Pontius Pilate in history and interpretation.* UK: Cambridge University Press, 1998.

Bornstein, Rabbi Shmuel. *Shem MiShmuel* [A Name Out of Samuel]. *VaYakhel* [And Moses Assembled]. *TAR'AV,* 1916.

Breitman, Richard and Allan J. Lichtman. *FDR and the Jews.* Cambridge, Massachusetts, U.S.: Harvard University Press, 2013.

Bunim, Rav Simcha of Peshischa. *Kol Mevaser.*

Cahill, Thomas. *The Gifts of the Jews: How a Tribe of Desert Nomads Changed the Way Everyone Thinks and Feels.* New York: Nan A. Talese/Anchor Books, 1998.

Connolly, Martin. *The Founding of Israel: The Journey to a Jewish Homeland from Abraham to the Holocaust.* US: Pen & Sword History, 2018. Kindle.

Dąbrowa, Edward, ed. *The Hasmoneans and Their State: A Study in the History, Ideology, and the Institutions.* Poland: Jagiellonian University Press, 2009.

Daniel-Nataf, ed. *Philo of Alexandria, Writings. Vol. 2.* Hebrew ed. Jerusalem 1951.

Derwhowitz, Alan M. *The Vanishing American Jew: In Search of Jewish Identity for the Next Century.* US: Touchstone, 1998.

Midrash Tanah De Bei Eliyahu, Seder Eliyahu Midrash Tanah De Bei. Rabbah.

Elon, Amos. *The Pity of it All: A Portrait of German Jews, 1743-1933.* US: Picador, 2002.

Feldman, Louis H., ed. *Jewish Life and Thought Among Greeks and Romans: Primary Readings.* With contributions by Meyer Reinhold. UK: Augsburg Fortress, February 23, 2009.

Fink, Carole. *West Germany And Israel: Foreign Relations, Domestic Politics, And The Cold War, 1965-1974.* New York: Cambridge University Press, 2019.

Ford, Henry. *The International Jew -- The World's Foremost Problem.* US: The Noontide Press, Early 1920s.

Frankel, Jonathan and Steven J. Zipperstein, eds. *Assimilation and Community: The Jews in Nineteenth-Century Europe.* UK: Cambridge University Press, 2004.

Friedlander, Saul. *Nazi Germany and the Jews: Volume 1: The Years of Persecution 1933-1939.* UK: Orion Books, 1997.

Gabai Ben, Rabbi Meir. *Avodat HaKodesh* [The Holy Work].

Galton, Francis. *Essays in Eugenics: The Eugenics Education Society.* UK: The Eugenics Education Society, 1909.

Gerber, Jane S. Introduction to *Jews of Spain: A History of the Sephardic Experience.* USA: Free Press, 1994.

Goldberg, Jonah. *Liberal Fascism: The Secret History of the American Left, From Mussolini to the Politics of Meaning.* U.S.: Doubleday, 2008.

Gordon, Sarah Ann. *Hitler, Germans, and the Jewish Question.* US: Princeton University Press, 1984.

Grant, Michael. *From Alexander to Cleopatra: the Hellenistic World.* New York: Charles Scribner & Sons, 1982.

Grill, Tobias, ed. "'Pioneers of Germanness in the East'? Jewish-German, German, and Slavic Perceptions of East European Jewry during the First World War." In *Jews and Germans in Eastern Europe: shared and comparative histories.* Germany: CPI books GmbH, Leck, 2018.

Guttstadt, Corry, Thomas Lutz, Bernd Rother, and Yessica San Román, eds. the International Holocaust Remembrance Alliance. *Bystanders, Rescuers or Perpetrators?: The Neutral Countries and the Shoah.* Berlin: Metropol Verlag & IHRA, 2016.

Haberer, Erich E. *Jews and Revolution in Nineteenth-Century Russia.* UK: Cambridge University Press, 2004.

HaCohen Kook, Rav Avraham Yitzchak (Raaiah). *Essays of the Raaiah.*

HaCohen Kook, Rav Avraham Yitzhak (the Raiah). *Orot* [Lights].

HaCohen Kook, Rav Avraham Yitzhak (the Raiah). *Orot HaKodesh.*

Halevi Epstein, Rabbi Kalonymus Kalman. *Maor VaShemesh* [Light and Sun].

Halevi Epstein, Rabbi Kalonymus Kalman. *Maor VaShemesh.* Portion *Nitzavim.*

Herodotos. Vol. 3, Book VII. Translated by A.D. Godley. US: Harvard University Press, The Loeb Classical Library, 1938.

Hitler, Adolf. *Mein Kampf.* US: The Noontide Press: Books On-Line, 2003.

Ingram, Kevin, ed. *Conversos and Moriscos in Late Medieval Spain and Beyond.* Vol. 1, *Departures and Change.* The Netherlands: Brill, 2009.

Jerusalem Talmud. *Masechet Nedarim.*

Jerusalem Talmud. *Rosh Hashanah*, 5b and *Shekalim*, 8a. Online version. Antwerp: Beit Daneil Bombergi, 1523. Shortened url. https://bit.ly/33gYtKF.

Johnson, Paul. *A History of the Jews.* New York: Harper Perennial, 1988.

Josephus, Titus Flavius. *The Antiquities of the Jews.*

Josephus, Titus Flavius. *The Wars of the Jews.*

Kern, Erich Kern, ed. *Verheimlichte Dokumente: Was den Deutschen verschwiegen wird.* Germany: FAZ-Verlag GmbH, 1988.

Kühl, Stefan. *The Nazi Connection: Eugenics, American Racism, and German National Socialism.* U.S.: Oxford University Press, 1994.

Landau, Ithak Eliyahu and Rabbi Shmuel Landau. *Masechet Derech Eretz Zutah.*

Laqueur, Walter, ed. Judith Tydor Baumel, assoc. ed. *The Holocaust Encyclopedia.* US: Yale University Press, 2001.

Lazare, Bernard. *Antisemitism: Its History and Causes.* U.S.: The International Library Publishing Co., September 12, 2013.

Leff, Laurel. *Buried by the Times: The Holocaust and America's Most Important Newspaper.* US: Cambridge University Press, April 10, 2006.

Luntchitz, Shlomo Ephraim ben Aaron. *Kli Yakar.*

Lurye, Solomon Yakovlevich. *Anti-Semitism in the Ancient World*. Translated by Michael Brushtein and Chaim Ratz. Berlin: Z.I. Grzhebina, 1923.

Luther, Martin. *The Jews and Their Lies*. Translated by Martin H. Bertram. Liberty Bell Publications, December 5, 2004. Kindle.

Marcus, Jacob Rader. *The Jew in the Medieval World: A Sourcebook: 315-1791*. US: Atheneum, 1974.

Matas, David. *Aftershock: Anti-Zionism & Anti-Semitism*. Toronto, Canada: Dundurn Press, September 3, 2005.

Medoff, Rafael. *Militant Zionism in America: The Rise and Impact of the Jabotinsky Movement in the United States, 1926–1948*. US: The University of Alabama Press, 2002.

Medoff, Rafael. *The Jews Should Keep Quiet: Franklin D. Roosevelt, Rabbi Stephen S. Wise, and the Holocaust*. US: University of Nebraska Press, 2019.

Midrash Rabbah. Beresheet.

Midrash Rabbah. Kohelet [Eccles.].

Midrash Tanhuma. Nitzavim.

Mishnah. *Mesechet Bikurim.*

Mommsen, Theodor. *The History of Rome*. Vol. IV. Translated by William Purdie Dickson. New York: Macmillan and Co., Limited, 1901.

Nahum, Rabbi Menahem of Chernobyl. *Maor Eynaim*. Portion *VaYetzeh*.

Nicosia, Francis R. and David Scrase, eds. *Jewish Life in Nazi Germany: Dilemmas and Responses*. NY: US: Berghahn Books, 2010.

Nicosia, Francis R. *The Third Reich and the Palestine Question*. 3rd paperback printing. US: New Brunswick, 2013.

Nicosia, Francis R. *Zionism and Anti-Semitism in Nazi Germany*. NY: Cambridge University Press, 2008.

Niewyk, Donald L. *The Jews in Weimar Germany*. Brunswick, New Jersey: Transactions Publishers, 2001.

Ogilvie, Sarah A. and Scott Miller. *Refuge Denied: The St. Louis Passengers and the Holocaust*. US: University of Wisconsin Press, 2006.

Pirkey de Rabbi Eliezer [Chapters of Rabbi Eliezer].

Porter, Anna. *Kasztner's Train: The True Story of an Unknown Hero of the Holocaust.* U.S.: Bloomsbury, 2009.

Raphael, David. *Expulsion 1492 Chronicles: An Anthology of Medieval Chronicles Relating to the Expulsion of the Jews from Spain and Portugal.* Translation of edict, David Raphael. USA: Carmi House Publishing. February 1, 1992.

Rapoport, Louis. *Shake Heaven & Earth: Peter Bergson and the Struggle to Rescue the Jews of Europe.* US: Gefen Publishing, May 1999.

Rawidowicz, Simon. *Israel, the Ever-Dying People, and Other Essays.* NJ, USA: Fairleigh Dickinson University, Pr, October 1, 1986.

Reinharz, Jehuda and Yaacov Shavit. *The Road to September 1939: Polish Jews, Zionists, and the Yishuv on the Eve of World War II.* Translated by Michal Sapir. US: Brandeis University Press, 2018.

Rockwell, George Lincoln. *White Power.* PDF file. Reproduced by the American Nazi Party. Chap. 15, "National Socialism."

Rose, Norman. *'A Senseless, Squalid War': Voices from Palestine; 1890s to 1948.* UK: Pimlico, 2010.

Roth, Cecil. *A History of the Marranos.* 5th ed. NY: Sepher-Hermon Press, 1992.

Roth, Norman. *Conversos, Inquisition, and the Expulsion of the Jews from Spain.* London, England: The University of Wisconsin Press, 2002.

Roth, Norman. *Jews, Visigoths, and Muslims in Medieval Spain: cooperation and conflict.* The Netherlands: E.J. Brill, 1994.

Shapira, Anita. "The Religious Motifs of the Labor Movement." In *Zionism and Religion.* US: Brandeis University Press, 1998.

Schiffman, Lawrence H. *From Text to Tradition, a History of Judaism in Second Temple and Rabbinic Times: A History of Second Temple and Rabbinic Judaism.* Hoboken, NJ: Ktav Publishing House, 1991.

Sefer HaYashar [The Book of the Upright One]. Portion Noah.

Shulgin, Vasily Vitalyevich. *What We Don't Like About Them...* Translated by Michael Brushtein and Chaim Ratz. St. Petersburg, Russia: Horse, 1992.

Sifrey Devarim (a *Midrash* attributed to Rabbi Akiva).

Solzhenitsyn, Aleksandr Isayevich. *Two Hundred Years Together: On Russian-Jewish Relations, 1795-1995.* Translated by Shelly Gaver. eBook.

Sternhartz, Rabbi Nathan. *Likutey Halachot* [Assorted Rules].

Tacitus. *The Histories.* Translated by Clifford H. Moore. Book V. VIII-IX. London: The Loeb Classical Library, William Heinemann LTD, 1914.

Rabbi Shimon bar Yochai, *The Book of Zohar* with the *Sulam* [Ladder] commentary by Rav Yehuda Ashlag. 10 Vol. ed., Vol. 4.

Rabbi Shimon bar Yochai, *The Book of Zohar* with the *Sulam* [Ladder] commentary by Rav Yehuda Ashlag. 21 Vol. ed. Vol. 19.

The First Book of the Maccabees (1 Macc).

The Second Book of the Maccabees (2 Macc).

Thomas, Gordon and Max Morgon-Witts. *Voyage Of The Damned: A Shocking True Story of Hope, Betrayal, and Nazi Terror.* US: Skyhorse Publishing, 2010.

Torat Emet. "The Days of Purim in the *Halacha* and *Agada*."

Weizmann, Chaim. *The Letters and Papers of Chaim Weizmann: August 1898-July 1931.* Vol. 1., edited by Barnet Litvinoff. New Brunswick, N.J.: Transaction Books, Rutgers University, 1983.

Wistrich, Robert S. *From Ambivalence to Betrayal: The Left, the Jews, and Israel.* USA: University of Nebraska Press, June 2012.

Yosef, Rav Ovadia. *Yalkut Yosef.*

Official Documents, Online Resources, Newspapers, and Academic Papers

Abramsky, Chimen. "Weizmann: A New Type of Leadership in the Zionist Movement." *Transactions & Miscellanies. Jewish Historical Society of England* 25. (1973): 137-49. http://www.jstor.org/stable/29778841.

Augstein, Rudolf. "Israel soll Leben." *Der Spiegel* 25. June 12, 1967.

Aide-Mémoire. "The British Embassy to the Department of State." *Foreign Relations of the United States: Diplomatic Papers, 1943, General.* Vol. 1. 840.48. Refugees/3633. https://history.state.gov/historicaldocuments/frus1943v01/d103.

"Anti-Semitism in Germany: Historical Background." *Minnesota State University.* http://web.mnstate.edu/shoptaug/AntiFrames.htm.

"Anti-Semitism: The Hep Hep Riots." *Jewish Virtual Library*. https://www. jewishvirtuallibrary.org/hep-hep-riots.

Bailin, Barbara L. "The Influence of Anti-Semitism on United States Immigration Policy With respect to German Jews During 1933-1939." (2011). *CUNY Academic Works*. 50. https://academicworks.cuny.edu/cc_etds_theses/262.

Battenberg, Friedrich. "Jewish Emancipation in the 18th and 19th Centuries." *European History Online*. August 25, 2017. http://ieg-ego.eu/en/ threads/european-networks/jewish-networks/friedrich-battenberg-jewish-emancipation-in-the-18th-and-19th-centuries.

Boas, Jacob. "A Nazi Travels to Palestine." *History Today* 30. No. 1. (January 1980). https://www.historytoday.com/archive/nazi-travels-palestine.

Bundestag, Deutscher. 5 Wahlperiode. 111 Sitzung. Bonn. StenBer. June 7, 1967: 5270, 5272 73, 5276 77, 5292, 5297, 5301 2, 5308 9, 5317 18, 5321, 5321, 5330.

"Complete List of Jewish Expulsions (908) (with explanations and sources)." *Internet Archive*. https://archive.org/details/900jewishexpulsions.

"Congress Gets Bill Opening Alaska to Settlement by Refugees of 16 to 45." *Jewish Telegraphic Agency Archive*. March 17, 1940. https://www.jta. org/1940/03/17/archive/congress-gets-bill-opening-alaska-to-settlement-by-refugees-of-16-to-45.

Culbertson, Katherine E. "American Wartime Indifference to the Plight of the European Jews." Hanover College – History Department. https://history. hanover.edu/hhr/94/hhr94_5.html.

"Das Protokoll der Wannsee-Konferenz." *House of the Wannsee Conference, Memorial and Educational Site*. https://www.ghwk.de/ fileadmin/user_upload/pdf-wannsee/dokumente/protokoll-januar1942_ barrierefrei.pdf.

Das Schwarze Korps. Jewish Virtual Library. https://www.jewishvirtuallibrary. org/das-schwarze-korps.

Dershowitz, Alan. "Dershowitz: Anti-Semitic cartoons, anti-Semitic synagogue shootings." *The Hill*. April 29, 2019. https://thehill.com/opinion/ civil-rights/441112-dershowitz-anti-semitic-cartoons-anti-semitic-synagogue-shootings.

"December 13, 1942, Goebbels complains of Italians' treatment of Jews," *This Day in History*, in *History*. https://www.history.com/this-day-in-history/ goebbels-complains-of-italians-treatment-of-jews.

Deutsch, Gotthard and Krauss, Samuel. "Procurators." *Jewish Encyclopedia*. 1906 ed. http://www.jewishencyclopedia.com/articles/12376-procurators.

Eshkoli Hava, "Zionism in the Land of israel and Its Relation to Nazism and the Third Reich: Historiographic Aspects (1932-1939)" [Hebrew]. *Yad Vashem—The World Holocaust Remembrance Center.*

"Establishment of Israel: The Declaration of the Establishment of the State of Israel." *Jewish Virtual Library.* https://www.jewishvirtuallibrary.org/the-declaration-of-the-establishment-of-the-state-of-israel.

"Evian Barred Mass Exodus, Rabbi Wise Declares." *Jewish Telegraphic Agency.* July 22, 1938. https://www.jta.org/1938/07/22/archive/evian-barred-mass-exodus-rabbi-wise-declares.

Fox News Videos. March 9, 2019, https://www.yahoo.com/news/alan-dershowitz-democrats-made-terrible-055238117.html.

Geggel, Laura. "1.32 Million Jews Were Killed in Just Three Months During the Holocaust." January 4, 2019. https://www.livescience.com/64420-holocaust-jewish-deaths.html.

Gelber, Yoav. "Zionist Policy and the Transfer Agreement 1933-1935." *Yalkut Moreshet* 17. February 1974.

Gottheil, Richard and Louis Ginzberg. "Archelaus." *Jewish Encyclopedia*. 1906 ed. http://www.jewishencyclopedia.com/articles/1729-archelaus.

Gottheil, Richard and Samuel Krauss. "Porcius Festus." *Jewish Encyclopedia*. 1906 ed. http://www.jewishencyclopedia.com/articles/6100-festus-porcius.

Gray, Eric William. "Pompey the Great, Roman Statesman." *Encyclopedia Britannica*. https://www.britannica.com/biography/Pompey-the-Great.

Grill, Tobias, ed. "'Pioneers of Germanness in the East'? Jewish-German, German, and Slavic Perceptions of East European Jewry during the First World War." In *Jews and Germans in Eastern Europe: shared and comparative histories*. Germany: CPI books GmbH, Leck, 2018.

"Günter Grass Says Jews Gain German Respect." *New York Times*. July 3, 1967: 5.

Haus Der Wannsee-Konferenz. "Dokumente zur Wannsee-Konferenz." https://www.ghwk.de/wannsee-konferenz/dokumente-zur-wannsee-konferenz.

Herodotos. Vol. 3, Book VII. Translated by A.D. Godley. US: Harvard University Press, The Loeb Classical Library, 1938.

Horsley, Richard A. "The Sicarii: Ancient Jewish 'Terrorists.'" *The Journal of Religion.* Vol. 59. No. 4. (October 1979): 435-458. University of Chicago Press. https://www.jstor.org/stable/1202887.

"Italy." United States Holocaust Memorial Museum. *Holocaust Encyclopedia* https://encyclopedia.ushmm.org/content/en/article/italy.

"Jewish Bodies See No Solution in Mass Emigration." *Jewish Telegraphic Agency Archive.* July 11, 1938. https://www.jta.org/1938/07/11/archive/jewish-bodies-see-no-solution-in-mass-emigration.

Jones, Nigel Jones. "The Assassination of Walther Rathenau." *History Today.* Vol. 63, No. 7. (July 2013). https://www.historytoday.com/archive/history-matters/assassination-walther-rathenau.

Kovac, Adam. "A New Plague at the Seder: Politics." *MEL.* (June 2019). https://melmagazine.com/en-us/story/a-new-plague-at-the-seder-politics.

Laffer, Dennis Ross. "The Jewish Trail of Tears The Evian Conference of July 1938." *Graduate Theses and Dissertations,* (2001). http://scholarcommons.usf.edu/etd/3195.

Lebovic, Matt. "How to explain the 'timid' reaction of American Jewish leaders to Kristallnacht?" *The Times of Israel.* November 10, 2018 https://www.timesofisrael.com/how-to-explain-the-timid-reaction-of-american-jewish-leaders-to-kristallnacht.

Letter from Stephen Wise, President, American Jewish Congress, to President Franklin D. Roosevelt; 12/2/1942; OF 76-c: Jewish 1942 - July 1943 (Church Matters). Collection FDR-FDRPOF: President's Official Files (Roosevelt Administration). Record Group Franklin D. Roosevelt President's Official Files, 1933 - 1945. Franklin D. Roosevelt Library. Hyde Park, NY. October 23, 2019. Online version. https://www.docsteach.org/documents/document/american-jewish-congress-fdr.

Link, Stefan. "Rethinking the Ford-Nazi Connection." *German Historical Institute. Washington, D.C.* https://www.ghi-dc.org/fileadmin/user_upload/GHI_Washington/Publications/Bulletin49/bu49_135.pdf.

Lipstadt, Deborah E. "Playing the Blame Game: American Jews Look Back at the Holocaust." Vol. 18. 2011 http://hdl.handle.net/2027/spo.13469761.0018.001.

Lowenstein, Steven M. "Jewish Intermarriage and Conversion in Germany and Austria." 24, https://www.researchgate.net/publication/265770066_Jewish_Intermarriage_in_Germany_and_Austria.

"Madagascar Plan." *Yad Vashem—The World Holocaust Remembrance Center.* https://www.yadvashem.org/odot_pdf/Microsoft%20Word%20-%206635.pdf.

Marr, Wilhelm. *The Victory of Judaism over Germandom.* March 1879 http://ghdi.ghi-dc.org/sub_document.cfm?document_id=1797.

Maryks, Robert A. "Purity of Blood." *Oxford Bibliographies.* DOI: 10.1093/OBO/9780195399301-0101. https://www.oxfordbibliographies.com/view/document/obo-9780195399301/obo-9780195399301-0101.xml.

Medoff, Rafael. "FDR Had His Kissinger, Too." The David S. Wyman Institute for Holocaust Studies. *Encyclopedia of America's Response to the Holocaust.* http://new.wymaninstitute.org/2010/12/fdr-had-his-kissinger-too.

Medoff, Rafael. "New York Times Column on Anti-Zionism a Reminder of its Own Publisher's Past." February 18, 2014. http://www.algemeiner.om/2014/02/18/new-york-times-column-on-anti-zionism-a-reminder-of-its-own-publisher's-past/.

Medoff, Rafael. "Why the Rabbi said: 'Eat bread on Passover.'" *Arutz Sheva – Israel National News.* April 21, 2016. http://www.israelnationalnews.com/Articles/Article.aspx/18754.

Medoff, Raphael. "A Thanksgiving plan to save Europe's Jews." *The Jewish Standard.* November 16, 2007 https://jewishstandard.timesofisrael.com/a-thanksgiving-plan-to-save-europes-jews.

Memorandum of Conversation. Under Secretary of State (Welles). *Office of the Historian, Foreign Relations of the United States Diplomatic Papers,* 1938, General. Vol. 1. November 17, 1938. https://history.state.gov/historicaldocuments/frus1938v01/d803.

Mikics, David Mikics. "The Jews Who Stabbed Germany in the Back." *Tablet.* November 9, 2017. https://www.tabletmag.com/jewish-arts-and-culture/books/248615/jews-who-stabbed-germany-in-the-back.

Naimark, Norman M. *Shofar* 16. No. 2. (1998): 117-19. http://www.jstor.org/stable/42942734.

"Nuremberg Race Laws." *United States Holocaust Memorial Museum* (USHMM). https://encyclopedia.ushmm.org/content/en/article/nuremberg-laws.

Palestine Royal Commission Report. PDF file. July 1937. https://palestinianmandate.files.wordpress.com/2014/04/cm-5479.pdf.

Perl, William R. "The Holocaust and the Lost Caribbean Paradise." *Foundation for Economic Education.* January 1, 1992. https://fee.org/articles/the-holocaust-and-the-lost-caribbean-paradise.

Perl. "The Holocaust and the Lost Caribbean Paradise." https://fee.org/articles/the-holocaust-and-the-lost-caribbean-paradise.

"Population of Chicago." *US Population. 2019.* https://uspopulation2019.com/population-of-chicago-2019.html.

Press Release: "The Big Lie Of Israeli 'Organ Harvesting' Resurfaces As YouTube Video On Haiti Earthquake Goes Global." *Anti-Defamation League.* January 21, 2010 http://www.adl.org/press-center/press-releases/miscellaneous/the-big-lie-of-israeli-organ.html.

"Principles." *The American Council for Judaism.* http://www.acjna.org/acjna/about_principles.aspx.

"Reich Migrants to Palestine Get Back 42% of Funds in Cash." Jewish Telegraphic Agency. May 25, 1936. https://www.jta.org/1936/05/25/archive/reich-migrants-to-palestine-get-back-42-of-funds-in-cash..

"Riots in Palestine." *The Sunday Times.* Perth, Western Australia ed. October 29, 1933: 3. https://trove.nla.gov.au/newspaper/article/58707344.

"Roosevelt Named to Receive American Hebrew's Good Will Medal." *Jewish Telegraphic Agency.* December 23, 1938. https://www.jta.org/1938/12/23/archive/roosevelt-named-to-receive-american-hebrews-good-will-medal.

"Rublee Sees 'unprecedented Difficulties' in Refugee Bureau's Task." *Jewish Telegraphic Agency.* September 22, 1938. https://www.jta.org/1938/09/22/archive/rublee-sees-unprecedented-difficulties-in-refugee-bureaus-task.

Shapira, Anita. "The Religious Motifs of the Labor Movement." In *Zionism and Religion.* US: Brandeis University Press, 1998.

Sharfman, Glenn R. "Jewish Emancipation." *Encyclopedia of 1848 Revolutions.* Ohio University. https://www.ohio.edu/chastain/ip/jewemanc.htm.

Shimon, Dr. Zvi. "The Exile in Egypt - Process or Punishment." *The Israel Koschitzky Virtual Beit Midrash.* https://www.etzion.org.il/en/exile-egypt-process-or-punishment.

Sokol, Sam Sokol. "'Institutional Anti-Semitism' Exists In the US, Expert Says." *JPost*. February 19, 2015. https://www.jpost.com/Diaspora/Institutional-anti-Semitism-exists-in-the-US-expert-says-391584.

Soresky, Aaron. "The ADMOR, Rabbi Yehuda Leib Ashlag ZATZUKAL—Baal HaSulam: 30ᵗʰ Anniversary of His Departure." *Hamodia*. Tishrey. TASHMAV. September 24, 1985.

"Spain Virtual Jewish History Tour." "Massacre of 1391." *Jewish Virtual Library*. https://www.jewishvirtuallibrary.org/spain-virtual-jewish-history-tour.

Stern, Marlow. "'Reporting on the Times' Calls Out New York Times Holocaust Coverage." *Daily Beast*. April 18, 2013. https://www.thedailybeast.com/reporting-on-the-times-calls-out-new-york-times-holocaust-coverage.

Stone, Kurt F. "The Amazing Sol Bloom." *The K.F. Stone Weekly*. https://kurtfstone.typepad.com/kurt_f_stone_speaks_/2006/07/the_amazing_sol.html.

"The 29ᵗʰ of November." *The Knesset, Occasions*. https://www.knesset.gov.il/holidays/eng/29nov_e.htm.

"The Chargé in Germany (Gilbert) to the Secretary of State." 840.48 Refugees/1381: Telegram, received February 4, 1939. *Office of the Historian*. https://history.state.gov/historicaldocuments/frus1939v02/d57.

The Editorial Board. "The Oldest Hatred." *The Wall Street Journal*. October 28, 2018. https://www.wsj.com/articles/the-oldest-hatred-1540760984.

The Editors of Encyclopaedia Britannica. "Anschluss." *Encyclopedia Britannica*. https://www.britannica.com/event/Anschluss.

"The Nazis & the Jews: The Madagascar Plan." *Jewish Virtual Library*. https://www.jewishvirtuallibrary.org/the-madagascar-plan-2.

"The Secretary of State to the Ambassador in the United Kingdom (Kennedy)." 840.48. Refugees/1662: Telegram. June 12, 1939. https://history.state.gov/historicaldocuments/frus1939v02/d100.

"The Secretary of State to the President." *Foreign Relations of the United States, Conferences at Washington and Quebec, 1943*. 840.48. Refugees/4034½. May 22, 1943. https://history.state.gov/historicaldocuments/frus1943/d142#fn:1.5.4.4.22.38.10.14.4.

"The Spanish Inquisition." *Encyclopedia Britannica*. https://www.britannica.com/place/Spain/The-Spanish-Inquisition#ref587472.

The United States Holocaust Memorial Museum. "The Weimar Republic." https://encyclopedia.ushmm.org/content/en/article/the-weimar-republic.

Tolstoy, Leo. "What is the Jew?" Quoted in "The Final Resolution." *Jewish World* (1908).

"Tomás De Torquemada." *Encyclopedia of World Biography.* The Gale Group Inc. 2004.), https://www.encyclopedia.com/people/history/spanish-and-portuguese-history-biographies/tomas-de-torquemada.

"'Transfer Agreement' and the Boycott of German Goods." *The National Library of Israel.* https://web.nli.org.il/sites/nli/english/collections/personalsites/israel-germany/world-war-2/pages/haavara-agreement.aspx.

Twain, Mark. "Concerning The Jews." *The Complete Essays of Mark Twain.* U.S.: Doubleday, 1963. Published 1899 by *Harper's Magazine.*

Verbovszky, Joseph. "Leopold von Mildenstein and the Jewish Question." Case Western Reserve University, May 2013: 6. https://etd.ohiolink.edu/!etd.send_file?accession=case1365174634&disposition=inline.

"Voyage of the St. Louis." *United States Holocaust Memorial Museum.* https://encyclopedia.ushmm.org/content/en/article/voyage-of-the-st-louis.

Vulliamy, Ed. "How Trump's presidency has divided Jewish America." November 14, 2018. https://www.theguardian.com/us-news/2018/nov/14/american-jewish-community-divisions-trump-pittsburgh.

Wallace, Donald Mackenzie. "Alexander II." *The Encyclopedia Britannica*, Vol. 1. UK: Cambridge, England, 1910.

"Wannsee Protocol." Based on the official U.S. government translation prepared for evidence in trials at Nuremberg, as reproduced in John Mendelsohn, ed. The Holocaust: Selected Documents in Eighteen Volumes. Vol. 11: The Wannsee Protocol and a 1944 Report on Auschwitz by the Office of Strategic Services. New York: Garland, 1982.

Wannsee Protocol. January 20, 1942. Translation based on the official U.S. government translation prepared for evidence in trials at Nuremberg. http://prorev.com/wannsee.htm.

Weiss, Yfaat. "The Transfer Agreement and the Boycott Movement: A Jewish Dilemma on the Eve of the Holocaust." Translated by Naftali Greenwood. *Yad Vashem—The World Holocaust Remembrance Center.* https://www.yadvashem.org/odot_pdf/Microsoft%20Word%20-%203231.pdf.

Wells, Summer. "The Hall of Holography Collection." *Abraham Lincoln Library and Museum*. Object ID:03.0003.140. https://www.lmunet.edu/uploads/OnlineResources/virtual_exhibit1/vex2/2910C8A7-DF50-4795-BF9C-234221359603.htm.

Whalen, Robert Weldon. "War Losses (Germany)." *International Encyclopedia of the First World War*. https://encyclopedia.1914-1918-online.net/article/war_losses_germany.

Yad Vashem—The World Holocaust Remembrance Center. https://www.yadvashem.org/odot_pdf/Microsoft%20Word%20-%201201.pdf.

Zalman, Amy. "The Sicarii: First Century Terrorists." *ThoughtCo*. July 3, 2019. https://www.thoughtco.com/sicarii-first-century-terrorists-3209152.

Ziri, Danielle. "D.C. Dyke March Bans Israeli and Jewish Symbols on Pride Flags, Sparking Criticism." *Haaretz*. June 6, 2019. https://www.haaretz.com/us-news/.premium-d-c-dyke-march-bans-israeli-and-jewish-symbols-on-pride-flags-sparking-criticism-1.7339707.

Notes

1   *Herodotos*, vol. 3, Book VII, 133 [trans. A. D. GODLEY] (US, Harvard University Press, The Loeb Classical Library, 1938), 435.

2   Recordings of my conversations and lectures from the October-November 2014 US tour are kept in the Bnei Baruch archive and will be given at no cost to anyone who asks for them.

3   Alan M. Dershowitz, *The Vanishing American Jew: In Search of Jewish Identity for the Next Century* (US: Touchstone, 1998), 6.

4   Ibid., 12.

5   Alan Dershowitz, "Dershowitz: Anti-Semitic cartoons, anti-Semitic synagogue shootings," *The Hill* (April 29, 2019), https://thehill.com/opinion/civil-rights/441112-dershowitz-anti-semitic-cartoons-anti-semitic-synagogue-shootings.

6   Mark Twain, "Concerning The Jews," in *The Complete Essays of Mark Twain* (published in *Harper's Magazine*, 1899) (U.S.: Doubleday, 1963), 249.

7   By: The Editorial Board, "The Oldest Hatred," *The Wall Street Journal* (October 28, 2018)https://www.wsj.com/articles/the-oldest-hatred-1540760984.

8   Press Release: "The Big Lie Of Israeli 'Organ Harvesting' Resurfaces As YouTube Video On Haiti Earthquake Goes Global," *Anti-Defamation League* (January 21, 2010), http://www.adl.org/press-center/press-releases/miscellaneous/the-big-lie-of-israeli-organ.html.

9   David Matas, *Aftershock: Anti-Zionism & Anti-Semitism* (Toronto, Dundurn Press, September 3, 2005), 118.

10 "The Jewish religion, mother of Christianity, grandmother of Mahometism, [was] beaten by her son and grandson." François Voltaire, *Le Sottisier de Voltaire* (Paris: Librairie des Bibliophiles, 1880), XXXIX. https://archive.org/details/lesottisierdevol00volt/page/n47.

11 Allan Arkush, "Voltaire on Judaism and Christianity." AJS Review18, no. 2 (1993): 223-43, p. 2, www.jstor.org/stabl e/1486572. "[Arthur] Hertzberg emphasizes that the misdeed for which Voltaire places the greatest blame on the Jews is the propagation of the Christian religion."

12 *Sefer HaYashar* [The Book of the Upright One], Portion Noah, *Parasha* 13, Item 3.

13 For much more on the dualism between egoism and altruism in nature and in human society, see my book from 2011, *Self-Interest vs. Altruism in the Global Era: How society can turn self-interests into mutual benefit.*

14 Rav Yehuda Ashlag (Baal HaSulam), *Ohr HaBahir: Entries in Kabbalah, Judaism, and Jewish philosophy* (Jerusalem: 1991), 212, 336.

15 Rav Yehuda Ashlag (Baal HaSulam), "The Peace" in *The Writings of Baal HaSulam*, vol. 1, trans. Chaim Ratz (USA, Laitman Kabbalah Publishers, 2019), 68.

16 Rav Moshe Ben Maimon (Maimonides), *Mishneh Torah*, Part 1, "The Book of Science," chap. 1, Item 1.

17 Maimonides, *Mishneh Torah*, Part 1, "The Book of Science," chap. 1, Item 10.3.

18 *Pirkey de Rabbi Eliezer* [*Chapters of Rabbi Eliezer*], chap. 24.

19 Ibid.

20 Rav Simcha Bunim of Peshischa, *Kol Mevaser*, Part 2, "Dictionary."

21 Thomas Cahill, *The Gifts of the Jews: How a Tribe of Desert Nomads Changed the Way Everyone Thinks and Feels* (New York: Nan A. Talese/ Anchor Books, 1998), 63-64.

22 Maimonides, *Mishneh Torah*, Part 1, "The Book of Science," chap. 1, Item 12.3.

23 *Midrash Rabbah, Beresheet*, Portion 38, Item 13.

24 Maimonides, *Mishneh Torah*, Part 1, "The Book of Science," chap. 1, Item 15.3.

25 Maimonides, *Mishneh Torah*, Part 1, "The Book of Science," chap. 1, Item 16.

26 Ibid.

27   Rabbi Meir Ben Gabai, *Avodat HaKodesh* [The Holy Work], Part 3, chap. 27.

28   *Midrash Rabbah, Kohelet* [Ecclesiastes], Portion 1, para. 34.

29   Rabbi Nathan Sternhartz, *Likutey Halachot* [*Assorted Rules*], "Blessings on Seeing and Personal Blessings," Rule no. 4.

30   Rabbi Shlomo Ben Yitzhak (RASHI), *The RASHI Interpretation on the Torah*, "On Exodus," 19:2.

31   Isaiah 42:6.

32   *Midrash Tanah De Bei Eliyahu, Seder Eliyahu Rabbah*, chap. 28.

33   Midrash *Tanhuma, Nitzavim*, chap. 1

34   Rabbi Kalonymus Kalman Halevi Epstein, *Maor VaShemesh* [Light and Sun], *Nitzavim*.

35   Ithak Eliyahu Landau, Rabbi Shmuel Landau, *Masechet Derech Eretz Zutah*, chap. 9, Items 28-29 (Vilna: Printer: Rabbi Hillel, 1872), 57-58.

36   Ashlag, *The Writings of Baal HaSulam*, vol. 1, "The Freedom," 95.

37   Henry Ford, *The International Jew -- The World's Foremost Problem* (US, The Noontide Press, Early 1920s), 8.

38   Ibid., 7.

39   Vasily Vitalyevich Shulgin, *What We Don't Like About Them...*, trans. Michael Brushtein & Chaim Ratz (St. Petersburg Russia, Horse, 1992), 209.

40   Shulgin, *What We Don't Like About Them...*, 219.

41   "JUIF? Selon Alain Soral," [trans. Noga Bar Noye], infolive tv, October 17, 2014, https://www.youtube.com/watch?v=PlBBZmLYTp4.

42   George Lincoln Rockwell, *White Power* (PDF reproduced by the American Nazi Party), chap. 15, "National Socialism," 263.

43   Paul Johnson, *A History of the Jews* (New York: Harper Perennial, 1988), 84.

44   Rabbi Shlomo Ben Yitzhak (RASHI), *The RASHI Interpretation on the Torah*, "On Exodus," 19:2.

45   Jerusalem Talmud, *Nedarim* 30b.

46   Sternhartz, *Likutey Halachot*, "Rules of *Tefilat Arvit* [Evening Prayer]," Rule no. 4.

47   Isaiah 42:6.

48   Genesis 37:7.

49 Dr. Zvi Shimon, "The Exile in Egypt - Process or Punishment," *The Israel Koschitzky Virtual Beit Midrash*, https://www.etzion.org.il/en/exile-egypt-process-or-punishment.

50 Rabbi Shimon bar Yochai, *The Book of Zohar* with the *Sulam* [Ladder] commentary by Rav Yehuda Ashlag (10 vol. ed.), vol. 4, Portion *Shemot*, Item 250, 78.

51 *Midrash Rabbah, Shemot* 1:8.

52 Rabbi Shimon bar Yochai, *The Book of Zohar* with the Sulam [Ladder] commentary by Rav Yehuda Ashlag (21 vol. ed.), *Beshalach*, Item 252, 73.

53 Johnson, *A History of the Jews*, 84.

54 Ibid.

55 Babylonian Talmud, *Masechet Yoma* 9b.

56 Ibid.

57 Titus Flavius Josephus, *The Antiquities of the Jews*, trans. William Whiston, Book IX, chap. 5.

58 Ibid., chap. 6.

59 Josephus, *The Antiquities of the Jews*, Book X, chap. 3.

60 Shlomo Ephraim ben Aaron Luntschitz, *Kli Yakar*, "About Shemot 17," Item 8.

61 Rav Ovadia Yosef, *Yalkut Yosef*, Mark 699, Item 4, "Rules of Mishloach Manot"[sending gifts on Purim].

62 Rav Chaim Yosef David Azulai (HaCHIDA), Pnei David – Al HaTorah, Ki Tissa.

63 Torat Emet, "The Days of Purim in the Halacha and Agada," chap. 7, "The Three Days of Fasting."

64 Babylonian Talmud, *Yoma* 9b.

65 Ashlag, "Exile and Redemption," in *The Writings of Baal HaSulam*, 1, 157.

66 Josephus, *The Antiquities of the Jews*, Book IV, chap. 8.

67 Mishnah, *Mesechet Bikurim*, chap. 3.

68 *Avot de Rabbi Natan*, chap. 35, 1.

69 Philo of Alexandria, "About the Laws and Their Details," Part 1, Items 69-70, in *Philo of Alexandria, Writings*, Hebrew ed., ed. Susan Daniel-Nataf, Jerusalem 1951, vol. 2, 245.

70   *Sifrey Devarim*, Item 354.

71   Johnson, *A History of the Jews*, 87.

72   *The Zohar* with the *Sulam* [Ladder] commentary (21 vol. ed.), vol. 14 [excerpt translated by Chaim Ratz], *Aharei Mot*, Items 65-66, 20-21.

73   Josephus, *The Antiquities of the Jews*, Book XII, chap. 2, Item 1.

74   Ibid.

75   Ibid.

76   Ibid.

77   Ibid.

78   Ibid.

79   Ibid.

80   *Philo*, vol. 1 [trans. F.H. Colson], "Moses" (U.S.: The Loeb Classical Library, Harvard University Press, 5th printing, 1984), 465.

81   Josephus, *The Antiquities of the Jews*, Book XII, chap. 2.

82   Ibid.

83   Babylonian Talmud, *Megillah*, 9a.

84   Josephus, *The Antiquities of the Jews*, Book XII, chap. 2.

85   Johnson, *A History of the Jews*, 2.

86   Josephus, *The Antiquities of the Jews*, Book XII, chap. 3.

87   Johnson, *A History of the Jews*, 98.

88   Johnson, *A History of the Jews*, 100.

89   Ibid., 101.

90   Ibid., 102.

91   Ibid., 102.

92   Josephus, *The Antiquities of the Jews*, Book XII, chap. 5.

93   Ibid.

94   Ibid.

95   Ibid.

96   Johnson, *A History of the Jews*, 103.

97   The First Book of the Maccabees (1 Macc), 1:10, 1, https://ebible.org/pdf/eng-kjv/eng-kjv_1MA.pdf.

98   1 Macc, 1:36, 4.

99   1 Macc, 1:41-43, 4.

100   The Second Book of the Maccabees (2 Macc), 4:50, 17, https://ebible.org/
        pdf/eng-kjv/eng-kjv_2MA.pdf.

101   Josephus, *The Antiquities of the Jews*, Book XII, chap. 6.

102   Ibid.

103   Ibid.

104   Ibid.

105   Ibid.

106   Edward Dąbrowa [Ed.], *The Hasmoneans and Their State: A Study in the
        History, Ideology, and the Institutions* (Poland: Jagiellonian University
        Press, 2009), 21.

107   Josephus, *The Antiquities of the Jews*, Book XII, chap. 7.

108   Ibid.

109   Lawrence H. Schiffman, *From Text to Tradition: A History of Second
        Temple and Rabbinic Judaism* Hoboken, (NJ: Ktav Publishing House,
        1991), 78.

110   Ibid.

111   Josephus, *The Antiquities of the Jews*, Book XII, chap. 9.

112   Ibid.

113   Ibid.

114   Ibid.

115   Ibid.

116   Johnson, *A History of the Jews*, 84.

117   Johnson, *A History of the Jews*, 108.

118   Ibid.

119   Ibid.

120   Josephus, *The Antiquities of the Jews*, Book XIII, chap. 16, Item 1.

121   Ibid.

122   Ibid., Item 2.

123   Ibid., Item 1.

124 Theodor Mommsen, *The History of Rome*, vol. IV [trans. William Purdie Dickson] (New York: Macmillan and Co., Limited, 1901), 424.

125 Johnson, *A History of the Jews*, 107.

126 Eric William Gray, "Pompey the Great, Roman Statesman," *Encyclopedia Britannica*, https://www.britannica.com/biography/Pompey-the-Great.

127 Mommsen, *The History of Rome*, vol. IV, 448.

128 Richard Gottheil, Louis Ginzberg, "Archelaus," *Jewish Encyclopedia* (1906 edition), http://www.jewishencyclopedia.com/articles/1729-archelaus.

129 Ibid.

130 Ibid.

131 Ibid.

132 Josephus, *The Antiquities of the Jews*, Book XIII, chap. 2, Item 2.

133 Gotthard Deutsch, Samuel Krauss, "Procurators," *Jewish Encyclopedia* (1906 edition), http://www.jewishencyclopedia.com/articles/12376-procurators.

134 Josephus, *The Wars of the Jews*, Book II, chap. 9, Item 2.

135 Philo, vol. X (trans. F.H. Colson), The Loeb Classical Library (London, England: Harvard University Press, 1962 [reprinted 1971, 1991]), 151.

136 Ibid.

137 Ibid., 151-152.

138 Ibid., 153.

139 Josephus, *The Antiquities of the Jews*, Book XX, chap. 5, Item 1.

140 Ibid.

141 Deutsch, Krauss, "Procurators," *Jewish Encyclopedia* (1906 edition), http://www.jewishencyclopedia.com/articles/12376-procurators.

142 Josephus, *The Wars of the Jews*, Book II, chap. 11, Item 6.

143 Josephus, *The Wars of the Jews*, Book II, chap. 12, Item 1.

144 Tacitus, *The Histories* [trans. Clifford H. Moore], Book V. VIII-IX (London: The Loeb Classical Library, William Heinemann LTD, 1914), 191.

145 Josephus, *The Wars of the Jews*, Book II, chap. 13, Item 1.

146 Ibid., Item 2.

147 Deutsch, Krauss, "Procurators," *Jewish Encyclopedia* (1906 edition).

148   This, and all the quotes in this paragraph are from Josephus, *The Wars of the Jews*, Book II, chap. 13, Item 3.

149   Amy Zalman, "The Sicarii: First Century Terrorists," *ThoughtCo* (July 03, 2019), https://www.thoughtco.com/sicarii-first-century-terrorists-3209152.

150   Richard A. Horsley, "The Sicarii: Ancient Jewish 'Terrorists,'" *The Journal of Religion*, vol. 59, No. 4 (Oct., 1979), 435-458, Published by: The University of Chicago Press, https://www.jstor.org/stable/1202887.

151   Josephus, *The Wars of the Jews*, Book II, chap. 13, Item 4.

152   Ibid.

153   Ibid., Item 5.

154   Ibid.

155   Ibid., Item 6.

156   Ibid.

157   Josephus, *The Wars of the Jews*, Book II, chap. 13, Item 7.

158   Ibid.

159   Richard Gottheil, Samuel Krauss, "Porcius Festus," *Jewish Encyclopedia* (1906 edition), http://www.jewishencyclopedia.com/articles/6100-festus-porcius.

160   Josephus, *The Wars of the Jews*, Book II, chap. 14, Item 1.

161   Ibid.

162   Ibid.

163   Ibid.

164   Tacitus, *The Histories*, Book V. IX-XI, 193.

165   Helen K. Bond, *Pontius Pilate in history and interpretation* (UK: Cambridge University Press, 1998), 61.

166   Josephus, *The Wars of the Jews*, Book II, Chapters 14-17.

167   Josephus, *The Wars of the Jews*, Book II, chap. 18, Item 1.

168   Johnson, *A History of the Jews*, 119.

169   *Masechet Yoma* 9b.

170   Josephus, *The Wars of the Jews*, Book VI, chap. 9, Item 1.

171   Ibid.

172   Johnson, *A History of the Jews*, 140.

173   Josephus, *The Wars of the Jews*, Book IV, chap. 6, Item 2.

174   All the quotes above are from Item 2 in Josephus, *The Wars of the Jews*, Book IV, chap. 6.

175   Josephus, *The Wars of the Jews*, Book IV, chap. 3, Item 2.

176   Johnson, *A History of the Jews*, 119-120.

177   Ibid.

178   Josephus, *The Wars of the Jews*, Book V, chap. 1, Item 5.

179   Josephus, *The Wars of the Jews*, Book VI, chap. 9, Item 3.

180   "Population of Chicago," *US Population, 2019*, https://uspopulation2019.com/population-of-chicago-2019.html.

181   Josephus, *The Wars of the Jews*, Book IV, chap. 3, Item 2.

182   Johnson, *A History of the Jews*, 138-139.

183   Josephus, *The Wars of the Jews*, Book V, chap. 1, Item 4.

184   Ibid.

185   Ibid.

186   Josephus, *The Wars of the Jews*, Book IV, chap. 3.

187   Ibid.

188   Josephus, *The Wars of the Jews*, Book IV, chap. 6, Item 3.

189   Ibid.

190   Josephus, *The Wars of the Jews*, Book V, chap. 1, Item 5.

191   Josephus, *The Wars of the Jews*, Book V, chap. 6, Item 1.

192   Ibid.

193   Ibid.

194   Josephus, *The Wars of the Jews*, Book V, chap. 10, Item 3.

195   Josephus, *The Wars of the Jews*, Book V, chap. 10, Item 2.

196   Josephus, *The Wars of the Jews*, Book V, chap. 10, Item 3.

197   Tacitus, *The Histories*, Book V, "Fragments of the Histories," 221.

198   Josephus, *The Wars of the Jews*, Book V, chap. 10, Item 4.

199   Josephus, *The Wars of the Jews*, Book V, chap. 13, Item 7.

200   Josephus, *The Wars of the Jews*, Book VI, chap. 3, Items 3-4.

201   Ibid.

202   Josephus, *The Wars of the Jews*, Book VI, chap. 3, Items 3-4.

203   Josephus, *The Wars of the Jews*, Book VI, chap. 9, Item 3.

204   Johnson, *A History of the Jews*, 148.

205   Johnson, *A History of the Jews*, 140.

206   *Jewish Life and Thought Among Greeks and Romans: Primary Readings* [ed. Louis H. Feldman, and Meyer Reinhold (Contributor)] (UK: Augsburg Fortress, February 23, 2009), 192.

207   Ibid.

208   Tacitus, *The Histories*, Book V. "Fragments of the Histories," 221.

209   Adolf Hitler, *Mein Kampf* (US: The Noontide Press: Books On-Line, 2003), 64.

210   Johnson, *A History of the Jews*, 142.

211   Maimonides, *Mishneh Torah*, "Introduction to Mishneh Torah (Passing the Oral Torah)," Item 9.

212   Babylonian Talmud, *Yevamot* 62b.

213   Jerusalem Talmud, *Rosh Hashanah*, 5b and *Shekalim*, 8a (Antwerp: Beit Daneil Bombergi, 1523). Online version (shortened url): https://bit.ly/33gYtKF.

214   Babylonian Talmud, *Masechet Shabbat* 31a.

215   Jerusalem Talmud, *Taanit*, chap. 4, Rule 5, 24a.

216   Johnson, *A History of the Jews*, 140-141.

217   *Midrash Rabbah, Eicha*, Portion 2, 5.

218   Solomon Yakovlevich Lurye, *Anti-Semitism in the Ancient World* [trans. Michael Brushtein & Chaim Ratz] (Berlin: Z.I. Grzhebina, 1923), 128.

219   Simon Rawidowicz, *Israel, the Ever-Dying People, and Other Essays* (NJ, USA: Fairleigh Dickinson University, Pr, October 1, 1986), 54.

220   Ibid., 61.

221   "Complete List of Jewish Expulsions (908) (with explanations and sources), *Internet Archive*, https://archive.org/details/900jewishexpulsions.

222   Jane S. Gerber, *Jews of Spain: A History of the Sephardic Experience*, "Introduction" (USA: Free Press, 1994), xi.

223   Yitzhak Baer, *A History of the Jews in Christian Spain*, vol. 1 [trans. Louis Schoffman] (Illinois: Varda Books, 1961), 16.

224   Norman Roth, *Jews, Visigoths, and Muslims in Medieval Spain: cooperation and conflict* (The Netherlands: E.J. Brill, 1994), 2.

225 Norman Roth, *Conversos, Inquisition, and the Expulsion of the Jews from Spain* (London, England: The University of Wisconsin Press, 2002), 9.

226 Josephus, *The Antiquities of the Jews*, Book XII, chap. 2, Item 1.

227 *Sifrey Devarim*, Item 354.

228 Solomon Yakovlevich Lurye, *Anti-Semitism in the Ancient World* [trans. Michael Brushtein & Chaim Ratz] (Berlin: Z.I. Grzhebina, 1923), 128.

229 Michael Grant, *From Alexander to Cleopatra: the Hellenistic World* (New York: Charles Scribner & Sons, 1982), 75.

230 Leo Tolstoy, "What is the Jew?" quoted in "The Final Resolution," 189, printed in *Jewish World* periodical, 1908.

231 Shulgin, *What We Don't Like About Them...*, 218.

232 Roth, *Conversos, Inquisition, and the Expulsion of the Jews from Spain*, 11.

233 "Spain Virtual Jewish History Tour," "Massacre of 1391," *Jewish Virtual Library*, https://www.jewishvirtuallibrary.org/spain-virtual-jewish-history-tour.

234 Gerber, *The Jews of Spain: A History of the Sephardic Experience*, 114.

235 Ibid.

236 "The Spanish Inquisition," *Encyclopedia Britannica*, https://www.britannica.com/place/Spain/The-Spanish-Inquisition#ref587472.

237 Tomás De Torquemada, *Encyclopedia of World Biography* (Copyright 2004 The Gale Group Inc.), https://www.encyclopedia.com/people/history/spanish-and-portuguese-history-biographies/tomas-de-torquemada.

238 Roth, *Conversos, Inquisition, and the Expulsion of the Jews from Spain*, 11-12.

239 Ibid.

240 Ibid., 12-13.

241 Ibid., 136.

242 Cecil Roth, *A History of the Marranos*, Fifth ed. (NY: Sepher-Hermon Press, 1992), IX.

243 Ibid.

244 Robert A. Maryks, "Purity of Blood," *Oxford Bibliographies*, DOI: 10.1093/OBO/9780195399301-0101, https://www.oxfordbibliographies.com/view/document/obo-9780195399301/obo-9780195399301-0101.xml.

245 Gerber, *The Jews of Spain: A History of the Sephardic Experience*, 124.

246 Ibid.

247 Roth, *Conversos, Inquisition, and the Expulsion of the Jews from Spain*, 133-134.

248 Ibid., 123-124.

249 Ibid., 129.

250 Ibid., 131.

251 Ibid., 131-132.

252 Ibid., 132.

253 Gerber, *The Jews of Spain: A History of the Sephardic Experience*, 136.

254 Ibid., 152-153.

255 Ibid., 284.

256 "Spain Virtual Jewish History Tour," "Inquisition & Expulsion," *Jewish Virtual Library*, https://www.jewishvirtuallibrary.org/spain-virtual-jewish-history-tour#5.

257 Jacob Rader Marcus, *The Jew in the Medieval World: A Sourcebook: 315-1791*, (US: Atheneum, 1974), 52-53.

258 Ibid., 53.

259 Ibid.

260 Gerber, *The Jews of Spain: A History of the Sephardic Experience*, 112.

261 All experts from the Edict of Expulsion are taken from David Raphael, *Expulsion 1492 Chronicles: An Anthology of Medieval Chronicles Relating to the Expulsion of the Jews from Spain and Portugal* [trans. of edict, David Raphael (USA, Carmi House Publishing, 1st ed. February 1, 1992), beginning on p. 189.

262 Friedrich Battenberg, "Jewish Emancipation in the 18th and 19th Centuries," *European History Online*, August 25, 2017, http://ieg-ego.eu/en/threads/european-networks/jewish-networks/friedrich-battenberg-jewish-emancipation-in-the-18th-and-19th-centuries.

263 Israel Bartal, *The Jews of Eastern Europe, 1772-1881* [trans. Chaya Naor] (US: University of Pennsylvania Press, 7 June, 2011), 63-64.

264 Ibid.

265 Ibid.

266 Ibid., 64.

267   Ibid., 66.

268   Ibid., 67.

269   Ibid.

270   Donald Mackenzie Wallace, "Alexander II," in *The Encyclopedia Britannica*, vol. 1 (UK: Cambridge, England, 1910), 559-560.

271   Ibid., 560.

272   Ibid.

273   Ibid.

274   Aleksandr Isayevich Solzhenitsyn, *Two Hundred Years Together: On Russian-Jewish Relations, 1795-1995*, [trans. Shelly Gaver], eBook edition.

275   Bartal, The Jews of Eastern Europe, 1772-1881, 97.

276   Ibid.

277   Ibid., 98.

278   Ibid., 108.

279   Ibid., 121-122.

280   Ibid., 53.

281   Erich E. Haberer, *Jews and Revolution in Nineteenth-Century Russia* (UK: Cambridge University Press, 2004), 67.

282   Ibid.

283   Ibid.

284   Ibid., 229.

285   Ibid., 56.

286   Solzhenitsyn, *Two Hundred Years Together: On Russian-Jewish Relations, 1795-1995*, eBook edition.

287   Ibid., 110.

288   Ibid., 149.

289   Ibid.

290   Norman M. Naimark, *Shofar* 16, no. 2 (1998): 117-19. http://www.jstor.org/stable/42942734.

291   Haberer, *Jews and Revolution in Nineteenth-Century Russia*, 13-14.

292   Haberer, *Jews and Revolution in Nineteenth-Century Russia*, 76.

293   Ibid., 66.

294   Ibid., 30.

295   Ibid., 143.

296   Solzhenitsyn, *Two Hundred Years Together: On Russian-Jewish Relations, 1795-1995*, eBook edition.

297   Ibid.

298   Haberer, *Jews and Revolution in Nineteenth-Century Russia*, 86.

299   Danielle Ziri, "D.C. Dyke March Bans Israeli and Jewish Symbols on Pride Flags, Sparking Criticism," *Haaretz* (June 06, 2019), https://www.haaretz.com/us-news/.premium-d-c-dyke-march-bans-israeli-and-jewish-symbols-on-pride-flags-sparking-criticism-1.7339707.

300   Ibid., 206.

301   Ibid., xi.

302   Ibid., 187.

303   Ibid., 203.

304   Bartal, *The Jews of Eastern Europe, 1772-1881*, 145.

305   Ibid., 142.

306   Shulgin, *What We Don't Like About Them...*, 218.

307   Ibid., 155.

308   Haberer, *Jews and Revolution in Nineteenth-Century Russia*, 206.

309   Ibid.

310   Ibid.

311   Ibid., 207.

312   Ibid.

313   Solzhenitsyn, *Two Hundred Years Together: On Russian-Jewish Relations, 1795-1995*, eBook edition.

314   Ibid.

315   Chimen Abramsky, "Weizmann: A New Type of Leadership in the Zionist Movement." *Transactions & Miscellanies (Jewish Historical Society of England)* 25 (1973): 137-49. http://www.jstor.org/stable/29778841.

316   Ibid.

317   Ibid.

318 Jehuda Reinharz, Yaacov Shavit, *The Road to September 1939: Polish Jews, Zionists, and the Yishuv on the Eve of World War II* [trans. Michal Sapir] (US: Brandeis University Press, 2018), 20.

319 Ibid.

320 Anita Shapira, "The Religious Motifs of the Labor Movement," in *Zionism and Religion* (US: Brandeis University Press, 1998), 252.

321 Ibid.

322 Ibid.

323 "Anti-Semitism: The Hep Hep Riots," *Jewish Virtual Library*, https://www.jewishvirtuallibrary.org/hep-hep-riots.

324 According to the *Jewish Virtual Library* (same link as in previous endnote), the words "Hep! Hep!" are either an acronym for *Hierosolyma est perdita*, a Crusader chant meaning 'Jerusalem is lost,' or simply an exhortatory cry for sheep-herders that Jew-baiters borrowed.

325 Ibid.

326 Amos Elon, *The Pity of it All: A Portrait of German Jews, 1743-1933* (US: Picador, 2002), 101.

327 Ibid., 102.

328 "Anti-Semitism: The Hep Hep Riots," *Jewish Virtual Library*.

329 Ibid.

330 "Anti-Semitism in Germany: Historical Background," Minnesota State University, http://web.mnstate.edu/shoptaug/AntiFrames.htm.

331 Jonathan Frankel, Steven J. Zipperstein [Eds.], *Assimilation and Community: The Jews in Nineteenth-Century Europe* (UK: Cambridge University Press, 2004), 62.

332 Ibid., 62-63.

333 Ibid., 63.

334 Dershowitz, *The Vanishing American Jew: In Search of Jewish Identity for the Next Century*, 6.

335 Sarah Ann Gordon, *Hitler, Germans, and the Jewish Question* (US: Princeton University Press, 1984), 7.

336 Ibid.

337 Glenn R. Sharfman, "Jewish Emancipation," *Encyclopedia of 1848 Revolutions*, Ohio University, https://www.ohio.edu/chastain/ip/jewemanc.htm.

338 Gordon, *Hitler, Germans, and the Jewish Question* (US: Princeton University Press, 1984), 7.

339 "Anti-Semitism in Germany: Historical Background," http://web.mnstate. edu/shoptaug/AntiFrames.htm.

340 Wilhelm Marr, *The Victory of Judaism over Germandom* (March 1879), http://ghdi.ghi-dc.org/sub_document.cfm?document_id=1797.

341 "Anti-Semitism in Germany: Historical Background," http://web.mnstate. edu/shoptaug/AntiFrames.htm.

342 Robert S. Wistrich, *From Ambivalence to Betrayal: The Left, the Jews, and Israel* (US: University of Nebraska Press, Lincoln and London, for the Vidal Sassoon International Center for the Study of Antisemitism, 2012), 41.

343 Francis R. Nicosia, David Scrase [Eds.], *Jewish Life in Nazi Germany: Dilemmas and Responses* (NY, US: Berghahn Books, 2010), 12.

344 Wistrich, *From Ambivalence to Betrayal*, 113.

345 Ibid., 124.

346 Elon, *The Pity of it All: A Portrait of German Jews*, 122.

347 Ibid., 122-123.

348 Adolf Hitler, *Mein Kampf* (The Noontide Press: Books On-Line), 217-219, url: www.angelfire.com/folk/bigbaldbob88/MeinKampf.pdf.

349 Steven M. Lowenstein, "Jewish Intermarriage and Conversion in Germany and Austria," 24, https://www.researchgate.net/publication/265770066_ Jewish_Intermarriage_in_Germany_and_Austria.

350 Ibid., 26.

351 Ibid., 26.

352 Ibid., 27.

353 Ibid., 31.

354 Ibid., 32.

355 Robert Weldon Whalen, "War Losses (Germany)," *International Encyclopedia of the First World War*, https://encyclopedia.1914-1918-online. net/article/war_losses_germany.

356 David Mikics, "The Jews Who Stabbed Germany in the Back," *Tablet* (November 9, 2017), https://www.tabletmag.com/jewish-arts-and-culture/ books/248615/jews-who-stabbed-germany-in-the-back.

357 Ibid.

358 Lowenstein, "Jewish Intermarriage and Conversion in Germany and Austria," 32.

359 Information on the Weimar Republic taken from *The United States Holocaust Memorial Museum*, "The Weimar Republic," https://encyclopedia.ushmm.org/content/en/article/the-weimar-republic.

360 Ibid.

361 Nigel Jones, "The Assassination of Walther Rathenau," *History Today*, Volume 63, Issue 7, July 2013, https://www.historytoday.com/archive/history-matters/assassination-walther-rathenau.

362 *The United States Holocaust Memorial Museum*, "The Weimar Republic," https://encyclopedia.ushmm.org/content/en/article/the-weimar-republic.

363 Edwin Black, *The Transfer Agreement: The Dramatic Story of the Pact Between the Third Reich and Jewish Palestine* (US: Dialog Press, August 16, 2009), 3.

364 Ibid., 8.

365 Ibid., 172.

366 Ibid., 173.

367 Francis R. Nicosia, *The Third Reich and the Palestine Question* (US: New Brunswick, Third paperback printing 2013), 55.

368 Black, *The Transfer Agreement*, 174.

369 The picture was taken in the Bundesarchiv at Bibliothek - StB 1, Finckensteinallee 63, box no. Z-F 4476, 12205 Berlin.

370 Harriet Scharnberg, *Die »Judenfrage« im Bild, Der Antisemitismus in nationalsozialistischen Fotoreportagen* (Germany, Hamburger Institus für Sozialforschung, September 24, 2018), 26.

371 Jacob Boas, "A Nazi Travels to Palestine," *History Today*, 30, no. 1 (January 1980), https://www.historytoday.com/archive/nazi-travels-palestine.

372 Ibid.

373 Ibid.

374 According to the Jewish Virtual Library. Reference: *Das Schwarze Korps, Jewish Virtual Library*, https://www.jewishvirtuallibrary.org/das-schwarze-korps.

375 "No Place for Jews in the Army!" *Das Schwarze Korps* (May 15, 1935).

376 Ibid.

377   "The Visible Enemy," *Das Schwarze Korps* (May 15, 1935).

378   Ibid.

379   Erich Kern [ed.], *Verheimlichte Dokumente: Was den Deutschen verschwiegen wird* (Germany: FAZ-Verlag GmbH, 1988), 184.

380   "Nuremberg Race Laws," *United States Holocaust Memorial Museum* (USHMM), https://encyclopedia.ushmm.org/content/en/article/nuremberg-laws.

381   Black, *The Transfer Agreement*, 175.

382   Black, *The Transfer Agreement*, 22.

383   "'Transfer Agreement' and the Boycott of German Goods," *The National Library of Israel*, https://web.nli.org.il/sites/nli/english/collections/personalsites/israel-germany/world-war-2/pages/haavara-agreement.aspx.

384   This is a summary of the agreement as presented in the essay (in Hebrew), *Heskem Haavara* ("The Transfer Agreement"), on *Yad Vashem—The World Holocaust Remembrance Center*, https://www.yadvashem.org/odot_pdf/Microsoft%20Word%20-%201201.pdf.

385   "Reich Migrants to Palestine Get Back 42% of Funds in Cash" (May 25, 1936), *Jewish Telegraphic Agency*, https://www.jta.org/1936/05/25/archive/reich-migrants-to-palestine-get-back-42-of-funds-in-cash.

386   Black, *The Transfer Agreement*, xv.

387   Yfaat Weiss, "The Transfer Agreement and the Boycott Movement: A Jewish Dilemma on the Eve of the Holocaust" [trans. Naftali Greenwood], *Yad Vashem—The World Holocaust Remembrance Center*, https://www.yadvashem.org/odot_pdf/Microsoft%20Word%20-%203231.pdf.

388   Weiss, "The Transfer Agreement and the Boycott Movement," 17.

389   Ibid.

390   Ibid., 2.

391   Yoav Gelber, "The Reactions of the Zionist Movement and the Yishuv to the Nazis' Rise to Power," *Yad Vashem Studies*, 18 (1987) 41-101, 51

392   Tobias Grill [ed.], "'Pioneers of Germanness in the East'? Jewish-German, German, and Slavic Perceptions of East European Jewry during the First World War," in *Jews and Germans in Eastern Europe: shared and comparative histories* (Germany: CPI books GmbH, Leck, 2018), 125.

393   Black, *The Transfer Agreement*, 4.

394   Ibid., 173.

395   Reinharz, Shavit, *The Road to September 1939*, 17.

396   Ibid., 52.

397   Ibid., 13.

398   Ibid., 13-14.

399   Ibid., 15.

400   Ibid.

401   Ibid., 272.

402   Weiss, "The Transfer Agreement and the Boycott Movement," 27.

403   Black, *The Transfer Agreement*, 311-312.

404   Ibid., 33.

405   Ibid.

406   Reinharz, Shavit, *The Road to September 1939*, 20-21.

407   Ibid., 21.

408   Israel Amikam, *The Attack on the Jewish Settlement in the Land of Israel, 1929* [excerpt trans. by Chaim Ratz], http://www.daat.ac.il/daat/vl/tohen.asp?id=36.

409   Norman Rose, *'A Senseless, Squalid War': Voices from Palestine; 1890s to 1948* (UK: Pimlico, 2010), 35.

410   Rose, *'A Senseless, Squalid War,'* 35.

411   Ibid., 36.

412   Ibid.

413   Ibid.

414   Ibid., 36-37.

415   Ibid., 37-38.

416   Black, *The Transfer Agreement*, 98.

417   "Riots in Palestine, *The Sunday Times, Perth*, Western Australia ed. (October 29, 1933), 3, https://trove.nla.gov.au/newspaper/article/58707344.

418   Chaim Weizmann, *The Letters and Papers of Chaim Weizmann: August 1898-July 1931*, vol. 1 (New Brunswick, N.J.: Transaction Books, Rutgers University, 1983), 124.

419   Ibid.

420   Anna Porter, *Kasztner's Train: The True Story of an Unknown Hero of the Holocaust* (U.S.: Bloomsbury, 2009), 94.

421   Ibid.

422   Black, *The Transfer Agreement*, 174.

423   Joseph Verbovszky, "Leopold von Mildenstein and the Jewish Question" (Case Western Reserve University, May 2013), 6, https://etd.ohiolink. edu/!etd.send_file?accession=case1365174634&disposition=inline.

424   Black, *The Transfer Agreement*, 174.

425   Francis R. Nicosia and David Scrase, eds., *Jewish Life in Nazi Germany: Dilemmas and Responses* (NY, US: Berghahn Books, 2010), 97-98.

426   Francis R. Nicosia, *Zionism and Anti-Semitism in Nazi Germany* (NY: Cambridge University Press, 2008), 134.

427   Martin Connolly, *The Founding of Israel: The Journey to a Jewish Homeland from Abraham to the Holocaust* (US: Pen & Sword History, 2018), Kindle.

428   Yehuda Bauer, *Jews for Sale? Nazi-Jewish Negotiations, 1933-1945* (US: Yale University Press, 1994), 174.

429   The Editors of Encyclopaedia Britannica, "Anschluss," *Encyclopedia Britannica*, https://www.britannica.com/event/Anschluss.

430   Corry Guttstadt et al., eds., the International Holocaust Remembrance Alliance, *Bystanders, Rescuers or Perpetrators? The Neutral Countries and the Shoah* (Berlin: Metropol Verlag & IHRA, 2016), 35-36.

431   Ibid., 36-37.

432   "Related Resources, Evian Conference," Yad Vashem—The World Holocaust Remembrance Center, http://www1.yadvashem.org/yv/en/ exhibitions/this_month/resources/evian_conference.asp.

433   Rafael Medoff, "FDR Had His Kissinger, Too," The David S. Wyman Institute for Holocaust Studies, *Encyclopedia of America's Response to the Holocaust*, http://new.wymaninstitute.org/2010/12/fdr-had-his-kissinger-too.

434   "Rublee Sees 'unprecedented Difficulties' in Refugee Bureau's Task," Jewish Telegraphic Agency (September 22, 1938), https://www.jta. org/1938/09/22/archive/rublee-sees-unprecedented-difficulties-in-refugee-bureaus-task.

435   Memorandum of Conversation, by the Under Secretary of State (Welles), Office of the Historian, Foreign Relations of the United States Diplomatic

Papers, General, vol. I (November 17, 1938), https://history.state.gov/historicaldocuments/frus1938v01/d803.

436 "The Secretary of State to the Ambassador in the United Kingdom (Kennedy)," 840.48 Refugees/1662: Telegram, June 12, 1939, https://history.state.gov/historicaldocuments/frus1939v02/d100.

437 "Evian Barred Mass Exodus, Rabbi Wise Declares," *Jewish Telegraphic Agency* (July 22, 1938), https://www.jta.org/1938/07/22/archive/evian-barred-mass-exodus-rabbi-wise-declares.

438 Ibid.

439 Summer Wells, "The Hall of Holography Collection," Abraham Lincoln Library and Museum, Object ID:03.0003.140, https://www.lmunet.edu/uploads/OnlineResources/virtual_exhibit1/vex2/2910C8A7-DF50-4795-BF9C-234221359603.htm.

440 "Jewish Bodies See No Solution in Mass Emigration," *Jewish Telegraphic Agency Archive* (July 11, 1938), https://www.jta.org/1938/07/11/archive/jewish-bodies-see-no-solution-in-mass-emigration.

441 Ibid.

442 "Roosevelt Named to Receive American Hebrew's Good Will Medal," *Jewish Telegraphic Agency* (December 23, 1938), https://www.jta.org/1938/12/23/archive/roosevelt-named-to-receive-american-hebrews-good-will-medal.

443 Ibid.

444 Saul Friedlander, *Nazi Germany and the Jews: The Years of Persecution 1933-1939* (UK: Orion Books, 1997), 248-249.

445 Ibid., 249.

446 Ibid.

447 Ibid., 312.

448 Ibid., 315.

449 "The Chargé in Germany (Gilbert) to the Secretary of State," 840.48 Refugees/1381: Telegram, received February 4, 1939, Office of the Historian, https://history.state.gov/historicaldocuments/frus1939v02/d57.

450 Ibid.

451 "Voyage of the St. Louis," United States Holocaust Memorial Museum, https://encyclopedia.ushmm.org/content/en/article/voyage-of-the-st-louis.

452   Gordon Thomas, Max Morgon-Witts, *Voyage Of The Damned: A Shocking True Story of Hope, Betrayal, and Nazi Terror* (US: Skyhorse Publishing, 2010), 23.

453   Sarah A. Ogilvie and Scott Miller, *Refuge Denied: The St. Louis Passengers and the Holocaust* (US: University of Wisconsin Press, 2006), 15.

454   Ibid., 18.

455   Ibid., 3-4.

456   Friedlander, *Nazi Germany and the Jews*, 299-300.

457   Rafael Medoff, *Militant Zionism in America: The Rise and Impact of the Jabotinsky Movement in the United States, 1926–1948* (US: The University of Alabama Press, 2002), 15.

458   Rafael Medoff, *The Jews Should Keep Quiet: Franklin D. Roosevelt, Rabbi Stephen S. Wise, and the Holocaust* (US: University of Nebraska Press, 2019), 88.

459   Ibid.

460   Ibid.

461   Matt Lebovic, "How to explain the 'timid' reaction of American Jewish leaders to Kristallnacht?," *The Times of Israel* (November 10, 2018), https://www.timesofisrael.com/how-to-explain-the-timid-reaction-of-american-jewish-leaders-to-kristallnacht.

462   Ibid.

463   "Congress Gets Bill Opening Alaska to Settlement by Refugees of 16 to 45," *Jewish Telegraphic Agency Archive* (March 17, 1940), https://www.jta.org/1940/03/17/archive/congress-gets-bill-opening-alaska-to-settlement-by-refugees-of-16-to-45.

464   Raphael Medoff, "A Thanksgiving plan to save Europe's Jews," *The Jewish Standard* (November 16, 2007), https://jewishstandard.timesofisrael.com/a-thanksgiving-plan-to-save-europes-jews.

465   William R. Perl, "The Holocaust and the Lost Caribbean Paradise," Foundation for Economic Education (January 1, 1992), https://fee.org/articles/the-holocaust-and-the-lost-caribbean-paradise.

466   Ibid.

467   Barbara L. Bailin, "The Influence of Anti-Semitism on United States Immigration Policy With respect to German Jews During 1933-1939" (2011). *CUNY Academic Works*, 50, https://academicworks.cuny.edu/cc_etds_theses/262.

468   Perl, "The Holocaust and the Lost Caribbean Paradise," https://fee.org/articles/the-holocaust-and-the-lost-caribbean-paradise.

469   Stephen S. Wise, The David S. Wyman Institute for Holocaust Studies, http://enc.wymaninstitute.org/?p=543.

470   Ibid.

471   Lipstadt, Deborah E., "Playing the Blame Game: American Jews Look Back at the Holocaust," vol. 18 (2011), http://hdl.handle.net/2027/spo.13469761.0018.001.

472   "Madagascar Plan," Yad Vashem—The World Holocaust Remembrance Center, https://www.yadvashem.org/odot_pdf/Microsoft%20Word%20-%206635.pdf.

473   "The Nazis & the Jews: The Madagascar Plan," *Jewish Virtual Library*, https://www.jewishvirtuallibrary.org/the-madagascar-plan-2.

474   Excerpt from Peter Longerich, *Politik der Vernichtung*, trans. Alex Stetter, (Germany: München, 1998), 273.

475   Ibid.

476   Ibid.

477   "The Nazis & the Jews: The Madagascar Plan," *Jewish Virtual Library*, https://www.jewishvirtuallibrary.org/the-madagascar-plan-2.

478   "Das Protokoll der Wannsee-Konferenz," House of the Wannsee Conference, Memorial and Educational Site, https://www.ghwk.de/fileadmin/user_upload/pdf-wannsee/dokumente/protokoll-januar1942_barrierefrei.pdf.

479   Wannsee Protocol, January 20, 1942; Translation, based on the official U.S. government translation prepared for evidence in trials at Nuremberg, http://prorev.com/wannsee.htm.

480   Ibid.

481   Haus Der Wannsee-Konferenz, "Dokumente zur Wannsee-Konferenz," https://www.ghwk.de/wannsee-konferenz/dokumente-zur-wannsee-konferenz.

482   Ibid.

483   All the quotes in the bullet list were taken from the above-cited translation of the Wannsee Protocol.

484   Laura Geggel, "1.32 Million Jews Were Killed in Just Three Months During the Holocaust" (January 4, 2019), https://www.livescience.com/64420-holocaust-jewish-deaths.html.

485 Judith Tydor Baumel, *The Holocaust Encyclopedia*, ed., Walter Laqueur (US: Yale University Press, 2001), 3-4.

486 Louis Rapoport, *Shake Heaven & Earth: Peter Bergson and the Struggle to Rescue the Jews of Europe* (US: Gefen Publishing, May 1999), 69.

487 Medoff, *Militant Zionism in America*, 85.

488 Ibid.

489 Letter from Stephen Wise, President, American Jewish Congress, to President Franklin D. Roosevelt; 12/2/1942; OF 76-c: Jewish 1942 - July 1943 (Church Matters); Collection FDR-FDRPOF: President's Official Files (Roosevelt Administration), Record Group Franklin D. Roosevelt President's Official Files, 1933 - 1945; Franklin D. Roosevelt Library, Hyde Park, NY, Online Version (October 23, 2019), https://www.docsteach.org/documents/document/american-jewish-congress-fdr.

490 Laurel Leff, *Buried by the Times: The Holocaust and America's Most Important Newspaper* (US:Cambridge University Press, April 10, 2006), 1.

491 Ibid., 16.

492 Marlow Stern, "'Reporting on the Times' Calls Out New York Times Holocaust Coverage," *Daily Beast* (April 18, 2013), https://www.thedailybeast.com/reporting-on-the-times-calls-out-new-york-times-holocaust-coverage.

493 Ibid.

494 "Principles," *The American Council for Judaism*, http://www.acjna.org/acjna/about_principles.aspx.

495 Rafael Medoff, "New York Times Column on Anti-Zionism a Reminder of its Own Publisher's Past" (February 18, 2014), http://www.algemeiner.com/2014/02/18/new-york-times-column-on-anti-zionism-a-reminder-of-its-own-publisher's-past/.

496 Ibid.

497 Baumel, *The Holocaust Encyclopedia*, 13.

498 Aide-Mémoire, "The British Embassy to the Department of State," Foreign Relations of the United States: Diplomatic Papers (1943), General, vol. I, 840.48 Refugees/3633, https://history.state.gov/historicaldocuments/frus1943v01/d103.

499 "The Secretary of State to the President," Foreign Relations of the United States, Conferences at Washington and Quebec (1943), 840.48 Refugees/4034½, May 22, 1943, https://history.state.gov/historicaldocuments/frus1943/d142#fn:1.5.4.4.22.38.10.14.4.

500 Rafael Medoff, "FDR Had His Kissinger, Too," The David S. Wyman Institute for Holocaust Studies, *Encyclopedia of America's Response to the Holocaust*, http://new.wymaninstitute.org/2010/12/fdr-had-his-kissinger-too/.

501 Ibid.

502 Rafael Medoff, "Why the Rabbi said: 'Eat bread on Passover,'" *Arutz Sheva – Israel National News* (April 21, 2016), http://www.israelnationalnews.com/Articles/Article.aspx/18754.

503 Ibid.

504 Kurt F. Stone, "The Amazing Sol Bloom," *The K.F. Stone Weekly*, https://kurtfstone.typepad.com/kurt_f_stone_speaks_/2006/07/the_amazing_sol.html.

505 Katherine E. Culbertson, "American Wartime Indifference to the Plight of the European Jews," Hanover College – History Department, https://history.hanover.edu/hhr/94/hhr94_5.html.

506 Jeremy Black, *The Holocaust: History and Memory* (US: Indiana University Press, 2016), 137.

507 Ibid., 138.

508 Ibid.

509 "Italy," *Holocaust Encyclopedia*, United States Holocaust Memorial Museum, https://encyclopedia.ushmm.org/content/en/article/italy.

510 "December 13, 1942, Goebbels complains of Italians' treatment of Jews" *This Day in History* (July 28, 2019), https://www.history.com/this-day-in-history/goebbels-complains-of-italians-treatment-of-jews.

511 Ibid.

512 "Oral history interview with Flory Jagoda," interview by Joan Ringelheim, *United States Holocaust Memorial Museum Collection*, RG Number: RG-50.030.0342 (August 10, 1995), min. 39:53, https://collections.ushmm.org/search/catalog/irn504836.

513 Pierre Birnbaum and Ira Katznelson, eds., *Paths of Emancipation: Jews, States, and Citizenship* (Princeton, NJ: Princeton University Press, 1995), 206-207.

514 Ibid., 207.

515 Ibid., 208.

516 Ibid., 225.

517 Ibid., 233.

518 Ibid., 234.

519 Ibid.

520 Ibid., 235.

521 "Italy," *United States Holocaust Memorial Museum* (*Holocaust Encyclopedia*), https://encyclopedia.ushmm.org/content/en/article/italy.

522 Ibid.

523 Ibid.

524 Birnbaum, Katznelsonm, *Paths of Emancipation*, 230.

525 Black, *The Transfer Agreement*, xxiii

526 Ibid.

527 "The 29th of November," *The Knesset, Occasions*, https://www.knesset.gov.il/holidays/eng/29nov_e.htm.

528 "Establishment of Israel: The Declaration of the Establishment of the State of Israel," *Jewish Virtual Library*, https://www.jewishvirtuallibrary.org/the-declaration-of-the-establishment-of-the-state-of-israel.

529 Ibid.

530 Deutscher Bundestag, 5 Wahlperiode, 111 Sitzung, Bonn (June 7, 1967), StenBer, 5270, 5272 73, 5276 77, 5292, 5297, 5301 2, 5308 9, 5317 18, 5321, 5321, 5330.

531 Ibid., 5304: "Unsere Nichteinmischung und damit Neutralität im völkerrechtlichen Sinne des Wortes keine moralische Indifferenz und keine Trägheit des Herzens bedeuten kann."

532 Both quotes taken from: Carole Fink, *West Germany And Israel: Foreign Relations, Domestic Politics, And The Cold War, 1965-1974* (New York: Cambridge University Press, 2019), 56.

533 Ibid.

534 "Günter Grass Says Jews Gain German Respect," *New York Times* (July 3, 1967), 5.

535 Rudolf Augstein, "Israel soll Leben," *Der Spiegel* 25 (June 12, 1967), 3.

536 Menachem Begin, "A City that Has Been Joined Together" [trans. Chaim Ratz], *Menachem Begin Heritage Center*, http://bit.ly/2QR007j.

537 Adam Kovac, "A New Plague at the Seder: Politics," *MEL* (June 2019), https://melmagazine.com/en-us/story/a-new-plague-at-the-seder-politics.

538   Ed Vulliamy, "How Trump's presidency has divided Jewish America" (November 14, 2018), https://www.theguardian.com/us-news/2018/nov/14/american-jewish-community-divisions-trump-pittsburgh.

539   Rabbi Kalonymus Kalman Halevi Epstein, *Maor VaShemesh*, Portion *Nitzavim*.

540   Rabbi Menahem Nahum of Chernobyl, *Maor Eynaim*, Portion *VaYetzeh*.

541   Rabbi Shmuel Bornstein, *Shem MiShmuel* [A Name Out of Samuel], *VaYakhel* [And Moses Assembled], *TAR'AV* (1916).

542   Rabbi Shlomo Ben Yitzhak (RASHI), *The RASHI Interpretation on the Torah, Beresheet* 19:2.

543   *The Book of Zohar* with the Sulam commentary, vol. 8, excerpt translated by Chaim Ratz, *BeShalach*, item 252 (printed in Jerusalem, Israel), 8:334.

544   *The Book of Zohar* with the *Sulam* commentary, Vol 14, *Aharei Mot*, items 65-66, 14:20-21.

545   Rav Moshe Ben Maimon (Maimonides), "The Book of Science," *Mishneh Torah*, part 1, chap. 1, item 1.

546   Norman M. Naimark, *Stalin's Genocides* (USA: Princeton University Press, 2010).

547   Donald L. Niewyk, *The Jews in Weimar Germany* (New Brunswick, New Jersey: Transactions Publishers, 2001), 95.

548   Rav Avraham Yitzhak HaCohen Kook (the Raiah), *Orot HaKodesh*, 2:415.

549   Rav Avraham Yitzhak HaCohen Kook (the Raiah), *Orot HaRaiah* [Lights of the Raiah], Shavuot, 70.

550   Rav Avraham Yitzhak HaCohen Kook (the Raiah), *Orot* [Lights], 16.

551   Rav Avraham Yitzchak HaCohen Kook (Raaiah), *Essays of the Raaiah*, 1:268-269.

552   Reinharz, Shavit, *The Road to September 1939*, 19.

553   Ibid., 15.

554   Aaron Soresky, "The ADMOR, Rabbi Yehuda Leib Ashlag ZATZUKAL— Baal HaSulam: 30th Anniversary of His Departure," *Hamodia*, 9, Tishrey, TASHMAV (September 24, 1985).

555   Yehuda Ashlag, "The Writings of the Last Generation," *The Writings of Baal HaSulam*, trans. Chaim Ratz, (U.S.: Laitman Kabbalah Publishers, 2019), 2:577.

5565 Ashlag, "Introduction to The Book of Zohar," *The Writings of Baal HaSulam*, items 66-71, 1:129-133.

557 Ashlag, "A Handmaid Who Is Heir to Her Mistress," *The Writings of Baal HaSulam*, 1:135.

558 Ashlag, "Introduction to The Book of Zohar," *The Writings of Baal HaSulam*, 1:130.

559 Henry Ford, *The International Jew -- The World's Foremost Problem* (US, The Noontide Press, Early 1920s), 7.

560 Ashlag, "Introduction to The Book of Zohar," *The Writings of Baal HaSulam*, 1:131.

561 Ibid.

562 Ibid., 132.

563 Ibid.

564 Babylonian Talmud, *Masechet Yevamot* 63a.

565 Ashlag, "Introduction to The Book of Zohar," *The Writings of Baal HaSulam*, 1:131.

566 Ibid., 133.

567 Ibid.

568 *Sifrey Devarim*, item 354.

Made in the USA
San Bernardino, CA
14 February 2020